1,000,000 Books

are available to read at

www.ForgottenBooks.com

Read online
Download PDF
Purchase in print

ISBN 978-1-331-68014-7
PIBN 10220557

This book is a reproduction of an important historical work. Forgotten Books uses state-of-the-art technology to digitally reconstruct the work, preserving the original format whilst repairing imperfections present in the aged copy. In rare cases, an imperfection in the original, such as a blemish or missing page, may be replicated in our edition. We do, however, repair the vast majority of imperfections successfully; any imperfections that remain are intentionally left to preserve the state of such historical works.

Forgotten Books is a registered trademark of FB &c Ltd.
Copyright © 2018 FB &c Ltd.
FB &c Ltd, Dalton House, 60 Windsor Avenue, London, SW19 2RR.
Company number 08720141. Registered in England and Wales.

For support please visit www.forgottenbooks.com

1 MONTH OF FREE READING

at

www.ForgottenBooks.com

By purchasing this book you are eligible for one month membership to ForgottenBooks.com, giving you unlimited access to our entire collection of over 1,000,000 titles via our web site and mobile apps.

To claim your free month visit:

www.forgottenbooks.com/free220557

* Offer is valid for 45 days from date of purchase. Terms and conditions apply.

English
Français
Deutsche
Italiano
Español
Português

www.forgottenbooks.com

Mythology Photography **Fiction** Fishing Christianity **Art** Cooking Essays **Buddhism** Freemasonry Medicine **Biology** Music **Ancient Egypt** Evolution Carpentry Physics Dance Geology **Mathematics** Fitness Shakespeare **Folklore** Yoga Marketing **Confidence** Immortality Biographies Poetry **Psychology** Witchcraft Electronics Chemistry History **Law** Accounting **Philosophy** Anthropology Alchemy Drama Quantum Mechanics Atheism Sexual Health **Ancient History Entrepreneurship** Languages Sport Paleontology Needlework Islam **Metaphysics** Investment Archaeology Parenting Statistics Criminology **Motivational**

SECRET MEMOIRS AND MANNERS

Of several

Persons of Quality,

OF

Both SEXES.

FROM THE

New *ATALANTIS*,

AN

Island in the *Mediteranean*.

Written Originally in ITALIAN.

LONDON:
Printed for *John Morphew* near Stationer's-Hall, and *J. Woodward* in St. Christopher's Church-yard, in Thread-needle-street. 1709.

To His Grace

HENRY

Duke of BEAUFORT,

Marquis and Earl of *Worcester*,

Earl of *Glamorgan*, Baron *Herbert*,

AND

Lord of *Chepstow*, *Ragland*, and *Gower*.

My LORD,

HOW vast must be the Ambition of an unknown and meer Translator, to dare to Hope from

A 2 *so*

The Dedication.

so Great a PRINCE, *his most Noble Protection for so small a Trifle? But as he who enters not the List, can never pretend to win the Race, this Attempt, how daz'ling soever, had never been mine, without a proportionate degree of Admiration for those Heroic Qualities conspicuous in Your Grace; thence Inspir'd, my Presumption may Hope to avoid Your Frowns, if the Performance be not so Happy to meet Your Smiles.*

The following Adventures First spoke their own mixt Italian, a Speech Corrupted, and

The Dedication. iii

and now much in Use thro' all the Islands of the Mediterranean; from whence some Industrious Frenchman soon Transported it into his own Country; and by giving it an Air and Habit, wherein the Foreigner was almost lost, seem'd to Naturalize it: A Friend of mine, that made the Campaign, met with it last Year at Bruxels, and thus, a la Francois, put it into my Hands, with a desire it might Visit the Court, and Great Britain.

That the unknown Translator has presum'd to lay it at Your

Your Grace's Feet, *proceeds not only from a long and profound Veneration to Your Grace's Family*, *and Your Own Eminent Vertues*, *and fix'd Heroick Principles*, *but he fancy'd so near a resemblance of Yours to the Young Prince in the* Prado, *pag.* 179. *And in the contiuuation of His Character in the Second Part, where Virtue and* Aftrea *repair to the Young Hero's Palace*, *That he thought in Justice it cou'd belong to none but Your Grace.*

If it be true, That a Resemblance, tho' never so much

to

to our Disadvantage, be said to make us wish better to the Resembler *than to another, who carries nothing about him of the same* Air *and* Feature, *we may* Hope *those favourable Sentiments will be no Strangers to* Your Grace's Breast; *which is a Repository for all* Things Great *and* Human, *for all* Things Just *and* Noble. *To speak* You *but to half the* Height *of* Your Own Elevated Character, *(to those who have not the* Honour *to know* You*) wou'd look like the* Daubings *of* Flattery *; and to those who are so* Blest, *an Attempt as utterly impossible, as it wou'd be to endeavour to make*

The Dedication.

make all Mankind Wise, or Honest, or Handsom: You will be better found in the Encomiums Astrea gives in her Visit to the Young Prince de Beaumond; thither I must refer my self, and once more implore Your Protection, and for Ever Your Pardon, for an Attempt so daring as is this of

My Lord,

May it please Your Grace,

Your Grace's

Most profoundly Obedient,
AND
Most Humble Servant,

(1)

ONCE upon a time, *Astrea* (who had long since abandon'd this World, and flown to her Native Residence above) by a new form'd Design and a Revolution of Thought, was willing to Revisit the Earth, to see if Humankind were still as defective, as when she in a Disgust forsook it. Her Descent was as soon perform'd as thought upon; the *European* World being the most Fam'd above for Sciences, she resolv'd her first Visit should be there. Accordingly (by a little too strong a Propension of one of the Winds that bore her) she alighted upon the Clifts of an *Island*, named *Atalantis*, situated in the *Mediteranean Sea*. Tho' her Design was rather for *Rome*, or the Metropolis of *France* or *Great Britain*, Places renown'd in the Court of *Jupiter*, for *Hypocrisy*, *Politicks*, *Politeness* and *Vanity*. No sooner did she re-tread that Ground, so long since abandon'd, but in a rapturous *Soliloquy*, thus she began: All hail thou beautiful Product of the Eternal Mind! How Enchanting are thy Prospects? How Generous is the Earth? How Charming her Fruits? How flowing the Waters? How cooling, how limpid the Streams? How Refreshing to the Taste and Limbs of Mortals? How pleasingly they wind to make fruitful the Neighbouring Meads? Those grassy Pastures, the aspiring shady Groves, and the whole ample Bosom of the Terrestial Globe.

B But

But Oh great *Jupiter!* who haft thus Richly endow'd Nature, the Off-spring of thy Power, so suited it for Admiration and for Use, so worthy of its Divine Original! to what a Race haft thou deliver'd these Enjoyments? How Corrupt, how unworthy of Benefits so Sweet, and of Posessions so Ravishing?

As she was continuing her Exclamations there arose, *Pensive,* and *Forlorn,* a *Beautiful Person* that sat near her, and who knowing the Divine *Astrea,* ran with open Arms to Embrace, and call her Daughter. She wonder'd at the Raptures of the *Stranger;* therefore repelling her eager Caresses, she ran over her Form, to see if she could recollect who this dejected Beauty was: Her *Habit Obsolete* and *Torn,* almost degenerated into Tatters: But her Native Charms, that needed not the help of Art, gave to *Astrea*'s returning Remembrance, that it could be no other than her Beautiful Mother *Virtue.* But Oh! how despicable her Garments! how neglected her flowing Hair! how languid her formerly animating Eyes! how pale, how withered the Roses of her lovely Cheeks and Lips! how useless her snowy Arms and polish'd Fingers! they hung in a melancholy Decline, and seem'd out of other Employment, but sometimes to support the Head of the dejected fair One; her Limbs enervated and supine, wanting of that Energy that should bear her from a Solitude so affrighting.

When *Astrea* had recovered her Astonishment, known and embraced her lovely Parent: For her Beauty being *Divine,* could degenerate no farther than a seeming *Impair,* she earnestly enquir'd into her Change of Habit and Appearance: To whom *Virtue* thus answered.

Astrea,

Virtue, Thou didst choose well in abandoning a World unworthy of thee: I had long since follow'd thee, if great *Jupiter* had not forbid my Flight, least these Creatures of his Fancy, clods of *Earth*, who, by his Command were impregnated by *Phœbus*, should be entirely destitute, even of the Pretence of those Ornaments which are call'd *Virtue*.

Thee they have not mourn'd, for since thy Flight, but have constituted a false Appearance in the Divine *Astrea*'s room, a mock sort of *Justice*, whom they invoke upon every Occasion, without any real regard to Right or Wrong. *Me* they have thrust out from *Courts* and *Cities*. *Cupid* (our little Relation) for a long time allow'd me a Refuge in the Heart of some of his Noblest Votaries, but even he is turn'd *Apostate*. I have no Sanctuary among the *Lovers* of this *Age*; the youngest *Virgin*, and the most ardent *Youth*, are contented to quote me only as a *Name*; something *Fine*, that their Histories indeed make mention of; a thing long since departed, and which at this Day is not to be found among 'em. *Innocence* is banish'd by the first dawn of early *Knowledge*; *Sensual Corruptions* and hasty *Enjoyments* affright me from their Habitation. They imbelish not the Heart to make it worthy of the *God*; their whole Care is outward, and transferr'd to the Person. By a Diabolical way of Argument they prove, the Body is only necessary to the Pleasures of Enjoyment; that Love resides not in the Heart, but in the Face, and as certain of their own Poets have it,

*To an exact Perfection they have brought
The Action Love, the Passion is forgot.*

 Hymen no more officiates at their Marriages, the *Saffron Robe* hangs neglected in the Ward-robe, the *Genuine Torch* is long since extinguish'd; the Glare only of a false Light appears: *Interest* is deputed in his Room, he presides over the *Feast*, he joins their Hands, and brings them to the sacred Ceremony of the *Bed* with so much indifferency, that were not Consummation a necessary Article, the *unloving Pair* could with the utmost Indifferency repair to their several Chambers. Guess then, my lovely *Astrea*, what must be the Off-spring of such an Union! How void of generous Fire, of that sparkling Genius, the product of noble free-born love. Hence it is, that the present Times are so defective of *Heroes*, and if some excel others, 'tis only like Trees planted in the same Soil. *Chance* gives them the Heighth over their Companions, or more properly speaking, a dextrous management of *Vice*; and *Dissimulation*, is sure to carry a Man through. in what ever he undertakes: what hope remains for so barren, so airy a Name as mine, of being so much as countenanc'd by Mankind; *Valour* and *Beauty*, formerly my two nearest Companions, do not so much as remember they were ever acquainted with me: I no longer (as in the Morning of the Creation) have Crowns and Garlands at my disposal, when Kingdoms and Lawrels were merited, and Virtue made the Choice.

 Quite exploded from *Courts* and *Cities*: I was reported to have refug'd among the *Villagers*, but alas! they knew less of me *there*, than in the Cabinets

inets of Princes. For Mortals being by Nature as well as Custom corrupt, the Lessons of *Philo-sophers* and *Humanity*, only refine and fit 'em for the Study of *Virtue*; a generous Education illuminates the *Clod-born-Birth*, without which, Man is the greatest Brute of the Creation; the Rustic Soul, looks out in *Native Ignorance, Cruelty, Avarice, Distrust, Fraud, Revenge, Ingratitude, Self-Interest*, the whole ignoble Train, that fly before the dawn of Knowledge, and the sweetness of Science. Thus may I well (neglected as I am) appear Disconsolate, Abandon'd, flying to the utmost Verge, to bewail my Misfortunes in those solitary Clifts, talking of my Woes to the sonorous Waves, who by the resounding of the Rocks eccho to my Wailings, and sometimes out-beat the remembrance of my Miseries: But you, my lovely *Astrea*, that are not condemn'd like me to wander, Exploded and Alone, what again has brought you to the Commerce of this despicable Race?

Astrea. You know the *Lunary World*, though Inferior to this in many things, yet are Professors of the same Manners, and are in short, a Twin-Creation. There was an Emperor, who [*K. James 2d*] gave Life to a Daughter, born a Master-piece of [*Lady Elizab.*] Nature for *Beauty*, *Virtue* and *Sorrows*. She was Married to a Neighbouring Prince, who had more [*K. Bohemia*] Ambition than Success: Puff'd up with the vain Hopes and Pride of his new Fathers Empire, he thought nothing too great for him to attempt; he put on the Royal Diadem, and call'd himself King of a People, who were Oppress'd and held in Slavery by a Nation more mighty than themselves; the Consequence of it was, his being forsaken, first by his Imperial Father-in-law, then

A 3

(6)

then by all his inferiour Allies: He lost not only his new assum'd Sovereignty, but his own Hereditary Principality. The Queen his Wife, a Miracle of suffering Goodness, wandered with her wretched Children from Territory to Territory; and at length refug'd in the Court where she was born: How often and how tenderly did this unhappy Queen invoke my Name, how did she appeal to *Justice*, whether she deserv'd those Miseries she suffer'd? How vainly did her Crys, her Tears and Beauty, excite her Countrymen to Arm in her Husband's Defence, and to reseat him in his native Rights? Those whom she implor'd, were deaf as Rage or Winds; it would indeed have been matter of Splenetick Laughter to *Momus*, as well as Wonder, if the Queen had succeeded, and that People void of *Religion*, open *Debauchees*, *Blasphemers* of *Great Jupiter* and all the *Gods*, *Gamesters*, *Userers*, should have Arm'd in the Defence of *Virtue*, with which they had no Acquaintance; it was not to be expected from them, and therefore my Votary was to sink under the Burthen of her Woes, hopeless of Redress. My Heart melted at the Complainings of this beauteous and upright Princess. I hastned to the heighth of *Olympus*, where great *Jove* holds his awful Residence; neither the Splendor of his Palace, nor the glorious brightness of his own Divinity, suspended in me, tho' for a moment the desire I had of redressing the Injur'd. I represented to great *Jupiter*, the Wrongs that were wrought in his *Lunary World*. The Father of Gods and Men, seeing me so nearly concern'd, receiv'd me to his Ambrosial Arms, wip'd off those Tears which Anguish had wrung from me, and bad me be Comforted; that the good Queen
should

should receive a double Portion of Bliss hereafter in the happy Regions, when her Years of wandring were accomplish'd; that she was not punish'd for her proper Crimes, but her Husband's Ambition, and her Fathers Supineness; that, since her own Country had refus'd to Arm in her Defence, *Bellona*, and the avenging Furies, *Fear* and *Death*, should take up their Residence among them, 'till a Prince descended from the Beautifullest of her Daughters, should obtain the Soveraignty over 'em; 'till then *Poverty* and *Captivity* should be the Lot of many, yet *Pride* and *Luxury* be abated in none; that they should Labour with endless Toil to Cultivate the Earth, and gather the Fruits she gave, and should compass their *Lunary Globe* for Gain, thro' the uncertain dangerous Ocean, and find the Profit lavish'd away in *War*, to save themselves from *destructive Violence*; that perpetual Terror of *Storms* and *Pirates* to the *Merchants* and *Mariners*; of *Captivity* and *Death* to the *Soldier*, the decline of Power in the *Statesmen*, ever trembling to descend a heighth were they can scarce maintain themselves from precipitately falling: The Debauches in the Young with *Wine* and *Love*; in the Old of *Hippocrisy*, *Avarice* and *Cruelty*, shou'd be the incessant Plagues, that should haunt their aching Thoughts, 'till the young Prince put an end to their Sufferings with their Vices, by his bright Example, leading 'em all into the glorious Path of Virtue and Renown, from whence they should begin to date their *Æra* of being a Happy People.

[marginal note: K. George 1st]

By this Sentence of *Jupiter's*, I grew well acquainted, that I was impotent of Power to assist the suffering Queen; she dy'd in Exile, the young

young Prince descended from her, born indeed with generous Inclinations, is in danger of suffering under the greatest of Misfortunes, the want of Royal Education; tho' Necessity be thought to be the best Instructor, especially to *Princes* (who, in a flowing Fortune are continually seduc'd, from without by Flatterers, from within by their own Pride, arising from the Homage of all about them) yet is it too apt to cramp the Soul, and to proportionate their Sentiments to their Fortune. To avoid either of these Extreams (in Gratitude to the Queen who was so true a Votary to me) I have resolv'd to be my self his Guide in Difficulties, his Leader to *Renown* and *Glory*, his Guard in *War*, his Assistant in *Peace*: my aim is to make him deserving to be Great, as well as to be so, and of the Two, rather to be Good than Mighty; I would fit him for all that Grandeur, which the Destinies have allotted him. I will have him merit the Empire over Mankind, not only fam'd for brutal Courage, as was *Alexander*, for Subtlety and Wisdom as *Cesar*, for being Invincible as *Achilles*, Fortunate as the most Fortunate; but all their particulars united in one, to render a Hero truly such, fond of the improvement of his People's Good, both in War and Peace, cautious of their Safety, and yet, wisely expensive of his own.

In this Task I have undertaken, I have thought it necessary to visit this lower Globe, where all the Arts and Virtues are profess'd with more Ostentation, than in the *Lunarary*, with my own Eyes to see the Change of Manners, that I may the better regulate his. I will go to the Courts, where *Justice*, is profess'd, to view the Magistrate, who presumes to hold the Scales in

my

my Name, to see how remote their profession is from their Practice; thence to the *Courts* and *Cabinets* of *Princes*, to mark their *Cabal* and *disingenuity*, to the *Assemblies* and *Alcoves* of the Young and Fair to discover their Disorders, and the height of their Temptations, the better to teach my young *Prince* how to avoid them, and accomplish him.

Virtue. The design is noble and worthy him you intend your exalted Favorite; but alass what can you do? You may indeed preach to him to avoid *Vice*, but then you must teach him to avoid *Mankind*; all are corrupt, and you will by this Visit only furnish your self with matter of Complaint to *Jupiter*, from ocular proof, when you have seen how abandon'd they are, it will excite your desire to destroy the Race; your cries, the cries of *Justice*, extorted by conscious resentment, will of necessity attack the greatest of all the Gods, even in his innermost retreat, and force him to blend the wretched Mortals with the Dust they were originally taken from; to destroy their very Beings, who dare thus contemptuously breath in defiance of all the *Virtues*: And fraught with *Vice*, fly full in the Face of the very power that form'd 'em, obeying none of the Precepts of their Wise Creator: Nay, in their proud vain Hearts, daring to question, if they and their World had an Original; or from all Eternity were not independant of, or Coequal with Omnipotence?

Astrea. I easily believe what you say, admirable Mother, but because out of multitudes of Evil still some good may be extracted, if you please to favour me me with your Company, I will proceed in my intended purpose.

Vir. Alas, *Virtue* will blush, and hang the Head, offended, and asham'd of the Pollutions of Mankind. Go on to the Capital, 'tis call'd *Angela*; I will expect your return upon the Brow of yon aspiring Clift.

[margin: *London.*]

Astrea. Mercy ever dwells with *Virtue*: Your Intercession may be necessary, (besides the ineffable Charms of your Conversation) lest *Justice* be too highly provok'd by those audacious Objects we may encounter, and, without waiting for the Sentence of *Jupiter*, be tempted to Punish, as well as Condemn; we will make us Garments of the ambient Air, and be invisible, or otherways, as we shall see convenient.

Vir. 'Tis hard to deny a Person so amiable; see, my dear *Astrea*, here is a Boat that belongs to Fishermen, the Sea falls at a little distance into a pleasant River, twelve Leagues in length, it will shorten our Passage; let us go Aboard, and commit our selves to the protection of the Gods.

Astrea. I cannot enough admire the Ingenuity of Mortals, the Art of Navigation is superior to all others; how early must they inure themselves to *Hardships*, contempt of *heat* and *cold*, *hunger*, *thirst*, intrepid in the midst of the most astonishing Dangers, when both the Winds and Seas are at War! Sheets of Light'ning descending! the Moon obscur'd! the Stars as it were extinguish'd! the rattling Thunder bellowing thro'out the Heavens! all things full of Horror and Despair! the dangerous Rocks, and devouring Sands, ready to receive 'em! yet Custom has rendred all these Evils familiar to 'em.

Vir.

Vir. And wou'd you believe, that ev'n in the very moment of destruction, when their Vessel strikes, and the rouling Waves rush greedily to devour 'em, their very Prayers are mingled with Blasphemies; a new invented Vice, since you abandon'd the Earth; they invoke the Name of *Jupiter*, and all the Gods, with horror calling on him at every trifling moment, to destroy and reprobate 'em to Eternity! You will have too many instances of this in viewing the Disorders of that Naval Preparation just before us. How proudly they Plough the Waves? See, can any thing be more magnificent? There are three hundred Ships of Burthen, some for Defence, and others for Traffick; but even the Merchant is not without her Beauty, the Poop and Stern glitters with Gold, the waving Streamers, and other imitated Ornaments, give us scarcely, but by her bulk, and number of her Men and Guns, to distinguish her from a Ship of War.

Astrea. O my Dear! Can there be a sight more beautiful? They all seem to be in a vast hurry, what are they doing? What use is so much Linen, fast'ned with Cords, that trembles in the Wind, and is but with strugling made obedient to the Hand?

Vir. To speak in Terms proper to the Sea, there's just sprung a Gale favourable to 'em; they have lain Wind-bound a considerable time, let us go Aboard the Admiral, she seems the Sovereign of the Seas. The Linen which you enquire after, are Sails, they spread their whiten'd Canvass before the Wind, which fill'd with an auspicious Gale, carries 'em swift, almost as imagination, to their desired Port, and,

for

for expedition, far exceeds any other mortal Invention of Journeying.

Astrea. Oh my dear Mother! I am ready to burst at the Pride and Oppression of Mortals, at their Riots, and Blasphemy; never will I go Aboard another Fleet, there is no manner of Entertainment there for us; I am glad we are got on shore, and releas'd from their Disorders. Good Heaven! how bountiful in Prospect? how detestable in Examination, is that gaudy, guilded, magnificent Prospect of a Fleet? How proud, how luxurious the Commanders? How dissolute, blasphemous, and servile, are the Crew? They bow lower to their Superiors, than ever they did to Heaven; whilst those elate and haughty, as if form'd of a peculiar Mould, look down with Contempt upon the fawning Company of Curs beneath 'em.

Vir. And which is yet more wonderful, some of the proudest, and yet bravest of these Commanders, were one day mean as the meanest of the Crew, crouching beneath the Burthen; yet, when once advanc'd, none more forward in imposing it upon others. Did you notice that old Seignior, stretch'd at his full length upon the crimson Damask Couch? That Youth he seem'd so fond of, was no other than a Woman so disguis'd. He was once in an Engagement with the Enemy, the young Creatures fears, amidst the Roaring of the Canon, the Cries of the Wounded, the Exultings of the Victors, disorder'd her into Fits. The Admiral, careless of Glory, or the preservation of that Renown he formerly had acquired, forgetful of his Nation's Interest, that was intrusted into Hands so feeble, forbid 'em to advance

vance, and so lost a considerable opportunity of taking or burning most of the Enemies Ships, and suffer'd 'em to make off with the reputation of Victory. So to quiet the fears of a Mistress belov'd how unpardonable was this? What had *Venus* to do amidst the rough Embraces of *Bellona*? She may indeed have a pretence, after the toil of Battle, the Fatigue of Fight, to congratulate the Deliverer, and applaud the Performance of her Warriour, to disrobe him of his cumbersome defensive and offensive Ornaments, to sweeten all his Pains, by the recompense of her Smiles; to lead him cover'd with slaughter, dust, and destruction, into the prepared Bath! but in the midst of danger there is no Business for her. The next eminent Commander that we saw, is a great Benefactor to the Ladies in the *Marine* Towns; he perpetually entertains them with Balls and Collations, as far as his Credit will stretch, tho' to the expence of the believing Tradesman, who may wait long enough, if they but wait, till their Bills come in course to be paid. These Disorders are generally the Entertainment of the Night, when the Old and the Wise are retired to that repose which they believe no Diversion can recompence the loss of; mean time the Virgin-Daughters are left an easie Conquest, to the flattery and vigour of these young *Neptunes*, eager as hungry Hawks upon their prey, they improve the coming moments; our young Commander, more inconstant than the Element on which he presides, makes every one of these guilty Meetings, subservient to the gratifying a fresh Inclination. The destin'd Damsel, at the breaking up of the Assembly,

is

is conducted by him to the place of her own abode; he 'is all the while protesting his never-dying Passion, slips in, and goes up to her Chamber with her: She dares make no noise, for fear of awaking her Parents; he improves the Hints, takes advantage of the silent opportunity, swears that he'll marry her, which the credulous Fair easily believes, because he has already two Wives, and does not know but he may as well have toleration to increase them to two hundred, and, without more difficulty, is robb'd of her Honour, and reputation of Honour.

E: of Berkeley
Ld Dursley
Mr Monfort

That very handsom Commander, that we visited next, has lately taken a Girl from the *Opera:* She it was that sat upon the Eminence on his right Hand, tho' there is none in the Company, but what were more beautiful than she: He has been what this Age calls it, a fortunate Man among the Ladies, they tell a great many pleasant Stories of him; pleasant I mean to the Ears of the vicious, who ever should see him, as we did, in his *Marine-room* of State, all dissolved in Luxury, would they readily believe, that this Mortal ought every Hour to be apprehensive of his Fate: Because he is every hour in danger of being Summon'd to pass in *Charons* Vessel instead of riding Triumphant in his own? Did you mark what a profuseness in eating, how his Table abounded, in what was nice as well as necessary; the extream delicateness of his own Taste, and the affected one of his Concubine; the debauch of the Glass after Dinner; the variety of rich Wines, and heightning Cordials; the *double Entenders* of their Conversation, where scarce good Manners, or the sacred Respect

spect due to our Sex was preserv'd; but these are Creatures that, with the real loss of their Modesty, have abandon'd the very appearance of it, and are never so well pleas'd, as when in their Discourse and Debauch, they confound Distinctions, and leave it only to their Dress to bespeak the Sex; the obscene Sports that succeeded, were but an accumulation of a riotous Life. Thus wasting the ebbing Sand! thus provoking Death! thus shaking the hasty Hourglass! neither taught to reflect by Tempests, or Thunder, by Canon, or Destruction! to prepare themselves for that dreadful Alteration, that Antipathy to Nature, that Antithesis of Life. You have not heard among those ten thousand Mariners, the name of *Jupiter*, but to blaspheme it! he is only invoked as a Witness to their Millions of Untruths and Vanities! how they deprecate and devote themselves, without remorse, to eternal Destruction? If great *Jove* be just; If yet he have attention for the Affairs of Mortals, will he not take 'em at their Word? Will he not hurl them into never-ending Destruction? How can they extenuate a Punishment themselves have invoked?

Astrea. With regret I beheld, that they made no Offerings to *Jupiter*, ev'n *Neptune* is neglected by them; *Bacchus* and *Venus* (in their most criminal Rites) are the only Deities that they reverence. It is my wonder that the Waves do not immediately swallow them alive! or that their Enemies do not perpetually vanquish them in Battle!

Vir. Human Nature is universally corrupted, those that fight against them, are as wicked as themselves; there is no sort of Justice in giving either the preeminence, and therefore generally
Chance

Chance decides it. Did you mark thro'out the whole Fleet (after their exorbitant Dinners were paſt) how they endeavour'd to waſte the time, not in improving Converſation, reading of meritorious *Authors*, the *Sciences*, even their own *Mathematicks*, or any other Entertainment that may better their *Lives*, *Philoſophy* and *Humanity*, to ſoften the rigidneſs of a ſtern, cruel *Education*, or to enable 'em to bear the Fatigues and Dangers of their Employment. The Glaſs only goes about, which makes 'em noiſy, vain-glorious, boaſting, ſevere, unmerciful. *That* is generally the time for puniſhing the Wretches beneath them. Dice and Cards have their turn: In this deteſtable Round of Wickedneſs they wear away their Lives; omitting no opportunity of defrauding the Seaman, that labours inceſſantly for a ſorry Subſiſtance; they adulterate even their Pulſe and Water, deputing damag'd in the place of good, which they can have at lower Prices; provided their Coffers are but repleniſh'd, they care not what he endures; The Diſeaſes that thro' unwholſome Food are contracted, the Enervating of their Youth and Vigour, and thouſand other Inconveniencies that ariſe from it. Then they are eminent in nothing more than in defrauding them of the ſweet Enjoyment and Fruit of their Labour; when by the undaunted Courage of the *Mariner*, their contempt of Death, and warrantable deſire to better their wretched Condition of Life, they attack a rich Prize, and take it, tho' all ought to have an equal ſhare in what they have equally purchaſed, at the expence of their Blood, the Commanders appropriate as well the Glory as the Purchaſe. The Wretches

dare

dare not murmur, for fear of that Discipline which was first design'd and term'd Martial, but is since degenerated, as the wild fancy of the cruel Man in Power suggests.

Astrea. But what remedy is there to all these Evils?

Virtue. If some great good Man should stand up and fearlessly regulate these Disorders, as is reported there is now such a one at their Head, if Corruptions were not above, these Inconveniences would not be below. Did only Service and true Merit recommend to Office, were not Bribery, and the Sollicitations of Friends, preferr'd to Duty and Worth; were severe Penalties inflicted upon these Blasphemers (the Commanders themselves first desisting from the use); were Dice, Cards, and an exorbitant Love of Wine, and the hotter Liquors taxed; were faithful Commissioners appointed to inspect the Provision of the Navy; were matter of lawful Complaint made free to the meanest Seamen, provided (upon pain of examplary Punishment) he advance nothing but the Truth; were it made capital to take a Bribe in the Service of their Country: The Regulation might be made easie, if the leading Men and Commanders, gave them but examples of *Sobriety*, *Justice* and *Morality*; but all is nothing but *Oaths*, *Drunkenness*, *burning Lust*, *Riots*, *Avarice*, *Cruelty*, and *Disorder*; they have got the better of a bad Reputation, and do not so much as care to dissemble a good: Hypocrisie is indeed banish'd far from them; Vice, with her many-headed Train, bare-fac'd and open, sits enthron'd, as in her proper *Sphere*; nay, so great a propension have the meanest of the Crew, so educated in harden'd Folly, that there's not a Wretch of them, tho' for three years he have gone tatter'd and almoſt naked, not knowing the uſe or benefit of Money, but, when he receives his Pay, ſhall never ſtir from the *Cabaret* (with a Gang of diſſolute Flatterers, and lewd Women about him) till the laſt Denier be expended.

Virtue. See, my dear *Aſtrea*, as we approach the *Capitol*, how buſie *Intelligence* appears, like a Courtier new in Office! ſhe buſtles up and down, and has a World of Buſineſs upon her hands; ſhe is firſt Lady of the *Bedchamber* to the *Princeſs Fame*, her Garments are all *Hieroglyphicks*; we'll ſtop her as ſhe goes by, but were we not inviſible to her, ſhe would not put us to the trouble, nor paſs us without either a good or bad Report, or poſſible a medium, and that would be the greateſt favour we could expect next to Truth; which ſhe is but rarely concerned with. Pray, Madam, may two Strangers of your own Sex make ſo bold with your Ladyſhip, as to enquire what great Affair ſits ſo buſie in your Face? Whether you can't afford a few moments of your precious time, to inform Foreigners of the *Temper, Genius*, and *Hiſtory* of this *Iſland* ?

Intell. You have hit, Ladies, upon my very Buſineſs; I entertain Strangers with vaſt Reſpect, they give me the greateſt attention; for all I ſay is generally new to Foreigners (when they appear in a Strange Court); my Name is *Intelligence*, I am *Groom* of the *Stole* to that omnipotent Princeſs *Fame*, of whom all the Monarchs on the Earth ſtand in awe. I would not fail to oblige your curioſity, were I not engag'd in a very preſſing Affair; to be ſhort,

between

between Friends, the King of this Island is just dead; 'tis yet a mighty Secret, but I must make what haste I can to divulge it, I have already been at the new Empress's Court, and left her to condole with her she Favorite over some Flasks of sparkling *Champaign*; so that you find 'tis not in my power at this time to oblige you, but if you please, Ladies, to let me know where you Lodge, I'll not fail to wait upon you, soon as this Business is dispatch'd.

Virtue. Leave the care of that to your Emissaries a Power more mighty than your own, controuls you at this time, you shall walk invisible with us; in the Name of *Jupiter* we Arrest you, to attend upon *Justice* and *Virtue*. You are to inform us of all we shall demand; *Truth* is summon'd to attend you on this occasion.

Intell. Having first (as I ought) paid my *Duty* and *Obeysance* to two such mighty Potentates as *Justice* and *Virtue*: I only beg, *Ladies*, a short absence of six moments, and then I will return as full, as proud of my desires to serve you.

Virtue. You are uneasie till you have divulg'd our Secret; but for once we will excuse the honour you design'd us, and are contented to pass unknown and unregarded among the croud of Mortals.

Intell. Your *Mightiness* has indeed guess'd at my Thoughts, I wou'd in a moment have dispatch'd your Affair, by a short whisper in the Ears of *Fame*; the honour of being let into so important a Secret sits heavy upon me, till I have disburthen'd my self, besides it is my Duty faithfully to report to her whatever is new, or of any seeming Importance.

Virtue.

(20)

Virtue. We difpenfe you from it at this time, But pray, Madam, how comes it, that a Perfon of your Importance finds Employment at above three Leagues diftance from the Metropolis?

Intell. This is a *Villa* of the *defunct-Monarchs*; let us ftrike down that Walk, and it brings us to the *Palace*, where all either are, or ought to be, in Tears, to fee him lie dead amongft them; that Chariot brings rouling on the young *Count Cornus*, his Father was Mafter of the Horfe to the King, and the moft accomplifh'd of all the Foreigners; the young Gentleman this Morning, upon the Death of his Mafter, (whom he unfeignedly lov'd) fell into Fits, beat his Breaft, tore his Shirt, and laid about fo handfomly in his Agony, that his Linen appears all bloody; they are carrying him to the *City*, he feems not to have recover'd his Senfes, a Servant fupports him (from finking) in the Chariot; there is a tincture of your *Ladyfhip*, fome fmall fhare of Virtue in the compofition of this young *Count*; but time, and the Air of the Court, will fpeedily deface it.

Aftrea. Who is that graceful Perfon that appears upon the high Loll in his Chariot and fix Horfes? They feem to cut the Air with the fwiftnefs of their motion, fcarce to touch the ground beneath, like flying Clouds, *Venus*'s Doves, or *Juno*'s Peacocks. There's fomething of a folemn Joy fits upon his Face, which flafhes out, notwithftanding his endeavours to the contrary.

Intell. That Gentleman is a *Hiftory*, a *Mignion* of *Fortune*! if your *Ladyfhips* pleafe to repofe your felves a little at the end of this *Vifta*, before we afcend the *Palace*, I will, in as few words as poffible, fatisfie your Curiofity. His

Name

Name is the *Count Fortunatus*, rais'd by the concurrent Favour of two Monarchs, his own, and his Sisters Charms, from a meer Gentleman to that Dignity he is posting now, to Congratulate the new *Empress*, who outstrips her Successors in esteem of him; his Wife is her *She-favourite*, all will be manag'd in the new Reign by their Advice; big with the coming Hopes of being at the Head of the Empire, you can't blame him if some of that abundant Joy that fills his Breast, sparkles from his Eyes and brightens o'er his Face.

Virtue. I never heard of him before; alas! what pity 'tis, that a Person of his graceful Appearance shou'd make no application at all to *Virtue.*

Intell. Fortune has been his *Deity*, and entirely propitious to him, when he was at the Age of sixteen. His Friends, out of their narrow Fortune, with much ado, purchas'd him a Standard in one of the Establish'd Regiments of Foot-Guards; his Mother's Sister was Surintendant of the Family of the Dutchess *De L'inconstant*, *Sultana* Mistress to *Sigismund the Second*: The Youth us'd to make Collations, and fill his Belly with Sweet-meats with his Aunt; the Dutchess came one day unexpectedly down the Back-Stairs to take Chair, and found 'em together; he had slip'd away, for fear of anger, but not so speedily but she had a glimpse of his graceful Person; she ask'd who he was; and being answer'd, she caus'd him to be call'd, and all full of native Love and high Desire, for an Object so entirely New and Charming, she bid him attend her after the King's *Couchee*, who that Night was to lie of his own side. The

Gover-

Governess knowing the Dutchess's amorous Star, was transported at the happy introduction of her Nephew, not doubting but he was design'd for her peculiar Pleasures; she caus'd him him to Bath in the Dutchess's Bathing-room; Perfumes being then much worn by People of Condition, she procur'd him the richest, scented his fine Linen, and all sweet and charming as an *Adonis*, introduc'd him to the Bed-side of the expecting *Venus*.

The Dutchess was enchanted with the pleasures of her new and innocent Lover, a Lover whom she had made such, and who first sigh'd and felt, in favour of her, those amiable Disorders, and transporting Joys, that attend the possession of early Love; she presented him with an unlimited Bounty. The lovely Youth knew punctually how to improve those first and precious Moments of good-fortune, whilst yet the Gloss of Novelty remain'd, whilst Desire was unsated, and Love in the high Spring-tide of full delight; having an early Forcast, a Chain of Thought, unusual at his Years, a length of View before him, not born a Slave to Love, so as to reckon the possession of the charming'st Woman of the Court, as the *Zenith* of his Fortune, but rather the first auspicious, ruddy Streaks of an early Morning, an earnest to the Meridian of the brightest Day; he bethought himself of establishing himself at Court, in a Post so advantagious, that even the Dutchess herself might not be able to hurt him, should she (as she had often done before) change her inclination. *Sigismund* the Second was then on the Throne, a Prince devoted to Pleasures, but he was Childless, and the Eyes, tho' not the Hearts of the

Island,

(23)

Island, were cast upon his Brother, the Prince of *Tameran*; he had had several Children, but only two surviv'd, and they Daughters; the eldest was marry'd, for Reasons of Religion, to a neighbouring Prince; but as it is not their History that I am now designing, I will only tell you that of the *Count*. The Dutchess gave six thousand Crowns for a Place in the Prince's Bed-chamber for him, and, by her favour with the King, procured him a rise in the Army; she call'd about her own Person his fair and fortunate Sister; but his Ambition would not rest there, he never left interceding with the Dutchess, nor the Dutchess with *Sigismund*, till she was receiv'd into the number of the Maids that attended the Princess of *Tameran*, when, by an overplus of Fortune, the Prince cast his Eyes upon her, so much to her advantage, that she became his Mistress confess'd, and had several Children by him. So great an Indulgence for the Brother, accompanied his Passion for the Sister, that he either found or fancy'd Merit in him superiour to all the Court; he gave him a considerable command in the Army, and call'd him into the Nobility; returning from an Expedition he had made by Sea, the Ship wherein the Prince was, struck upon a dangerous Sand; it was inevitable Death to all but those cou'd save themselves in the Long-Boat; the awe of Royalty is such, even in the Breasts of the Vulgar, that the ignoble Crew willingly devoted themselves to the *Sea-green Deity*, to secure the Life of their Master; not one of them, tho' to avoid hasty destruction, pressed forward to secure themselves by entring the Boat, nor all of 'em together, by an eager precipitation, attempted, as in such

C 4   cases

cafes, to jump by confent into it, by overfetting it with numbers, to render their deftiny more inevitable, but one and all calling upon the Royal Brother, put him to defcend, with the good Wifhes and dying Prayers of the remaining Wretches. No fooner was the Prince feated, but he tenderly call'd for his dear Count, and commanded that not one, upon pain of immediate Death from his own Hand, fhould dare to come down till he was placed by him. How tenderly he embrac'd him! I knew not, my faithful Friend, faid the Prince, how dear you were to me till this ugly profpect of lofing you! how many have I difoblig'd by the open preference my Heart forc'd me to, in your advantage? Cou'd Life have been valuable to me, when you were out of it! I never lov'd any fo tenderly as you, nor you fo much as now! What can a Creature (owing all to his great Mafter) return for fuch an ineftimable Diftinction! anfwer'd the Count, happily bleft in your exalted Favour! unhappy in defpairing ever to have an opportunity of fhowing the leaft grain of my abundant Gratitude! fince when I have return'd you all; even to my Life, it is but what was your Highnefs's before; the beft gift of Nature I have this moment receiv'd from your Royal Favour; there will be no happinefs for me, nor an equality in my Deftiny, unlefs fome means be found to lofe in your Service (by an eminent Occafion) that Breath you have beftow'd upon me; but I, *more faithful than fortunate,* can only wifh, not expect a Deftiny fo Glorious.

Aftrea.

Astrea. Methinks I shudder with the dread or apprehension of the Count's Ingratitude! How do I foresee that he deserv'd not that distinction? Put me out of pain; has he not been ungrateful to the Royal Bounty?

Intell. More than all Mankind, because he was more beloved and trusted; but he has rose by it, and will in a moment (so favourable are the disposition of his Stars) touch the tallest Dignities of the Empire.

Astrea. Can *Great Jupiter* permit it? Methoughts long since (when in *Egypt*) I was pleased with that show of Justice in the *Egyptians*, their contempt of Ingratitude, in which they held all Wickedness was contained. 'Tis counted meritorious to forgive Injuries, but the most gentle Nature is permitted (with applause) to retain the memory of an ungrateful Act; it ought hardly ever to be forgotten, and 'tis as certain, that we shall find no Goodness in him that is ungrateful, as we are sure to find but little Evil in the grateful. Mankind wou'd in part avoid that shameful Vice, if they did but esteem the Benefits that they receive greater than they are, and those which they confer, less than in reality they be; but in moralizing I interrupt your Story, let me mark him down the foremost in my Pocket-Book, I will claim an especial Audience of *Jupiter*, in relation to the particular good Fortune of the Favourite *Count*, and resolve to lead my Prince wide of the Road he has travell'd in.

Intell. 'Tis time we should now return to shew how he lost the favour of the Dutchess, the first step upon which he mounted from Obscurity. *Fortune*, When she intends to go through
with

(26)

with a Hero, what ever would in an other be a falſe Step, is but in him, an Advance, conducing to her end. He fell paſſionately in love, with young *Jeanitan*, a Companion of his Siſters, and in the ſame Service about the Princeſs: Here all his Precaution forſook him, that *coolneſs* of *Temper*, that *allay* of *Fire*, that *paſſive Moderation*, ever uppermoſt, and to which he has ow'd his greateſt Succeſs; by this he has acquir'd thoſe appearances of *Virtue*, that are found in him; 'tis his *eaſy Phlegm*, that has ſuffer'd him, when at a Council, either of *War* or *State*, to permit, without the leaſt ſhow of Uneaſineſs, even the loweſt and worſt favour'd Perſon, to deliver his Opinion at length, tho' never ſo oppoſite to his own: He weighs 'em all with Deliberation, and yet remain fix'd to his firſt form'd Deſigns : Hence it is, that even in the heat of Fight he is not tranſported beyond his uſual Moderation; neither his Griefs upon a Diſapointment are exceſſive, nor the exaltings of his Joy upon a Victory: He neither *Cruelly* puniſhes nor *generouſly* forgives; 'tis all a *Medium*, and conſidering the extent of his Power, he has both done the leaſt Miſchiefs, and the ſmalleſt Good, of any that ever poſſeſs'd it. His *Flatterers* cry up his *Courage*, but it ſeems to me not to be *inborn* to him, but *acquir'd*; for certainly we may as well learn to be Valiant as Judicious. A proof of what I advance, may be taken from always ducking his Head at the noiſe of a Bullet, the firſt apprehenſion is in his *Nature*, and only to be controul'd not prevented by *Reaſon*: That immediately comes in for a Second, and carries him ſafely through to Glory, which all Hero's ſhould chiefly aim at; in ſhort he is

Ex-

Exceſſive in nothing, but his love of *Riches*; whether *Ambition* lies ſmothered beneath, and that he has ſome diſtant Views, a depth of Deſign, which none has yet had Line enough to fathom. *Mony* is the only means to carry on ſucceſſively the greateſt Enteprize; perhaps he may one Day, find our *Royal Ball*, the ſport of *Fortune*, a *Kingdom* at her diſpoſal, and to be obtain'd by the higheſt bidder; ſuppoſe him *Canditate* for the Crown of *Poland*, if among the many *Pretenders (Foreigners or others)* he have the *deepeſt* Purſe? 'Tis more than probable, his Succeſs will be the *higheſt*, either to conceal'd *Ambition*, or native *Covetouſneſs*, we muſt attribute his unbounded, unwearied deſire of *Wealth*; will he one Day ſet it all at Stake upon a *Royal Caſt*, or an *Imperial Squander*? Or deſcend to his Grave, choak'd with greedineſs of Gain, and a moſt prodigious, accumulated maſs of Wealth.

But to return to his Amours, what would have ruined another Man, ſerv'd but to advance him; his Love for a young Girl then without Intereſt, or the appearance of any, a Maid of Fortune, that was ſent to Court, and plac'd among the Rank of thoſe who generally owe their Eſtabliſhment to their Beauty, from whence the young unthinking Men of *Quality* and *Eſtates*, chooſe themſelves Wives of Fancy; 'tis well enough for thoſe, whoſe Affairs will permit them to Marry for *Inclination*, though it ſurvives not the *Hymenial Moon*; but for the *Count*, who depended for moſt of his great Expence upon the Dutcheſs, and to whom he ow'd all his Fortune, 'twas Ruin inevitable, 'twas Deſtruction bare-fac'd; yet Love, aſſiſted by his ever propitious Fortune, carried him through; his *Siſter*

lay

lay in his *Master's* Bosom, to protect him against the ill Effects of the Dutchesses Resentment, should she animate *Sigismund* against him; *Love* gave him this for Reason, *Love* is the Master of *Boldness*, he carries us fearless on to the greatest Attempts, and is ever most Fortunate where the Courage is most Resolute; *Love*, finds nothing difficult that leads to the Possession of what is *Beloved*. Young *Jeanitin* had a Mother, whose Cunning assisted the *Count* in the management of this Affair, she foresaw glorious Things for the *Hero*; the Publick would have it that she knew more than the common Race of Mortals; in short, that she was conversant with a *Dæmon*, who gave her to understand the Future. I do not report this as matter of *Faith*, but rumor has it, that she foretold the *Count's* rising to this heighth, when there was scarce a prospect of it: She bid him to rest there, and be contented to possess *Honour* and *Wealth* to an extream old Age; but if he advanc'd a step further, his *Glory* shou'd be *short*, and his *Death* violent. Time only can determine the *Oracle*; but this I believe, the *Count* will scarce consult it, or any thing else that seems a stop in his way to the *Goal* of *Grandeur*. But to return, he got his Master's Consent for Marrying the young *Jeanitin*, and the promise of his Protection against the Dutchess; who when she heard she was going to lose her *dear Count*, or at best, divide him with a Wife of *Inclination*, her haughty Soul, conscious of Beauty and superior Charms, resolv'd to revenge the neglect of 'em; he had lately (by quite an other pretence than that of his Marriage) drawn the last, and most considerable Sum from her; 'tis affirm'd that besides what she did for his

Sister,

Sister, and the Honours and Places of Profit she procur'd for him, out of her own Cash, she at times had presented him to the value of One Hundred and Forty Thousand *Crowns*; but what could he do? He had never lov'd her, cover'd with Charms as she was, 'tis only to be suppos'd that he well dissembled it, and in that point the *false* Lover, has a thousand Advantages over the true, they can personate all that's *necessary*, and are in no danger of the *Superfluons*; can imitate the *Transports*, and avoid the *Digustive* part; *Jealousy*, *Disquiets*, *Upbraidings*, are very well exchang'd, for perpetual *Applause*, *Flattery*, *Raptures*, pleasing *Sighs*, and never-ceasing *Joys*; the Dutchess was a Mistress in the Art of Distinction, as to the Merit of a Lover, and 'tis to be thought, that if the *Count* had not been a Masterpiece, he could not have *tallied* her Excellence: But (Ladies) in the pursuit of my Story, perhaps there may be somethings that are not very proper for so nice an Ear as *Virtue*, and 'till I receive your Commands in that point, however prompted as you see, by *Truth*, I am at a loss how to behave my self.

Virtue. Oh! my dear *Astrea*, this I foresaw in returning to the bad World; and if I did not urge it more to you at first, it was because I too willingly gave it to the Pleasure of accompanying you.

Astrea. *Justice* must impartially decide, to fit the *Person* for a *Judge*, he must be inform'd of the most minute particular, neither can we be polluted but by our *own*, not the Crimes of *others*. They stain nor reflect back upon us; but in our approbation of them. In the design I have form'd, 'tis necessary I should be throughly instructed; and

and you my Lady *Intelligence*, may if you please proceed, without any other Caution, than avoiding Terms unfit for you to explain by, or we to understand.

Intell. There was a young *Cavalier* just then come to Court (allied to a preceeding Favourite, which was his Introduction) named *Germanicus*, well *Form'd*, *Graceful*, and might very well be Candidate for the manly Beauties with the *Count*: The Dutchess had seen him in the *circle* with Approbation, as yet she had only heard of her Favourite's Marriage, as a thing intended, not resolv'd on: One Day she expostulated thus with her *Ingrateful*, Is it true, Monsieur *le Count*, that in neglect of all my Bounties, you dare to throw away a Heart I esteem, and have so dearly purchas'd, upon a Girl, who scorns to receive it at a lesser price than your perpetual Slavery? have I neglected the most agreeable Monarch upon Earth! have I bestow'd my Heart intirely upon you! and brought you in [a Glorious Rival] to divide with him the Possession of a Person, that all the World says is not unlovely? Have I call'd you from *Obscurity* and *Want*, to *Light* and *Riches*, thus to be rewarded? ah *Ungrateful!* Why am I form'd of the softer Passions? Why is not my Soul fir'd, as it ought, by the *rough* and *bold?* Why has not Anger and Revenge the ascendant of *Love* and *Joy?* Why am I more tempted to *Embrace* than Kill a Monster so Ingrateful! Here she cast her tempting Arms about the *Count's* Neck, and wet his Cheeks with drops of Love, (the overflowings of Desire) that fell from her fine Eyes; the *Count* overcome by the amorous pressure, took the Charmer in his Arms, and by reconciling himself to her

Re-

Resentment, made himself dearer to her Pleasures. 'Twas impossible she could part with what so luxuriously gave her Joys; no, my charming *Count*, we must never lose you, you must ever thus be renewing your Interest in my Heart, always be thus intolerably Engaging; will you leave me for another? Will you carry my Rights to the detested Arms of a Rival? Do I Breath? Do I Live? answer'd the *Count*; am I insensible of *Beauty* or of *Benefits*? Do I possess the *greatest*, and can I stoop to any *second*? Can I be more than bless'd? More than entirely happy! Wou'd I exchange all this *Elysium* of *Joys* for Ingratitude? Baseness, Inconstancy! never, my charming Dutchess! never believe so wrongfully of your truest Votary. *Jeanitin* is a little Creature I sometimes divert my self with at my Sisters, when you are otherways engag'd. *Vanity*! for she's a perfect *Coquet*; has made her report, (I'm sure she can't believe) that I am her *Conquest*; she that more than suspects I am favour'd by you, and must for ever despair of gaining so much as a glance from any Lover that you are pleased to make happy. I believe you, my Dear, answer'd the Dutchess, overcome with transport, you shall live only for me, and in return, take, take all that an over-indulgent Monarch has enrich'd me with! these *Jewels*! these *Bills* must be yours! I know nothing so valuable as your self, all my Treasure is at your Devotion, be you but mine. The King Hunts to Morrow, and will not be in Town till Night, let us pass the Afternoon at your House, in a waste of Joy, let us *live* whilst *Life* is pleasing, whilst there's a *poinancy* in the Taste, desire at heighth, the Blood in perfection, and all our Senses fitted for those Raptures you know so well how to receive and give.

The *Count* wou'd have very gladly componnded any thing (unless it were Treasure) that the Dutchess wou'd abate of her fondness, but, by a relief of Thought, he quickly guess'd his only way to come off with honour, was to make her the Aggressor; cou'd he but fit her with a new Lover, and catch her in the Embrace, he shou'd have a good pretence for his Marriage with *Jeanitin*; he had made a strict Friendship with *Germanicus*, from his first coming to Court, as he left the Dutchess's Appartment, he met the young Gentleman; happy Count, said he to him, from what Joys are you come? To possess the *Heart* and *Person* of the finest Woman of her Age! What wou'd I not do for one hour so bless'd? Nay, for but one moment of inexplicable Rapture! You may have thousands, my lovely Youth, answer'd the *Count*, if they are so necessary to your quiet, I'll make you entirely easie, if you'l but rely on me. Can you divide? Can you part with all that Heaven of Beauty? interrupted he, to a Friend, replied the Count, I can do any thing, to a Friend so much belov'd as your self; but how is it possible, you can give away such Joys? I could never do it! you speak the Language of a Lover, answer'd the Count, not yet obtaining, and that of *one* in full possession, and cloy'd with the too luscious Entertainment, there's a vast difference between *Desire* and *Enjoyment*, the *full* and *vigorous light* of the *Sun* compar'd with the *pale Glimers* of the *Moon*, is no ill Emblem of what I advance, yet tho' we surely know we shall be

Sated

Sated, we can't help desiring to *eat*, 'tis the Law of *Nature*, the pursuit is pleasing, and a Man owes himself the Satisfaction of gratifying those Desires that are importunate, and important to him.

 Here they debated, and at last concluded upon a Method to oblige *Germanicus*; the Dutchess went to the Count's the next Day, immediately after she had Din'd, she scarce allow'd her self time to eat, so much more valuable in her Sense were the Pleasures of Love; the Servants were all out of the way as usual, only one *Gentleman*, that told her, his Lord was lain down upon a Day-bed that join'd the *Bathing-Room*, and he believed, was fallen a Sleep since he came out of the *Bath*; the Dutchess softly enter'd that *little Chamber* of *Repose*, the Weather violently hot the *Umbrelloes* were let down from behind the Windows, the Sashes open, and the Jessimine that cover'd 'em blew in with a gentle Fragrancy; *Tuberoses* set in pretty *Gilt* and *China Posts*, were placed advantageously upon Stands, the Curtains of the Bed drawn back to the *Canopy*, made of yellow Velvet embroider'd with white *Bugles*, the Panels of the Chamber Looking-Glass, upon the Bed were strow'd with a lavish Profuseness, plenty of *Orange* and *Lemon Flowers*, and to compleat the Scene, the young *Germanicus* in a dress and posture not very decent to describe; it was he that was newly risen from the *Bath*, and in a lose Gown of *Carnation Taffety*, stain'd with *Indian Figures*, his beautiful long, flowing Hair, for then 'twas the Custom to wear their own, tied back with a Ribbon of the same Colour, he had thrown himself upon the Bed, pretending to Sleep, with nothing on but his Shirt and Night-Gown, which he had so indecently dispos'd, that slumbring as he appear'd, his whole Person stood confess'd to the Eyes of the Amorous Dutchess, his Limbs were exactly form'd, his Skin shiningly white, and the Pleasure the Ladies graceful entrance gave him, diffus'd Joy and Desire throughout all his Form; his lovely Eyes seem'd to be closed, his Face turn'd on one side (to favour the Deceit) was obscur'd by the Lace depending from the *Pillows* on which he rested; the Dutchess, who had about her all those *Desires*, she expected to employ in the Embraces of the Count, was so blinded by 'em, that at first she did not perceive the Mistake, so that giving her Eyes, time to wander over Beauties so inviting, and which encreased her Flame; with an amorous Sigh, she gently threw her self on the Bed close to the desiring Youth; the Ribbon of his Shirt-Neck not tied, the Bosom (adorn'd with the finest Lace) was open, upon which she fix'd her charming Mouth, impatient and finding that he did not awake, she rais'd her Head, and laid her Lips to that part of his Face that was reveal'd: The burning Lover thought it was now time to put an end to his pretended Sleep, he clasp'd her in his Arms, grasp'd her to his Bosom, her own Desires help'd the Deceit; she shut her Eyes with a languishing Sweetness, calling him by intervals, her dear Count, her only Lover, taking and giving a thousand Kisses, he got the possession of her Person, with so much transport, that she own'd all her former Enjoyments were imperfect to the Pleasure of this.

Still

Still *Charm'd* and *Breathless* with the Joy, he grasp'd her to his ravish'd Bosom: Glorious Destiny, cry'd he, with a transported Tone, by what means, Fortune, hast thou made me thy happy Darling? I am in possession of greater Joys then mortal Sense can bear. The Dutchess awak'd from her amorous Lethargy, by a Voice entirely strange, open'd her languishing Eyes, and seeing his charming Face, which she had often admir'd, and perhaps secretly Sigh'd for, stifl'd with his repeated Kisses, and charm'd with the strenuous Embrace, which held her, as a drowning Wretch is said to grasp the last thing he has hold of, new desire for so new and lovely an Object seiz'd her, she darted back his Kisses, return'd his Pressure, and in short, bestow'd upon *Germanicus*, what she before in her own Opinion had bestow'd upon the Count.

When they had lavishly sacrific'd to Love, the Dutchess, with a feigned Confusion, ask'd what was become of the Count, and whether he were such a Villain to depute another in his Place? So far from it, Madam, answered *Germanicus*, that I must expect to defend my Life, should he know of my good Fortune, for he would certainly put me to it. But where is he then ask'd the inquisitive fair One? Did you not receive a Letter from him? Heavens! I receive a Letter from him, for what? when he expected my self, what is the Mystery of all this? Ah! return'd the dissembling Lover, the Count is posess'd, he knows not what he does, his Affairs call'd him another way, he writ you an Excuse, not doubting but it would come early enough, and see if the Hair-brain'd Creature have not left it behind him; the Paper that I see lie upon yonder Stand, must certainly be that. The impatient Dutchess made but two steps from the Bed before she got it in her Hand, and finding it was really addressed to herself, she hastily broke the Seal, and read these Words.

Till Night at ten a Clock, my lovely Dutchess, I can't be happy in your Charms; at that hour I'll wait on you, with a Heart full of impatient Love, to complain to you of what has detain'd me from my happiness.

The Traitor's Sense is degenerated, as well as his Kindness, continu'd the Dutchess; but you, my fortunate Lover, can, if you please, unriddle this Affair: Have you the Power to refuse me? Cannot my Kindness triumph over your Fidelity to the *Count*? Let it get the better of your Confusion? Must I ask you twice? How *irresistable*, and how *dangerous* are you, Madam, answer'd *Germanicus*, I sacrifice my Friend! after that, never doubt, but I wou'd sacrifice my Life. *Jeanatin* has sent for him. How! that *little Creature* interrupted the Dutchess, Heavens! am I betray'd for so worthless a Baggage? Henceforward I'll hate him more than I ever lov'd him; I'll be reveng'd, his Life shall answer it: But you! how came you by the liberty of the Apartment, thus undress'd, thus ruinously tempting? The *Count* sometimes makes me his Bedfellow, Madam, last Night I was so; the Weather being extremely hot, after Dinner we went into the Bath; he expected your Excellence, and intended to receive you in his own Bed-chamber; by that means this little Room of Repose was left to me, where I was to suffer the killing Rack of knowing the *Count* more happy than I could ever pretend to be:

Jeanatin

Jeanatin sent him a flight Invitation to make one at *Ombre* this Afternoon; the ill-Judging Madman preferr'd the dull diverfion of Cards, with a worthlefs Girl, before the moſt tranfporting Joys in Nature, with the moſt lovely of her Sex: He writ that Letter, and it feems, in the hurry of his Thoughts, (fortunately for me) forgot to fend it. He went down the Backſtairs, and crofs'd the Gardens to her Lodgings, by which means, I fuppofe the Gentleman in waiting did not fee him; all his other People, as expecting your Excellence after Dinner, were order'd to depart the Houfe: But how happy have I been made by his neglect? It can receive no addition, but from the affurance that my lovely Dutchefs does not repent the Favours fhe has fuffer'd me to take. But what Excufe does the *Villain* intend to make me at ten a Clock, anfwer'd the Lady, both the *King* and his *Mafter* are in the Country, and even their Service ought, in his efteem, to yield to mine? How blinded have I been? He faid, Madam, that Love wou'd be propitious, (reply'd *Germanicus*) and before ten a Clock furnifh him with a current Excufe for your Excellence: Never, never, will I any more hear the Traytor; you fhall take his place in my Arms and Heart. The happy Youth was dazzled at this affurance, and, after they had lov'd away three or four hours, fhe was preparing to depart: The new Lover refolv'd to pufh for the continuation of his good Fortune, and to merit her Favour by excefs of Love, prevail'd with her for one more tempting Embrace: The Lady yielded with a pleafing willingnefs, furpriz'd and charm'd by a Lover that then even exceeded himfelf. In that dan-

dangerous moment the *Count* (as they had agreed) with softly treading steps enters the Chamber, and finds the happy Pair at the *ultimate* of all their *Joys*. The Scene was admirable; *Germanicus* counterfeited Confusion, the *Count* a transport of *Anger*; the Dutchess, without counterfeiting, was really so, and, by an admirable *Boldness* and *Haughtiness* of Nature, ask'd him how he durst presume to enter a Place where his Gentleman must tell him she was, without giving notice at the Door? He indeed ask'd her pardon, for, knowing the warmth of her Constitution, he said, he might well conclude, she cou'd not be long in a Bed-chamber, with a handsom young Gentleman, without Consequences; favour'd by his *Disabilly*, all tempting, the Bed, and her more *favourable Inclination*. Be gone, cry'd the Dutchess, I banish you for ever; you that can prefer *Jeanatine* to me! I banish my self, Madam, answer'd the *Count*, from the most *immoderate* of her Sex; what the first moment to bestow your self upon another! whilst my Image yet wanton'd before your Eyes! whilst your Blood yet mantled by those desires my Idea had mingled with it! you that know how nice I am in Point of *Amour*! that for all the Treasure the Sea and Earth can boast, wou'd not divide the Heart I adore with any other. I suffer'd the concurrence of a potent Monarch (who had a prior right) but with *regret*, and sometimes *indignation*, tho' I never suspected that he rival'd me in your *Heart*, but *Person*; but this *tempting Youth*, this *pollish'd Adonis*, is too perfect not to have touch'd your *Heart*, as well as your *Desires*; yet it had been *Modesty*, as well as *Prudence*, to defer his Joy till

till you had given him time to sigh after the Bleffing, is too great to be fo eafily obtain'd; I am undone by your killing Perfidy, I can never forgive it, neither can I ceafe to love you! I'll this Night Marry *Jeanatine* (a Creature I before contemn'd) to be reveng'd of your Infidelity if it be true that you have any remains of that Favour you formerly honoured me with, at leaft, I fhall *pique* your *Pride*, when in your turn you fhall findy ourfelf forfaken, for a thing of not the tenth part of your value. Here he flung out of the Chamber. The Dutchefs, ftung with his threatning, and not yet refolv'd to part with him, efpecially to her Rival, attempted to ftop him; but he broke with precipitation from her. Ah, the *Traitor*! faid fhe, how glad his Ingratitude is of this occafion! my lovely Youth, what have we not to fear? He will ruin us with *Sigifmund*, but I fhall take care to prevent him.

What fhe forefaw came to pafs exactly: He took his Meafures fo well (tho' his Friend were facrific'd by it) that it was *Sigifmund*'s own fault he did not twice, at her Lodgings, find *Germanicus* in Bed with her; but he was a a Prince perfectly good-natur'd, full of *Love* and *Inconftancy*, and made ftrange allowances for the Frailties of Flefh and Blood. Thus Indulgent he fuffer'd a great Belly of the Dutchefs (due to that happy amorous Rancounter of the Bugle-Bed) to pafs in the efteem of the World (as the reft of hers had done) for his. Indeed he got him another Miftrefs whom he entirely devoted himfelf to, without quarrelling with the Dutchefs; he fometimes faw her in turn, but never after with Efteem. Thus you find how grateful the *Count* was to her, the Foundation

(40)

of all his Fortune. He immediately Marry'd *Jeanatine*, and from that moment difus'd all Converfation with the Dutchefs. The new *Bride*, well inftructed by her *Husband* and her *Mother*, made her Court fo fuccefsfully to the Princefs of *Invernefs*, that fhe became her profeffed Favorite. [P.ᵉ of Denmark / Qu.ⁿ Anne] The young Princefs had admirable good Inclinations, but without confulting them, they had marry'd her, according to *Royal Cuftom*, to the Prince of *Invernefs*, before fhe had ever feen him. Count *Lofty*, whofe good Senfe was totally obfcur'd by *Pride*, caft his ambitious Thoughts fo high, as to pretend to pleafe the Princefs, whilft yet fhe was a Maid. [D. of Buckᵐ / D. of Buckingh Sheffield] The *Favorite Countefs*, for fo we fhall call her now, no longer *Jeanatine*, took the alarm at his being fo tenderly receiv'd by the Princefs; fhe put his Poetical Declaration of Love into her Husband's Hand; her Policy fuggefted to her, that fhe ought not to fuffer a Rival Favorite, efpecially one of the Heart; in difcharge of Duty pretended, but in reality of Intereft, advis'd him to acquaint his Mafter with it. 'Twas done as defign'd, the audacious Lover forbid the Court, and the Lady immediately Betrothed to the Prince of *Invernefs*: [Pr. of Denk / P. of Denmark] Some time after he arriv'd, and they were publickly Marry'd. The Princefs has fince been an Example of Conjugal Happinefs, they have lov'd and deferv'd each other; nor cou'd there be any objection againft her, but in fo entirely refigning herfelf up to the Countefs's Management, who introduc'd the *Count* to her Miftrefs with fuch fuccefs, that nothing was refolv'd on in that little Court, without firft confulting and having their approbation.

Thus

(41)

Thus Time roul'd on in an uninterrupted Series of good Fortune for the *Count*; *Sigismund* dy'd, and he was, by a most advantagious Remove, drawn nearer to the Throne. A Natural Son of *Sigismund* pretended to succeed; but the Prince of *Tameran*, with the Fears, more than Acclamations of the People, was Crown'd. There was no Honours that the *Count* and his Sister might not expect in this new Reign; but he immediately saw that the Monarch had not the Hearts of his Subjects; he was a Bigotted Christian, a different Religion from that Establish'd in *Atalantis*. The *Count* dreaded falling (as a Favorite) a Sacrifice to the incens'd Rabble. His Master, wholly guided by his too zealous Priests, totter'd in the Throne. Young *Casario*, *Sigismund*'s Natural Son, was belov'd: He had been banish'd by his Father, and was refug'd in Prince *Henriquez*'s Court, who had marry'd the new King of *Atalantis*'s Daughter. The Peoples Wishes call'd aloud for him, to secure their Fears against the growing Tyranny of the Priests. The Count had no Interest in the young *Casario*, a Prince of little depth, entirely in the Hands and Interest of a Factious Party: He trembled to think, if he once prevail'd, himself must either fall, as a Favorite of the foregoing Monarchs, or waste the remainder of his Life in inglorious Obscurity; he therefore cast about, and, with the Cabal of the principal Lords of *Atalantis* in concert, sent to Prince *Henriques*, to invite him over to their Relief, from Oppression, and *holy Fears* of Slavery. 'Tis true, he betray'd in this a Master who tenderly lov'd him, but a Master *Indiscreet* and *Bigotted*, that cou'd not in all probability long support

port himſelf, ond therefore he held it wiſe to evade a falling Ruin. Prince *Henriquez* had a conſummate Courage, deep Diſſimulation, under which he conceal'd the moſt towring Ambition. The *Count* advis'd that he ſhou'd lend Aid to *Cæſario*, who implor'd it, to Invade *Atalantis*, where the Hearts and Hands of the People were ready to aſſiſt him: Aid not ſufficient to ſerve, but to betray him. 'Twas done as projected; *Cæſario*'s Enterprize miſcarry'd, and his Life fell a Sacrifice to the Laws that he had broken. After which *Henriquez* was conſider'd as the Succeſſor: He came over with a much more powerful Army. The *Count* had a tender Conſcience, and cou'd not act to the prejudice of his Intereſt; he left an indulgent Maſter, and went to *Henriquez*, who was ſhortly after Crown'd, with the Acclamation and Approbation of the major part, by the Name of *Henriquez* the Ninth.

In this Warlike Reign, the Count ſupported himſelf in the King's Favour and Eſteem by his natural and acquir'd Merit, he ſhared in all his Secrets of *War* and *Government*; 'tis this Prince who is now Dead, after a long and troubleſome Reign, turmoil'd with *Factions*, and involv'd in a perpetual Foreign *War*: The Count is the only Perſon that will be thought fit to purſue the Deſigns, *Henriquez* had form'd, the Empreſs will undoubtedly make him her *General*, what may he not expect? What will he not perform?

Germanicus made an ample Fortune by the Dutcheſſes Favour, but diſliking all Court Factions, he wiſely Married and retir'd himſelf from
Govern-

Government remote from *Courts*, he ended his Days in a pleasing *Obscurity*.

The Dutchess by her Prodigality to Favourites, fell into extream neglect, her Temper was a perfect Contradiction, unboundedly *lavish*, and sordidly *Covetous*, the former to those who administer'd to her particular Pleasures, the other, to all the rest of the World, when Love began to forsake her, and her Charms were upon the turn, because she must still be a Bubble, she fell into Gamester's Hands, and play'd off that Fortune *Sigismund* had enrich'd her with; she drank deep of the bitter Draught of Contempt, her successive Amours, with mean ill form'd Domesticks, made her abandon'd by the esteem and pity of the World; her Pension was so ill pay'd, that she had oftentimes not a Pistole at Command, then she solicited the Count (whom she had rais'd) by his Favour with the Court, that her Affairs might be put into a better posture, but he was Deaf to all her Intreaties; nay, he carried his Ingratitude much further; one Night at an Assembly of the best Quality, where the Count *Tallied* to 'em at *Basset*, the Dutchess lost all her Mony, and beg'd the favour of him, in a very civil Manner, to lend her twenty Pieces, which he absolutely refus'd, tho' he had a thousand upon the Table before him, and told her coldly the Bank never lent any Mony: Not a Person upon the Place but blam'd him in their Hearts; as to the Dutchesse's part, her Resentment burst out in a Bleeding at her Nose, and breaking of her Lace, without which aids, it is believ'd her Vexation had kill'd her upon the Spot.

Astrea

Astrea. We are entertain'd with an other Object, who is that Person not very *young* nor *handsome*, yet something august and solemn in his *Mien*, he that walks up the *Vista*? He sees us not, 'tis certainly one that lov'd the departed Monarch, his Handkerchief is in his Hand, his Eyes red and full of Tears; he comes hither doubtless to weep in Solitude, a Master upon whom his Fortune probably depended.

Intell. He weeps indeed, and he lov'd his Master, but his Fortune is the greatest of all the Favourites, therefore are his Tears the more Merritorious, yet is he not free from the Vices of Men in Power; the greediness of Gain and unbounded Ostentation, in expending with Noise and Splendor, in Foreign Courts, what he by Cunning had aquir'd in this. Love has had his turn, in a fatal manner! Fatal I mean to the unhappy Object of his Flame, rais'd from a mean degree, 'tis no wonder his Head is guidy with the heighth; if Pride and Contempt of those beneath them, be fashionable Manners, worn ev'n by those that are born Great, we need not wonder to find 'em assum'd by Persons that oftner by Chance, than true Merit, touch a Fortune unexpected; yet is the Duke's Fidelity to his Master to be applauded, and as well as he loves *Riches*, he could never be bought to depart from the King's Interest; he has been bred to the business of the State and Cabinet, he perfectly knows the management of Affairs, the posture of his own and that of his Neighbour-Nations; their true and their false Interests. He is not Eloquent but Wise; to be short, few Princes but would be glad of such a Servant, for since in the Composition of the Human Frame,

Frame, Vices are generally blended with the Vertues, we are to Reverence that Man, who suffers not, to the Prejudice of his Master, the former to get the ascendant.

If I be not tiresome, I design a short Sketch of the Amour he had with a Lady, truly named Unfortunate, I will take the Duke as high as from his first coming to Court a Boy, to attend Prince *Henriquez*, as his Page of *Honour*; when Persons have their Fortune to make, and are born with little or no Estate, 'tis necessary that they have a lucky hit, a happy Introduction, a leading Card to make a prosperous Game; Such the Duke met with, and had the Courage and Address to lay hold of the opportunity. Prince *Henriquez* fell ill of a malignant Distemper, Medicine was at a loss, it seem'd as if Art were no more, the *Physicians* could find no Drugs of sufficient Heat to throw out the Distemper; without which, inevitable Death was all that could be expected. One of those Sons of *Esculapius*, propos'd, that a Youth of Warmth and Vigour, should be put to Bed to him, by that natural glow of Body, to call out the Malignancy of the Distemper; the Duke was the only Person, that with Pleasure and Boldness, offer'd his own, to save the Life of his Master, he would not ev'n stay to take his leave of any of his Friends, but with the greatest Bravery throwing off his Cloaths got into Bed to the *Prince*, embracing closely his Feverish Body, from whence he never stirr'd, 'till the happy Effects of his kind Endeavours, were visible; the Disease past from the *Heart* into the *Blood*, from thence by the Application of a kindly warmth, 'twas thrown into the Flesh and Skin;

after

after which the Symptoms being favourable, they no longer doubted the Life of the Prince; but the generous Youth cou'd not escape the Infection, it seiz'd him in such a terrible manner, that Destiny was expected to be fatal to him. They remov'd him to another Bed. The Prince tenderly regreted his Sufferings, assur'd him, that he hop'd he wou'd Live, to find in his *Friendship* and *Gratitude* the rewards of *Fidelity* and *Generosity*. The Gods were too well pleas'd at so glorious an Action to let him sink under it, after an unusual and bitter Conflict, they restor'd him to his former Health and Vigour; and if he still wear the cruel Marks of so malignant a Distemper, they are in him but glorious Proofs of *Love* and *Duty* to his Prince; no less to be rever'd than the most flourishing Laurels of others.

Not one of the most fortunate Courtiers but dreaded the tow'ring Genius of the Youth; they saw he was resolv'd to push, tho' at the expence of Life, rather than not to make his Fortune to sink under the endeavour. *Henriquez* was young, *Human*, dispos'd by Nature (all Heroe as he was) to the soft trusts and joys of Friendship: He call'd the Youth nearer to his Confidence, found in him a strength of Mind, a Capacity far above his Years, a projecting Brain, with a height of Courage, able to put in practice the boldest Resolutions. The Prince had in his Nonage been oppressed by a potent Faction, that left him only a titular Sovereignty; he had no longer the Command of his own Fleet and Armies, all were at the disposal of those who pretended to Administer to the

the Publick Good. He wou'd often lament with his young Favorite the oppression: His inborn Courage, and boiling Youth, made him long to rush into the Field of Glory, to snatch from thence those Laurels that were not to be attain'd but with the greatest difficulty! At the Head of his own Armies, to meet the Enemy of his Country, who with hostile Fire, and cruel Slaughter had successfully Invaded it. The young Statesman (by his intriegue and management with some of the Head Officers) procured that a Battle shou'd be lost. The Event was fatal to the two Brothers that opposed the Prince, and were at the Head of the State: The People (dreading the approach of the Conqueror call'd aloud for their own Sovereign to defend 'em. They rush'd unanimously upon the two Usurpers, with as much ease and fierceness, as a hungry Lyon, the devouring Woolf, or Tyger, falls upon the harmless Flock; and, with the same expedition (animated by the Intriegues, Cabals, and Spirit of our young Favorite) rends 'em piecemeal! scatters their Body small as the Dust thrown into the Air! swift as destruction, and mortal Plagues fall from the Hands of the avenging Deities, when by the accumulated Sins of Mortals they are justly provok'd.

This was no sooner perform'd, but they rush into the Palace, seize upon *Henriquez*, bear him (with exultings of rapturous Joy) upon their Shoulders, force open the Door of the *Divan*, and with Acclamations that pierced the Skies! seat the Prince upon the Royal Throne! Invest him with the Purple Robe, the Sword of Defence, the awful Diadem, and all other
Ensigns

Stadholder — Enſigns of Sovereignty! take a voluntary Oath of Fidelity! perform their Homage! and then with the ſame Exclamations (of rude and haſty Joy) preſent him to the Army! who eccho'd back (with loud Shootings) their Approbation of what was done. The *Prince* and his *young Favorite*, harangue and careſs the Soldier and People; he tells 'em (like his glorious Anceſtors) he longs to loſe his Blood in defence of his Country! that he will either die or relieve 'em from the Oppreſſion of the Invader! They one and all demand him to lead 'em on to Conqueſt and Revenge.

No Age has ever ſhown us a Hero made up of greater Compoſitions! *Henriquez* was ardent for Battle, yet cautiouſly prudent to watch all the Advantages of it: His young Favorite, with his Valour, maintain'd that Opinion he had acquir'd; by Conduct and politick Management, they put a ſtop to the rapid Courſe of the Enemy's Victories, and regain'd the Towns that were loſt. The progreſs of the young Hero's Arms, rais'd a jealouſie in all his Neighbours; they envy'd him the greenneſs of his Laurels; and to put a ſtop to that Glory, which elſe had known no bounds, they force him to a *Treaty* with the Enemy. Whilſt the Peace was concluding, by their dreaming Plenipotentaries, a Peace diſpleaſing to the Prince and his Favorite, and which nothing but their newneſs in Power cou'd force 'em to ſubmit to, he let all *Europe* ſee how much in the wrong they were, in impoſing it upon him now, when he was in a condition to force the Enemy to yield the Allies their own Terms. He fell upon their *General* ſo haſtily and unexpectedly (tho' he were the

Hero

Hero of his Age) that he put him into an irretrievable Disorder. The Battle was Glorious for *Henriquez*; but the less so, for that it was no sooner decided to his advantage, but the repeated Thund'ring of the Canon gave him to know that the Peace was Publish'd, and that those he had so lately fought with, were no longer his Enemies. The Dispatch was brought him at the Head of his Army, when he was just going to engage. The Courier knew nothing of the Contents, or did not report 'em. The Prince wou'd not delay attacking the Enemy: They were then (knowing the Peace was concluded) upon their March; he resolv'd to fall in with their Rear. Should he have staid to open the Pacquet, the opportunity would have been lost; and possibly guessing what it imported, he order'd the Courier to his Tent, there to expect his return. Envy (that is always busie in blotting the Actions of Hero's) has made ours reflected on, for a Breach of the Law of Nations; they rob him of the Glory of his Conquest, by condemning the unlawfulness of the Occasion.

After this the young Favorite (tho' formerly but of his Pleasures) became his first Minister. He was always trusted, and extreme *habile* in the Affairs of State; he follow'd the wise Maxims of *Machiavel*, who aim'd to make his Prince Great, let what wou'd be the price. He it was that encourag'd *Count Fortunatus*, and the Disaffected Lords of *Atlantis*, to expel their Bigotted Monarch: By his politick Management the young *Cæsario* was sacrific'd; and the Prince call'd to take possession of the Government; without such a Head as his (cunning to conceal, crafty

(50)

to foresee, wise to project, and valiant to undertake) the whole Fabrick had totter'd. He was the solid Foundation upon which the greatest *Hero* of the Age has rais'd himself to be such; tho' in all his Advices the finishing Stroke still came from *Henriquez*.

Now rais'd to be Earl and *Peer*, *General* of the *Army*, in possession of the Ear and Cabinet of the Prince, whom we must henceforward (if we have occasion to speak of him) call King. He gave up himself to amass Riches! his Ambition was not satisfied! he aim'd at something more! 'Twas Glorious to be a Sovereign Prince, tho' but of a Petty State! He offer'd sixteen hundred thousand Crowns for the Succession, where only a Princess Dowager was in Possession, and to become her Husband. Affairs of that Consequence, that depend not upon Action but Treaty, are generally tedious: Whilst it was depending, our Duke felt the Sting of a Passion, which (at the expence of the Ladies) he had hitherto only play'd with. There was a young Girl, nam'd *Madmoisel Charlot*, left to his Care by her Father, for whom he had had as great a Friendship, as a Statesman can be suppos'd to have. The young *Charlot* had lost her Mother long before: Her Dowry amounted to forty thousand Crowns; the Family was Noble, and there was almost nothing but what she might pretend to. The Duke had been some considerable time a Widower; his Wife was of the Family of the Favorites, naturally Born to the soothing Arts of Courts. 'Fame is not afraid to speak aloud, that *Henriquez* saw what was agreeable in her; and when wearied with the Fatigues of Hunting, wou'd go to Bed between

tween her and her Husband; but you may be sure all very innocent, especially where such a witness was in place. When she dy'd, he transferr'd his Esteem, with an additional Tenderness, to her Sister. She affected first to be in Love with the *Hero*, not the *Prince*. Personal Lovers are so rarely found among People of their Station; so few are acquainted with the delicacy of dividing the *Monarch* from the *Man*, that out of gratitude he gave into those Endearments that were necessary to bespeak a reciprocal Passion: And as his Temper to his Favorites was magnificiently Lavish, she tasted all the Sweets of unlimited Majesty, and the charming Effects of unbounded Generosity!

But to return to the Duke. He spar'd for no expence in the Education of young *Charlot*; she was brought up at his own House with his Children; but having something the advantage in Age of his Daughters, the Precepts were proportionably advanced. He design'd her (in those early Days of his Power) as a Wife for his Son, before the increase of his own Ambition, and Riches taught him other desires; that is to say, to look out a Lady for the young Lord with more than six times *Charlot's* Fortune: And indeed he was not to blame in that, for certainly all that Fable has ever reported of *Adonis*, *Narcissus*, the most beautiful of the *Hero's*, the united Sweetness and Graces of Mankind, are to be found in his Person! with an unknown Goodness of Temper! an Air of perfect Behaviour and accomplish'd Courtship! neither has he shown us an Inclination to any Vice, that might balance these Perfections! but as Malice loves to mingle in the Characters ev'n

of

of the most deserving; not being able to find a fault from without, have recourse to the inside, and assure us there of a Genius no way proportionable to the Greatness of his Fathers; a softness of Conversation, which they otherways term a weakness of Intellects. But the Ladies find no such fault with the charming Youth; he has all things in his Person, Voice and Discourse, that prove him indeed irresistable! besides, occasion calls not upon him to exert his Faculties, as they did the Duke; his Fortune is made, his Father was Born before him, and so happily too, as from a meer Gentleman to make himself one of the Richest and most Potent Subjects in *Europe*.

Charlot was no great Beauty, her Shape was the best; but Youth and Dress make all things agreeable. To have prepossessed you in her favour, I shou'd, as I was inclin'd, have advanc'd a System of her Charms; but *Truth*, who too well foresaw my Intentions, has repell'd 'em with a Frown; not but *Charlot* had many Admirers; there's something so touching in the *agreeable*, that I know not whether it does not enchant us deeper than Beauty; we are oftentimes upon our guard against the attack of that, whilst the unwary Heart, careless and defenceless, as dreading no surprize, permits the *agreeable* to manage as they please.

The Duke had a seeming Admiration for Virtue, wherever he found it, but he was a Statesman, and held it incompatible (in an Age like this) with a Mans making his Fortune, *Ambition, desire of Gain, Dissimulation, Cunning,* all these were meritoriously serviceable to him: 'Twas enough he always applauded Virtue, and in his Discourse decry'd Vice; as long as he stuck close in his Practice, no matter what became of his Words, these are not times where the Heart and the Tongue do not agree! However, young *Charlot* was to be educated in the high road to applause and Virtue, he banish'd far from her Conversation whatever would not edify, Airy *Romances*, *Plays*, dangerous *Novels*, *loose* and *Insinuating Poetry*, artificial Introductions of *Love*, well-painted Landskips of that dangerous Poyson; her Diversions were always among the sort that were most Innocent and Simple, such as Walking, but not in publick Assemblies; Musick in Airs all Divine; reading and improving Books of Education and Piety; as well knowing, that if a Lady be too early us'd to violent Pleasures, it debauches their Tastes for ever to any others, he taught her to beware of *Hopes* and *Fears*; never to desire any thing with too much eagerness; to guard herself from those dangerous Convulsions of the Mind; that upon the least Disappointment precipitates into a Million of Inconveniencies; he endeavour'd to cure her of those number of Affections and Aversions so natural to young People, by shewing her that nothing truly deserved to be passionately belov'd, but the *Gods*, because they alone were perfect, though nothing on the other Hand ought to be hated but Vice, because we are all the Image of their Divinities; he wisely and early forewarn'd her, from what seem'd too natural to her, a desire of being applauded for her Wit; she had a brightness of Genius, that would often break out in dangerous Sparkles; he shew'd her that true Wit consisted not in much speaking, but in speaking much

much in a few Words, that whatever carried her beyond the knowledge of her Duty; carried her too far; all other Embelishments of the Mind were more dangerous than useful, and to be avoided as her Ruin; that the possession of 'em was attended with *Self-Love*, *Vanity* and *Coquettry*, things incomparable and never mingled in the Character of a Woman of true Honour; he recommended *Modesty* and *Silence*; that she should shun all occasions of speaking upon Subjects not necessary to a Ladies Knowledge, tho' it were true that she spoke never so well; he remembred her, that so Great, so Wise a Man as *Zeno*, of all the Virtues made choice of Silence, for by it he heard other Mens Imperfections, and conceal'd his own; that the more Wit she was Mistress of, the less occasion she had to show it; that if want of it gave a disgust, too much does not generally please better, *That* assuming Air that generally accompanies it, is distatsteful to the Company, where all pretend an equal right to be heard; the weakness of Human Nature is such, the chiefest Pleasure of Conversation lies in the speaking, not the hearing part, and if a presumptious Person (though with never so great a Capacity) pretends to usurp once upon that Priviledge, they look upon her as a Tyrant, that would ravish from 'em the Freedom of their Votes. But his strongest Battery was united against *Love*, that invader of the *Heart*; he show'd her how shameful it was, for a young Lady ever so much as to think of any tenderness for a Lover, 'till he was become her Husband; that true Piety and Duty would instruct her in all that was necessary for a good Wife to feel of that dangerous Passion; that she should not

so

so much as ever seek to know what was meant by that shameful Weakness call'd Jealousy; 'twas abominable in us to give others occasion to be Jealous, and painful to be so our selves; that 'tis generally attended with *Slander* and *Hatred*, two base and contemptible Qualities; That that violent *inborn* desire of pleasing so natural to Ladies is the pest of Virtue, they would by the Charms of their Beauty, and their sweet and insinuating way of Conversation, assume that native Empire over Mankind, which seems to be politically deny'd them, because the way to Authority and Glory is stop'd up: Hence it is that, with their aquir'd Arts and languishing Charms, they risque their *Virtue* to gain a little contemptible Dominion over a Heart that at the same time it surrenders it self a Slave; refuses to bestow esteem upon the Victor; that Friendship was far nobler in its Nature, and much to be prefer'd to Love; because a *Friend loves always, a Lover but for a time*; that under the most flattering appearances is conceal'd inevitable Ruin; the very first Impressions were dreadful, and to be carefully suppressed. *Pythagoras, Taught, the assaults of Love were to be beaten back at the first Sight, least they undermine at the second. And* Plato *that the first step to Wisdom was not to love ; the second so to love, as not to be perceived.*

Fraught with these, and a number more of such Precepts such as these, the young *Charlot* seem'd to intend her self a Pattern for the Ladies of this degenerate Age, who divide their Hours between the *Toylet* and *Basset* Table; wich is grown so totally the Business of the Fair; that even the Diversions of the *Opera, Gallantry* and *Love,* are but secondary Pleasures: A Person who

who has once given her felf up to Gaming, neglects all her Duties, diforders her Family, breaks her Reft, forgets her Husband, and by her Expence often inconveniences him irreparably, together with their wafte of time: The Paffions of Anger and Avarice, concur to make her odious to all, but thofe who ingage with her at that dangerous Diverfion; not to inftance, who have compounded for the lofs of Mony, with the lofs of their Chaftity, and Honour; nor is it a new, tho' frequent, way of paying of Play-Debts, in this entirely corrupted Age.

Bulstrode The Duke had a magnificent *Villa* within five Leagues of the Capital, adorn'd with all that's imaginable Beautiful, either in Art or Nature; the pride of Conqueft, the plunder of Victory, the homage of the Vanquifh'd, the prefents of Neighbouring Monarchs, and whatever Curiofity could inform, or Mony recover, were the Ornaments of this Palace. *Henriquez* had received a new Favourite into his Bofom, but it was a Favourite not at all interfering with the Duke; who was ever trufted and efteemed; by this means he oftner found a recefs from Court; his great Mafter would fometimes in Goodnefs difmifs him to his *Villa*, to tafte a reft from Power, a calm of Greatnefs, a fufpenfe of Bufinefs, a refpiration of Glory; here it was, that he us'd to confirm the young *Charlot* in that early love of Virtue that had been taught her, to unbend her Mind from the more ferious Studies; he fometimes permitted her thofe of *Poetry*, not loofe Defcriptions, lafcivious Joys or wanton heightnings of the Paffions; they fung and acted the Hiftory of the *Gods*; the Rape of *Proferpine*, the defcent of *Ceres*, the Chaftity of *Diana*, and

such

such pieces that tended to the instruction of the Mind. One Evening at a Representation, where *Charlot* personated the Goddess, and the Duke's Son *Acteon*, she Acted with so animated a Spirit, and cast such Rays of Divinity about her, gave every Word so twanging, yet so sweet an Accent, that awaken'd the Duke's Attention; and so admirably she varied the Passions, that gave Birth in his Breast, to what he had never felt before; he applauded, embrac'd, and even kiss'd the charming *Diana*; 'twas Poyson to his Peace, the cleaving sweetness thrill'd swiftly to his Heart, thence tingled in his Blood, and cast Fire throughout his whole Person; he Sigh'd with Pleasure! he wondered what those Sighs meant! he repeats his Kisses, to find if *Charlot* were the occasion of his Disorder. Confirm'd by this new taste of Joy, he throws the young Charmer hastily from him, folds his Arms, and walks off with continu'd Sighs! the innocent Beauty makes after him modest and afraid, insinuatingly and with trembling she enquires, if she have not offended? Begs to know her Fault, and that she will endeavour to repair it. He answers her not but with his Eyes, which have but too tender an Aspect; the Maid (by them) improving her Courage, comes nearer, spreads her fond Arms about him, and in her usual fawning Language calls him dear *Pappa*, joins her Face, her Eyes, her Cheeks, her Mouth close to his; by this time the Duke was fallen upon a Chair that stood next him, he was fully in her reach, and without any opposition she had leisure to difuse the irremediable Poison through his Veins: he sat immoveable to all her Kindness, but with the greatest taste of Joy, he had ever been sensible

sible of. Whilst he was thus dangerously entertain'd, the young *Acteon*, and the rest of the Company, join 'em, the Duke was forc'd to rouze himself from his Love-sick Lethargy; *Charlot* wou'd leave him, till he wou'd tell her in what she had done amiss? He only answer'd her, that he had nothing to object; she had acted her part but too well. The young Lady had been taught (in her cold Precepts of Education) that it was a degree of fault to excel, even in an' Accomplishment. Occasion was not to be sought of eminently distinguishing one's self, in any thing but solid Virtue; she fear'd she had shown too great a Transport in representing *Diana*; that the Duke wou'd possibly think she was prepossessed more than she ought with that diversion; and in this despondence she took resolutions to regulate herself hereafter, more to his satisfaction.

That fatal Night the Duke felt hostile Fires in his Breast; *Love* was entred, with all his dreadful Artillery; he took possession in a moment of the Avenues that lead to the Heart! neither did the resistance he found there serve for any thing but to make his Conquest more illustrious. The Duke try'd every corner of his uneasie Bed! whether shut or open, *Charlot* was still before his Eyes! his Lips and Face retain'd the dear Impression of her Kisses! the Idea of her innocent and charming Touches, wander'd o'er his Mind! he wish'd again to be so bless'd, but then, with a deep and dreadful Sigh, he remembred who she was, the Daughter of his Friend! of a Friend who had at his Death left the charge of her Education to him! his Treaty with the Princess Dowager, wou'd not admit him

him to think of marrying of her, Ambition came in to rescue him (in that particular) from the Arms of Love. To possess her without, was a villanous detestable Thought! but not to possess her at all, was loss of Life! was Death inevitable! Not able to gain one wink of Sleep, he arose with the first Dawn, and posted back to *Angela*. He hop'd the hurry of Business, and the Pleasures of the Court, wou'd stifle so guilty a Passion; he was too well perswaded of his Distemper, the Symptoms were right, the Malignity was upon him! he was regularly possess'd! Love, in all its forms, had took in that formidable Heart of his! he began to be jealous of his Son, whom he had always design'd for *Charlot*'s Husband; he cou'd not bear the thoughts that he shou'd be belov'd by her, tho' all beautiful, as the lovely Youth was. She had never had any tender Inclinations for him, nothing that exceeded the warmth of a Sister's love! whether it were that he were designed for, or that the Precepts of Education had warn'd her from too precipitate a liking: She was bred up with him, accustom'd to his Charms, they made no impression upon her Heart! neither was the Youth more sensible. The Duke cou'd distress neither of 'em by his love of that side, but this he was not so happy to know. He wrote up for the young Lord to come to Court, and gave immediate orders for forming his Equipage, that he might be sent to Travel: Mean time *Charlot* was never from his Thoughts. Who knows not the violence of beginning Love! especially a Love that we hold opposite to our Interest and Duty? *'Tis an unreasonable excess of Desire, which enters swiftly, but departs slowly.*

The

The love of Beauty, is the loss of Reason. Neither is it to be suppress'd by Wisdom, because it is not to be comprehended with Reason. And the Emperor *Aurelius*; "*Love is a cruel Impression of that wonderful Passion, which to define is impossible, because no Words reach to the strong Nature of it, and only they know which inwardly feel it.*"

The Duke vainly strugled in the Snare; he wou'd live without seeing *Charlot*, but then he must live in Pain, in inexplicable Torture! he applies the relief of Business, the Pleasures of Woman! *Charlot*'s Kisses were still upon his Lips, and made all others insipid to him. In short, he try'd so much to divert his Thoughts from her, that it but more perfectly confirm'd him of the vanity and the unsucuesfulness of the attempt: He could neither eat or sleep! love and restlesness rais'd Vapours in him to that degree, he was no longer Master of his Business! Wearied with all things, hurry'd by a secret Principle of *Self-Love*, and *Self-Preservation*, the Law of Nature! he orders his Coach to carry him down once more to his *Villa*, there to see his Dear! this dangerous *Charlot*! that little innocent Sweetness! that imbitter'd his Happiness. She lov'd him tenderly, as a Benefactor, a Father, or something more; that she had been us'd to love without that severe mixture of Fear that mingles in the love we bear to Parents: She ran to meet him as he alighted; her young Face, over-spread with blushing Joys! his transport exceeded hers! he took her in his Arms with eagarness! he exchang'd all his Pains for Pleasures! there was the Cure of his past Anguish! her Kisses were the Balm to his wounded Mind! he wonder'd at the immediate

diate alteration! she caress'd and courted him; shew'd him all things that cou'd divert or entertain. He knew not what to resolve upon; he cou'd not prudently marry her, and how to attempt to corrupt her! those excellent Principles that had been early infused into her, were all against him; but yet he must love her! he found he cou'd not live without her! he open'd a *Machiavel*, and read there a Maxim, *That none but great Souls can be compleatly Wicked*: He took it for a kind of Oracle to him! He wou'd be loath to tell himself, his *Soul was not great enough for any attempt*. He clos'd the Book, took some turns about the Gallery to digest what he had read, and from thence concluded, that neither *Religion*, *Honour*, *Gratitude*, nor *Friendship*, were ties sufficient to deprive us of an essential Good! *Charlot* was necessary to his very Being! all his Pleasures faded without her! and, which was worse, he was in torture! in actual pain as well as want of pleasure! therefore *Charlot* he would have; he had strugled more than sufficient, Virtue ought to be satisfied with the terrible Conflict he had suffered! but Love was become Master; and 'twas time for her to abscond. After he had settled his Thoughts, he grew more calm and quiet; nothing shou'd now disturb him, but the manner how to corrupt her. He was resolv'd to change her whole Form of Living, to bring her to Court, to show her the World; *Balls*, *Assemblies*, *Opera's*, *Comedies*, *Cards*, and *Visits*, every thing that might enervate the Mind, and fit it for the soft play and impression of Love! One thing he a little scrupled, lest in making her susceptible of that Passion, it shou'd be for another, and not for him; he did not doubt,

doubt, but upon her firſt appearance at Court ſhe wou'd have many Admirers; Lovers have this opinion peculiar to themſelves, they believe that others ſee with their Eyes: He knew that were ſhe leſs agreeable, the gloſs of Novelty was enough to recommend her; but the remedy he found for this, was, to careſs and pleaſe her above all others; to ſhew ſuch a particular regard for her, that ſhou'd frighten any new pretender. Few are willing to croſs a firſt Miniſter, eſpecially in ſuch a tender Point, where all Mankind are tenacious of their Pretenſions.

He had obſerv'd, that *Charlot* had been, but with diſguſt, deny'd the gay Part of reading: 'Tis natural for young People to chuſe the diverting, before the inſtructive; he ſent for her into the Gallery, where was a noble Library in all Languages, a Collection of the moſt valuable Authors, with a mixture of the moſt Amorous. He told her, that now her Underſtanding was increas'd, with her Stature, he reſolv'd to make her Miſtreſs of her own Conduct; and as the firſt thing that he intended to oblige her in, that *Governante* who had hitherto had the care of her Actions, ſhould be diſmiſs'd; becauſe he had obſerv'd the ſeverity of her Temper had ſometimes been diſpleaſing to her; that ſhe ſhou'd henceforward have none above her, that ſhe ſhou'd need to ſtand in awe of; and to confirm to her that good opinion he ſeem'd to have, he preſented her with the Key of that Gallery, to improve her Mind, and ſeek her Diverſion, amongſt thoſe Authors he had formerly forbid her the uſe of: *Charlot* made him a very low Curtſie, and, with a bluſhing Grace, return'd him Thanks for the two favours he beſtow'd stow'd upon her. She assur'd him, that no Action of hers shou'd make him repent the distinction; that her whole endeavour should be to walk in that Path he made familiar to her; and that Virtue shou'd ever be her only Guide. Tho' this was not what the Duke wanted, 'twas nothing but what he expected: He observ'd formerly, that she was a great lover of Poetry, especially when 'twas forbid her; he took down an *Ovid*, and opening it just at the love of *Myrra* for her Father, conscious red overspread his Face; he gave it her to read; she obey'd him with a visible delight; nothing is more pleasing to young Girls, than in being first consider'd as Women. *Charlot* saw the Duke entertain'd her with an Air of Consideration more than usual, passionate and respectful; this taught her to refuge in the native Pride and Cunning of the Sex, she assum'd an Air more haughty. The leaving a Girl just beginning to believe herself capable of attaining that Empire over Mankind, which they are all born and taught by Instinct to expect. She took the Book, and plac'd herself by the Duke, his Eyes Feasted themselves upon her Face, thence wander'd over her snowy Bosom, and saw the young swelling Breasts just begining to distinguish themselves, and which were gently heav'd at the Impression *Myrra*'s Sufferings made upon her Heart, by this dangerous reading, he pretended to shew her, that there were Pleasures her Sex were born for, and which she might consequently long to taste! Curiosity is an early and dangerous Enemy to Virtue, the young *Charlot*, who had by a noble Inclination of Gratitude a strong propension of Affection for the Duke, whom she call'd and estem'd her *Papa*, being a Girl of wonderful reflection, and consequently

quently Application, wrought her Imagination up to such a lively heighth at the Fathers Anger after the possession of his Daughter, which she judg'd highly unkind and unnatural, that she drop'd her Book, Tears fill'd her Eyes, Sobs rose to oppress her, and she pull'd out her Handkerchief to cover the Disorder. The Duke, who was Master of all Mankind, could trace 'em in all the *Meanders* of Dissimulation and Cunning, was not at a loss how to interpret the Agitation of a Girl who knew no Hipocrisy, all was Artless, the beautiful product of Innocence and Nature; he drew her gently to him, drunk her Tears with his Kisses, suck'd her Sighs and gave her by that dangerous Commerce (her Soul before prepar'd to softness) new and unfelt Desires; her Virtue was becalm'd, or rather unapprehensive of him for an Invader; he prest her Lips with his, the nimble beatings of his Heart, apparently seen and felt thro' his open Breast! the glowings! the tremblings of his Limbs! the glorious Sparkles from his guilty Eyes! his shortness of Breath, and eminent Disorder, were things all new to her, that had never seen, heard, or read before of those powerful Operations, struck from the Fire of the two meeting Sex; nor had she leisure to examine his disorders, possess'd by greater of her own! greater! because that Modesty opposing Nature, forc'd a struggle of Dissimulation. But the Duke's pursuing Kisses overcame the very Thoughts of any thing, but that new and lazy Poison stealing to her Heart, and spreading swiftly and imperceptibly thro' all her Veins, she clos'd her Eyes with languishing Delight! deliver'd up the possession of her Lips

Lips and Breath to the amorous Invader; return'd his eager grasps, and, in a word, gave her whole Person into his Arms, in meltings full of delight! The Duke by that lovely Extasie, carry'd beyond himself, sunk over the expiring Fair; in Raptures too powerful for description! calling her his admirable *Charlot*! his charming Angel! his adorable Goddess! but all was so far modest, that he attempted not beyond her Lips and Breast, but cry'd that she shou'd never be anothers. The Empire of his Soul was hers; enchanted by inexplicable, irresistable Magick! she had Power beyond the Gods themselves! *Charlot* return'd from that amiable Disorder, was a new charm'd at the Duke's Words; Words that set her so far above what was mortal, the Woman assum'd in her, and she wou'd have no notice taken of the Transports she had shown. He saw and favour'd her modesty, secure of that fatal Sting he had fix'd within her Breast, that Taste of delight, which powerful Love and Nature wou'd call upon her to repeat. He own'd he lov'd her; that he never cou'd love any other; that 'twas impossible for him to live a day, an hour, without seeing her; that in her absence he had felt more than ever had been felt by Mortal; he begg'd her to have pity on him, to return his Love, or else he shou'd be the most lost, undone thing alive. *Charlot*, amaz'd and charm'd, felt all those dangerous perturbations of Nature that arise from an amorous Constitution, with Pride and Pleasure, she saw herself necessary to the happiness of one, that she had hitherto esteemed so much above her, ignorant of the Power of Love, that Leveller of Mankind; that blender of Distinction

stinction and Hearts. Her soft Answer was, That she was indeed reciprocally Charm'd, she knew not how; all he had said and done was wonderful and pleasing to her; and if he wou'd still more please her (if there were a more) it shou'd be never to be parted from her. The Duke had one of those violent Passions, where, to heighten it, resistance was not at all necessary; it had already reach'd the ultimate, it cou'd not be more ardent; yet was he loth to rush upon the possession of the Fair, lest the too early pretension might disgust her: He wou'd steal himself into her Soul, he wou'd make himself necessary to her quiet, as she was to his.

From the Library he led her to his Cabinet, from forth his strong Box he took a set of Jewels that had been her Mothers; he told her, she was now of an Age to expect the Ornaments, as well as Pleasures of a Woman. He was pleas'd to see her look down, with a seeming contempt, upon what most other Girls wou'd have been transported with: He had taught her other Joys, those of the Mind and Body. She sigh'd, she rav'd to herself, she was all charm'd and uneasie! The Duke casting over the rest of his Jewels, made a Collection of such as were much more valuable than her Mothers; he presented her with, and wou'd force her to accept 'em; but *Charlot*, as tender and gallant as the Duke, seeing his Picture in little, set round with Diamonds, begg'd that he wou'd only honour her with that mark of his Esteem. The ravish'd Duke consented, conditionally, that she wou'd give him hers in return.

After

After this tender, dangerous Commerce, *Charlot* found every thing infipid, nothing but the Duke's kiffes cou'd relifh with her; all thofe Converfations fhe had formerly delighted in, were infupportable: He was oblig'd to return to Court; and had recommended to her reading the moft dangerous Books of Love, *Ovid*, *Petrarch*, *Tibullus*, thofe moving Tragedies that fo powerfully expofe the force of Love, and corrupt the Mind; he went even farther, and left her fuch as explain'd the Nature, Manner, and Raptures of Enjoyment. Thus he infus'd Poifon into the Ears of the lovely Virgin. She eafily (from thofe emotions fhe had found in herfelf) believ'd as highly of thofe Delights as was imaginable; her waking Thoughts, her golden Slumber, ran all of a Blifs only imagin'd, but never prov'd: She even forgot, as one that wakes from fleep, and the Viffions of the Night, all thofe Precepts of airy Virtue, which fhe found had nothing to do with Nature: She long'd again to renew thofe dangerous Delights. The Duke was an Age abfent from her, fhe cou'd only in imagination poffefs what fhe believ'd fo pleafing. Her Memory was prodigious, fhe was indefatigable in Reading. The Duke had left orders fhe fhou'd not be controul'd in any thing: Whole Nights were wafted by her in that Gallery; fhe had too well inform'd herfelf of the fpeculative Joys of Love. There are are Books dangerous to the Community of Mankind; abominable for Virgins, and deftructive to Youth; fuch as explain the Myfteries of Nature, the congregated Pleafures of *Venus*, the full Delights of mutual Lovers, and which rather ought to pafs the Fire than the Press. The Duke had laid in her way such as made no mention of *Virtue* or *Hymen*, but only advanced native, generous and undissembled Love. She was become so great a Proficient, that nothing of the Theory was a stranger to her.

Whilst *Charlot* was thus employ'd, the Duke was not idle; he had prepar'd her a Post at Court with *Henriquez*'s Queen. The young Lady was sent for; neither Art, Money, nor Industry was wanting, to make her appearance glorious. The Duke aw'd and trembling with his Passion, approach'd her as a Goddess; conscious of his and her own desires, the mantling Blood wou'd smile upon her Cheeks, sometimes glowing with delight, then afterwards, by a feeble recollection of Virtue, sink apace, to make room for a guilty succeeding Paleness. The Duke knew all the motions of her Heart, he debated with himself, whether it were best to attempt the possession of her whilst so young, or permit her time to know and set a value upon what she granted. His Love was highly impatient, but respectful; he long'd to be happy, but he dreaded to displease her. The Ascendant she had over him was wonderful; he had let slip those first Impressions, which strike deepest in the Hearts of Women, to be successful; *One ought never to allow 'em time to Think, their vivacity being prodigious, and their forsight exceeding short, and limited; the first hurry of their Passions, if they are but vigorously follow'd, is what is generally most favourable to Lovers.* *Charlot* by this time had inform'd herself, that there were such terrible things as Perfidy and Inconstancy, in Mankind; that even the very Favours they receiv'd, often disgusted ed; and that to be entirely Happy, one ought never to think of the faithless Sex. This brought her back to those Precepts of Virtue that had embellish'd her dawn of Life; but alas! these Admonitions were too feeble, the Duke was all submissive, passionate, eager to obey, and to oblige. He watch'd her uprisings, scarce cou'd eat without her; she was Mistress of his Heart and Fortune; his own Family, and the whole Court, imagin'd that he resolv'd her for his Dutchess; they almost look'd upon her as such; she went often to his Palace, where all were devoted to her Service; the very glance of her Eyes commanded their attention, at her least request; assoon as her Mouth was open'd to speak, before her Words were half form'd, they started to obey her.

She had learnt to manage the Duke, and to distrust herself; she wou'd no more permit of Kisses, that sweet and dangerous Commerce. The Duke had made her wife at his own cost, and vainly languish'd for a repetition of Delight. He guess'd at the Interest he had in her Heart, had prov'd the warmth of her Constitution, and was resolv'd he wou'd no more be wanting to his own Happiness; he omitted no occasion by which he might express his love; pressing her to crown his Longings. Her courage did not reach to ask him that honourable Proof of his Passion, which 'tis believ'd he wou'd not have refused, if she had but insisted of it. The Treaty was still depending, he might marry the Princess Dowager; *Charlot* tenderly drop'd a word that spoke her apprehensions of it; he assur'd her there was nothing in it, all he aim'd at was to purchase the Succession, that he might

F 3 make

make her a Princefs, as fhe deferv'd. Indeed the hopes his Agent had given the Lady, of becoming her Husband, was not the fmallest inducement to the Treaty; therefore he delay'd his Marriage with *Charlot*; for if that were but once confirm'd, the Princefs (by refenting, as fhe ought, the abufe that had been lain upon her) wou'd put an end to it, infinitely to his prejudice.

Charlot, very well fatisfied with thefe Reafons, and unwilling to do any thing againft the Intereft of a Man whom fhe tenderly lov'd, accuftom'd herfelf to hear his eager Sollicitations: He cou'd no longer contend with a Fire that confumed him, he muft be gratified, or die. She languifhed under the fame difquiets. The Seafon of the Year was come that he muft make the Campaign with the King; he cou'd not refolve to depart unblefs'd; *Charlot* ftill refus'd him that laft proof of her Love. He took a tender and paffionate Farewel. *Charlot*, drown'd in Tears, told him, 'twas impoffible fhe fhou'd fupport his abfence; all the Court wou'd ridicule her Melancholy. This was what he wanted; he bid her take care of that, a Maid was but an ill Figure, that brought herfelf to be the fport of Laughters; but fince her Sorrow (fo pleafing and glorious to him) was like to be vifible, he advifed her to pafs fome days at his *Villa*, till the height of Melancholy fhou'd be over, under the pretence of Indifpofition; he wou'd take care that the Queen fhou'd be fatisfied of the neceffity of her abfence; he advis'd her even to depart that hour; fince the King was already on his Journey, he muft be gone that moment, and endeavour to overtake him. He

affur'd

assur'd her be wou'd write by every Courier, and beg'd her not to admit of another Lover, tho' he was sensible there were many (taking the advantage of his absence, wou'd endeavour to please her). To all this she answer'd so as to quiet his distrust and fears, her Tears drowned her Sighs, her Words were lost in Sobs and Groans! The Duke did not show less concern, but led her all trembling, to put her in a Coach that was to carry her to his *Villa*; where he had often wish'd to have her, but she distrusted her self, and wou'd not go with him, nor had she ventur'd now, but that she thought he was to follow the King, who cou'd not be without him.

Charlot no sooner arriv'd, but the Weather being very hot, she order'd a Bath to be prepar'd for her. Soon as she was refresh'd with that, she threw her self down upon a Bed, with only one thin Petticoat and a loose Night-gown, the Bosom of her Gown and Shift open; her Night-cloths tied carelesly together with a Cherry-colour'd Ribon, which answer'd well to the yellow and silver Stuff of her Gown. She lay uncover'd, in a melancholy careless Posture, her Head resting upon one of her Hands, the other held a Handkerchief, that she employ'd to dry those Tears that sometimes fell from her Eyes; when raising herself a little, at a gentle noise she heard from the opening of a Door that answer'd to the Bed-side, she was quite astonished to see enter the amorous Duke. Her first emotions were all Joy, but in a minute she recollected herself, thinking he was not come there for nothing: She was going to rise, but he prevented her, by flying to her Arms, where, as we may call it, he nail'd her down to the Bed with Kisses; his love and resolution gave him a double vigour, he wou'd not stay a moment to capitulate with her; whilst yet her surprise made her doubtful of his designs, he took advantage of her confusion to accomplish 'em; neither her prayers, tears, nor struglings, cou'd prevent him, but in her Arms he made himself a full amends for all those pains he had suffer- for her.

Thus was *Charlot* undone! thus ruin'd by him, that ought to have been her Protector! 'Twas very long before he cou'd appease her; but so artful, so amorous, so submissive was his Address, so violent his Assurances, he told her, that he must have dy'd without the Happiness. *Charlot* espous'd his Crime, by sealing his Forgiveness. He pass'd the whole Night in her Arms, pleas'd, transported, and out of himself; whilst the ravish'd Maid was not all behind-hand in Extasies and guilty Transports. He staid a whole Week with *Charlot*, in a Surfeit of Love and Joy! that Week more inestimable than all the Pleasures of his Life before! whilst the Court believed him with the King, posting to the Army; he neglected *Mars* to devote himself wholly to *Venus*; abstracted from all Business, that happy Week sublim'd him almost to an Immortal. *Charlot* was form'd to give and take all those Raptures necessary to accomplish the Lover's happiness; none were ever more Amorous! none were ever more Happy!

The two Lovers separated, the Duke for the Army, *Charlot* return'd to Court; one of the Royal-Secretaries fell in Love with her, but his being

being of the precise Party, and a marry'd Man, it behov'd to carry himself discreetly: He omitted no private Devoirs to please her, but her Heart entirely fix'd upon the Duke, neglected the Attempt. She had made an intimate Friendship with a young Countess, who was a lovely Widow, full of Air, Life and Fire; her Lord purchas'd her from his Rival, by the Point of his Sword, but he did not long survive to enjoy the Fruits of his Victory; he made her Circumstances as easie as he cou'd, but that was not extraordinary, however, she appear'd well at Court, knew the Management of Mankind, and how to procure her self universal Love and Admiration, *Charlot* made her the unwary Confidant of her Passion for the Duke; the Countess had the Goodness, or Complaisance, which you please, to hearken to the over-flowings of a Love-sick-Heart: She imparted to her all the Letters she receiv'd from him, and took her Approbation for the Answer; that *never dying Fire!* those *racking Uneasiness's! Languors! Expectations! Impatiencies!* that the two Lovers express'd, were all *Greek* and *Hebrew* to the Countess, who was bred up in the fashionable way of making Love, wherein the Heart has little or no part, quite another turn of Amour. She would often tell *Charlot*; that no Lady ever suffer'd her self to be truly touch'd, but from that moment she was blinded and undone; the first thing a Woman ought to consult was her Interest, and Establishment in the World; that Love shou'd only be a handle towards it; when she left the pursuit of that to give up her self to her Pleasures, Contempt and Sorrow were sure to be her Companions: No Lover was yet ever known so ardent, but

time

[marginalia: Lady Berkeley of Stratton.]

time abated of his Transport; no Beauty so ravishing, but that her Sweetness wou'd cloy; nor did Men any longer endeavour to please, when nothing was wanting to their Wishes: Love the most generous, and yet the most mercenary of all the Passions, does not care what he lavishes, provided there be something still in view to repay his Expence; but that once over, the Lover possess'd of whatever his Mistress can bestow, he hangs his Head, the *Cupid* drops his Wings, and seldom feels their native Energy return, but to carry him to new Conquests.

Charlot knew not how to digest this System of Amour; she was sure the Countess knew the World, but thought she knew not the Duke, who had not a Soul like other Men: She said, she would, at his return, convince her, (all Infidel as she was) that he had not the same Gaft of Mind as the rest of his Sex; the Countess said she should be glad to see it, but that he had took exactly the same Methods to make his Fortune: She would advise her as a good Friend, (if it were strangely true, that his Ardors were yet unallayed) to push her Interest with him, that he might marry her; advis'd her to bestow no more Favours, till he paid her price; made her read the History of *Roxalana*, who by her wise Address, brought an imperious *Sultan*, contrary to the establish'd Rules of the *Seraglio*, to divide with her the Royal Throne. *Charlot* said she would try what she could do; at the same time she receiv'd certain Advice, that the Treaty was broke off with the *Princess Dowager*. *Charlot* thought it was for her sake, and from thence (flatter'd by Love) took it into her Head, that

it

it would not be long before she should be the Dutchess of —— *Countess of Portland*

The Queen prepar'd a Ball to be danced the King's Birth-Night, which happned to be that of his Return from a fortunate Campaign. *Charlot* had, since the Duke's absence, to render her self conspicuous to him) been practising an Accomplishment, which a certain great Author calls *excelling in a Mistake*. She danc'd that Night to the satisfaction of all who beheld her; the Duke's Return and Presence re-animated her; she seem'd born to new Life, and more Vivacity: He was charm'd with the Performance, and long'd for nothing so much, as to tell her he was more in Love with her than ever. Those *Duena's* that guard the fair Maids belonging to the Queen, would not permit him all the Happiness he wish'd: How impatient they were to lose themselves in unnumber'd Kisses and Joys! the Duke proposed to her to go down to his *Villa* the next Day; that he would ask the King's leave to retire to put his Affairs in order, and immediately follow. There was no Body that wonder'd she shou'd pay her Compliment whilst he was in the Country, her Guardian, the Trustee of her Family; all the Duke's Children caress'd and lov'd her; they even wish'd their Father would marry her; for so 'twas receiv'd and believ'd at Court, that she shou'd be the Dutchess of —— They were no Strangers to his Love; he never pretended to dissemble; but not one imagin'd his guilty Passion had carry'd him that length it had: He was so charm'd with her, that he told her, she must resolve to pretend a distant Journey to her Relations, and remain conconceal'd near *Angela*, where he might have the

freedom

freedom of seeing her twice a Day, at least, unknown to all the Court; that if she could devote her self to such a Solitude, he would endeavour to do all things that were in his power to make it agreeable to her; the Love-sick Maid consented with joy; then was her time to push for what he possibly might have consented to, rather than not have possessed her undisturbed; but she was afraid that he shou'd think her Love was the result of Interest, and believ'd so well of his Honour, as not to distrust his Care of hers.

Behold her then settled in a pleasing Solitude, within a short Mile of the *Capitol*; the Servants that were put about her were all Strangers, her Name chang'd; and not a Mortal suspected but *Charlot* was gone into the Country to her Relations. The Duke saw her twice or thrice every Day, sometimes eat with her, and because he could not be so often lost, without being found by some body, they reported that he had a new Mistress, and had sent *Charlot* away, not to discompose her with the Report; no body could tell who she was, yet many pretended to have seen her, and ev'n gave Descriptions of her Height, Features, and Complexion, all by guess, and not likely to agree; some would have her the *fair*, some the *brunet*, and not a few the *black* Beauty. Every one spoke of what was most agreeable to themselves, but a Beauty to be sure she must be; because the Duke was so attach'd to her.

Charlot, tho' she possess'd all she cou'd desire in the Duke's Company, yet had many Hours of Solitude upon her Hands, the great Hurry of Affairs, the Business of the State, which lay heavy vy upon the Duke, engross'd too much of his time: To alleviate the Pains his Absence gave her, *Charlot* begg'd the Countess might be let into the Secret, to help her pass away, more agreeably those Moments that he was not with her: She urg'd this so earnestly, that the Duke knew not how to deny her, but bid her take it for her pains, if she one day repented of it; that if he was not mistaken in the Countess, she was none of those few Ladies that possess the retentive Faculty; but shou'd their Secret not suffer by her Tongue, (which indeed wou'd be wonderful) her being known to visit there, (as all things of that Nature are quickly known) wou'd blow the Suspicion of it abroad, to the prejudice of *Charlot*'s Honour, which was dearer to him than his Life. She might easily have believ'd this last Asseveration, if he had had any Sense of his own, for there's no body but what would condemn him for corrupting hers.

Charlot cou'd not evade her Destiny; she wou'd have the Countess with her. Pride concurr'd with Diversion; she long'd to shew the Countess (who had so slender an Opinion of the Constancy of Mankind) how much and faithfully she was belov'd. The Countess came, and they met on both sides over-joy'd; she boasted of her good Fortune; the Widow told her, all that was very fine, but why did she not think of marrying of him, then they might be all Day and Night, and every Day and Night together, without interruption, and hiding; that other Diversions ought to have their turn with a Lady of her age. *Charlot* told her, she found all she desir'd in the Duke's Love, and her Friendship, she had nothing further to wish, if she wou'd but have the Goodness

to

to see her as often as she cou'd. The Countess pitied the Love-sick Maid, but finding she was incorrigible, resolv'd to speak to her no more of her marrying the Duke: She saw, by his Delays, that he did not design it, and look'd upon *Charlot* as a *pauvre Fille trompez*.

Almost the whole Winter pass'd away in an agreeable Cabal; the Countess had Wit enough, and a pleasant manner of relating things; her Intelligence was universal; she knew all that was done both at Court, and in the City: The Duke, who came to unbend himself with these two fair Ladies, seem'd to relish the Countess's Conversation: Not to disgrace Love, he was sometimes beholden to this gay Widow, for keeping up the Diversion. 'Tis not possible always to love, or to bear up to the extravagant height of a beginning Flame, without new Supplies it must decay, at least abate of its first Vigour, when not a Look, or Touch, but are Fuel to it. The Countess was not displeas'd at being heard; she remark'd his Attention; saw his Eyes were less on *Charlot*, and more on her; that he wou'd turn away, with a gentle Sigh, when she catch'd him looking at her; who does not know that undisturb'd possession makes Desire languish. *Charlot* believ'd nothing of this, but the Countess knew all the Maxims of Mankind. She presently guess'd how things went, and was not supriz'd to hear the Duke tell the young Lady, that the time drawing on to take the Field, he would have her think of returning to Court; but that she might do it with the more Honour, and free from all suspicion of their Commerce, he advis'd her, in reallity, to take a Journey down to her Relations, from whence she might give

notice

notice of her return, as if she had been there the whole Winter. *Charlot* look'd tenderly upon the Duke, her Eyes fill'd with Tears; some drops of Blood fell from her Nose upon her Handkerchief, as she was reaching it to her Eyes, the Omen startled her, she was going to withdraw, to weep alone, when her Spirits fail'd her, and she fell in a fainting Fit upon the Countess's Bosom; the Duke had Affairs that urg'd his departure; he call'd her Women, and left her to their Care: Nothing is able to express the Despair she was in, when she found he could depart and leave her in that Condition. His date of Love is out, says the unfortunate *Charlot*, Oh Madam! that I had but believ'd you! What is to be done? Shall I see my self complaining, and neglected, scorn'd, and yet fawning upon my Undoer? tho' my Heart burst with Grief and Tenderness, I will never have that little Spirit. The Countess confirm'd her in those Heroick Thoughts, and ev'n advis'd her to depart as soon as she cou'd, and without taking her Leave of him; for if he still lov'd her, that Indifferency would distract him, and cause him to fetch her back; if otherwise, prevent her from being his Triumph. *Charlot* judg'd the Advice good, and order'd all things for her departure on the morrow: She might, and ought to have gone early in the Morning, as the Countess would have had her, but lazy, lingering Love, made her trifle away the time, till the usual hour of the Duke's Visit. As he entred the Chamber, a mortal Paleness, and universal Trembling was seen in poor *Charlot*: He tenderly ran to support her; when she was a little recover'd, he ask'd her what those Preparations meant?

meant? She told him 'twas for her Journey, as he had advis'd her. The Duke told her be was glad of it, 'twas prudently resolv'd, but he wish'd, for both their sakes, she wou'd make no long stay in the Country, because he hop'd to be thus bless'd again, before he departed. She burst out into a Passion of Tears, at his approbation of a thing, when she thought the suddenness of it would have startled him. Let us go, let us go for ever, said she, sobbing, my Lord Duke, I wish your Eminence all Happiness, wretched *Charlot* shall never disturb it. Farewel, my dear Countess, I was not born to taste the Sweets of Love and Friendship: Here she hasted out of the Room, and got into the Coach that waited, without taking her Leave in Form, either of the one or the other. They made after her to the Gate; she briskly order'd the Coachman to drive on, and with six good Horses was presently out of sight.

The Duke gave his Hand to the Countess, to lead her back into the House; they continued in mutual Silence till the Duke broke it, by Words to these effect. " You doubtless con-
" demn me, Madam, for my Indifferency to
" *Mademoiselle Charlot*, I would remove so strong
" an Evidence as your self, by making you
" equally guilty. I know you are a Woman of
" the World, fully acquainted with your own
" Charms, and what they can do upon the
" Hearts of others. You have Wit, understand
" your own Interest, therefore if you have no
" Aversion for my Person, 'tis in your power
" to do what you please with me. For your
" sake I have advis'd *Mademoiselle* to this Jour-
" ney: I cou'd not say what I wou'd before so
" trouble-

" troublesome a Witness; I have good Nature,
" and cou'd not see a Creature who loves me in
" pain, when nothing but Esteem and Pity re-
" main for her: Not that I am naturally In-
" constant, but your superior Charms have im-
" perceptibly made their way, I had doubtless
" lov'd her a long time, if the Vivacity of your
" Wit and Conversation had not interfer'd:
" However, I will omit nothing for her Estab-
" lishment in the World. Her Fault is yet a
" Secret between us Two, and that I may bribe
" you to keep it inviolably, I offer to share In-
" terests; whatever is mine may be yours, nay
" Honour as well as Interest will oblige you
" to it, for it cannot be unknown, that we see
" one another often at this House, when we
" are married, that will be suppos'd to be the
" Secret: 'Tis your own Fault if it be not done
" this Night: In giving you that ultimate Proof
" of my Love, I spare both you and my self
" the trouble of Words: I have took time to
" weigh the Design, all things plead for you,
" *Beauty*, *Merit*, *Sense*, and every thing that can
" render a Woman charming, whilst I pretend
" nothing to plead for me, but making it your
" own Interest to make me happy. As I have
" avoided the tedious Forms, by which our Sex
" think they must engage yours, so I beg that
" you will use none to me, that relate in any
" sort to *Mademoiselle Charlot*, that is a tender
" Point, I wou'd not so much as remember, (in
" the Joys I prepare my self for with you) that
" there is such a Person in the World.

This Harangue put the Countess to her Reflections. She begg'd his Eminency wou'd be
pleas'd to give her time till to morrow Night,

before she pretended to answer him; and then she would do herself the Honour to expect him alone at her House to Supper. The Duke kiss'd her Hand with a respective Assent to what she had said, then led her to her Chair, and departed to prepare himself for his Marriage with the Countess.

He did not fail to wait upon her at the usual Hour: The Lady was in a gentile *Dishabile*, ev'n to the very Night-cloaths that she intended to lie in. After a well order'd Supper, she carry'd him into a little Drawing-Room, and told him, in a few Words, she was ready to receive the Honour of what he had offer'd; his Inconstancy had held her for some Moments in suspence, but as to that, she assur'd her self, that religiously performing her own Duty, would oblige his Eminence to a Tenderness in his; that as the Distance was so infinitely great, both in their Title, and other Circumstances, she would not pretend to capitulate with him, but left all her Interest in his, as the best Hands, who was so much her Friend, as to raise her to a Rank and Fortune she could not without the highest Vanity have expected. The Duke receiv'd her Consent with a wonderful deal of Joy and Gallantry; they were immediately marry'd, and bedded That very Night 'twas known at Court, and some of poor *Charlot*'s Friends, did her the Diskindness to send the News of it into the Country, already Heart-broke with the Imagination of the Duke's Indifferency. This but confirm'd her in her Resolution, of not surviving the Loss of his Kindness: Her Solitude was Nourishment to those black and corroding Thoughts that incessantly devour'd her: We may be sure she often

ten exclaim'd against *breach* of *Trust*, and *Friendship* in the Countess, as well as Ingratitude and Faithlesness in the Duke: The remainder of her Life was one continu'd Scene of Horror, Sorrow, and Repentance: She dy'd a true Landmark: to warn all believing Virgins from shipwracking their Honour upon (that dangerous Coast of Rocks) the Vows and pretended Passion of Mankind.

Astrea. Your Story has two Morals, one you have your self remark'd, the other is, " That " no Woman ought to introduce another to " the Man by whom she is belov'd; if that had " not happen'd, the Duke had not possibly " been false. Those dangerous Intimacies dis- " cover Charms, that are not reveal'd but by " Conversation. I do not so much condemn the " Duke for quitting as corrupting her; one is " natural, and but the consequence of the other; " methinks it shou'd not be the least Induce- " ment for Ladies to preserve their Honour, that " let 'em be never so ill used by the Person " that robs 'em of it, by any Art or Pretence " whatsoever, tho' the World may condemn " and call him a Villain, yet they never pity " her; the reason is plain, Modesty is the *Principle*, the *Foundation* upon which they ought to " build for *Esteem* and *Admiration*, and that " once violated, they totter, and fall, dash'd in " pieces upon the obdurate Land of Contempt, " from whence no kind Hand can ever be put " forth, either to rescue or to compassionate 'em. " Men may regain their Reputations, tho' after " a Complication of Vices, *Cowardice*, *Robbery*, " *Adultery*, *Bribery*, and *Murder*, but a Woman " once departed from the Road of Virtue, is

" made incapable of a return; Sorrow and Scorn
" overtake her, and, as I said before, the World
" suffers her to perish loath'd, and unlamented.

Having done moralizing upon that Story, they follow'd the Lady *Intelligence* into the Palace. She e'en ascended the Stairs, and cross'd the Lodgings, to the Apartment where the King's Body lay, but all was a Desart; the numerous Croud of Guards and Attendance, nay even his menial Servants were vanish'd; they enquir'd the reason of this, to whom *Intelligence*.

Intel. Alas! this is nothing new, were you to peruse History, you wou'd find few faithful to the Dead. I have read of Kings that have dy'd in peace, amidst a great and flourishing People, yet have not found any to bestow the decent Rites of Washing or Covering to the Royal Carkass, till the Embalmers, who are paid for what they do, come two or three Days after, to find if 'tis time for them to fall to work. The Lesser follow the Example of the Greater, these run to make their Court to the new Successor, (whom, perhaps, they had not seen in an Age before, but *en passant*) for fear of disobliging the reigning Monarch; the little People in that hurry of Affairs, secure what they can get; they know the dead are provided for, that they can have no real Wants, and therefore never trouble themselves to stay in a Place no longer significant to 'em. This very Morning, the youngest and most beloved of all the Favourites, as soon as ever he saw that his Master cou'd not live, accepted of the Key he gave him to his strong Box, to secure for himself, in Bills and Gold, Seventy eight thousand Crowns, which was all the personal Wealth the Monarch was possess'd

of:

of: His extreme Sorrow for losing so good a Prince did not prevent him from doing all that was necessary to hinder that Money from falling into the Successors Hands, to whom of right it belong'd.

Were you to see, as I did, that great Croud of Flatterers that immediately flock'd about the new Empress, before the last Breath had carry'd the departing Monarch to the happy Regions, you wou'd have sworn they had ever tenderly adored her: She receiv'd them, with a solemn Grace no way displeasing. Methinks 'twou'd have put 'em to a stand, shou'd she have ask'd 'em, how it came to pass, that they cou'd let her wear away whole Days and Years, without once taking notice, that there was such a Person in the World, than when she amus'd herself in the Nursery, and at Cards with her Domesticks, to pass away the tedious time? But this is the way of the World; all that's past of that kind must be forgotten. Count *Orgueil* has already touch'd *D. of Bucks* the Skies in his Imagination; he depends much upon the merit of his former Admiration for the Empress, and does not doubt but to rival the most fortunate in her Favour. For matter of Entertainment, she said to him this Morning, after he had mad his congratulary Court, *that 'twas a very fine Day.* He answer'd, with presence of Mind, and no ill turn of Thought, *Yes, it was the finest Day he ever saw in his Life.* Seldom are Women renown'd for Constancy, but if she do persevere in her former good Opinion of him, now she has power, so to trust and raise him as he expects, 'twill scarce be grateful, to those who love *Virtue*, or *Moderation*. He affects to be Head of a Party, which in a little time

G 3

(86)

time, will be found opposite to the true Interest of the Court, than his Pride and Narrowness of Soul, are intolerable. There is no excess in vicious Love that he has not been guilty of, even to the lowest and most despicable part of Womankind, and those in numbers. Tho' thrice advantagiously Marry'd, all of 'em Ladies of *Beauty* and *Merit*, he has us'd two of 'em with very little Deference. Ill-nature is his Province, Sarcastical Wit his delight, Luxury his Practice, animated by Pride, and devoted to Covetousness. I never yet heard of any good or generous Action perform'd by him.

Virtue. Here lies the departed Monarch, who after a Reign full of Perturbation and Anxiety; applauded by most, yet condemn'd of many; is summon'd by *Minos*, to give an account of his Administration. By this time he has receiv'd his Sentence, and knows whether he were in the right or wrong, who can decide, if his ambition or love to Mankind were his chief motive to Good? Wou'd he have reliev'd the Oppressed, combated Tyranny and Arbitrary Government? So often hazarded his Life in Battle, if his own particular had not been involv'd with the Publick? Yet shall his Memory ever be dear to those People he has delivered, rank'd amongst their best and most fortunate Monarchs, having fewer of their *Vices*, and more of their *Virtues*. *War* was his Pleasure, *War* was his Employment. Whilst he follow'd the true Interest of his Country, at the Head of his Armies, he suffered two potent and opposite Factions to break themselves against one another; calm and serene, like great *Jove* upon *Olimpus* top, he wisely involv'd himself with neither; free from

the

the servile Arts with which other Monarchs have been forc'd to cajole their People; he yet found the happy Secret to draw from 'em, with alacrity and good-will, more Treasure than in some Ages had been bestow'd upon the whole Series of Kings his Predecessors, rest in peace, oh glorious Shade! may all thy defects, as thou wer't mortal, be atton'd for by those Performances of thine, that were more than Mortal. O *Astrea*! may your Prince imitate his Conduct, Courage, Fortitude, and Wisdom; and let us pray the Gods that he have but part of his good fortune.

Astrea. But, my Lady *Intelligence*, pray what will become of the late Favourites, in this new Reign?

Intell. Why they will be Favourites still; it is not as in former times, when down go the Kings, down go the Favourites. They take example by their Predecessor's Failings, avoiding the umbrage of great Crimes, they find little Villains to support the calumny of Male-Administration, who are perpetually sacrific'd to their safety; the Servant often dies for his Master. This is a new and wise Scheme of Management, whilst the Favourite takes care to get him an Estate sufficient to make him formidable, and to perswade the new Successor, and People, to leave him in repose, to taste the Sweets of ease and pleasure.

Virtue. Pray, my Lady *Intelligence*, let us have some of your assistance, to explain to us that Parade that appears yonder.

Intell. O, my good Ladies, if you please to step into this Balcony, you will see it at your ease; 'tis the Funeral Solemnity of the richest Widow

England Widow in all *Atalantis*, that but six Months, or thereabouts, surviv'd her Husband.

Vir. A Widow, and rich, and yet die so soon! was it of Love, Grief, or Old-age?

Intell. Young and Blooming; I'll entertain your Divinities with the whole Affair, assoon as the Procession's past.

Astrea. There cannot sure be greater vanity, than the Pomp they bestow upon the Dead; 'tis all superfluous, True Grief consists not in Ceremony.

Intell. There's no such thing among those that appear in these Cavalcades; there's scarce any 'em that ever saw the Person deceas'd; nay often they don't so much as know the Name of him whose Corps they accompany, or whether it be a Man or a Womans. 'Tis none of their Business, they are paid for what they do; a formal Cast of Face, a Down-look, immovable and demure, is all that is required of them. 'Tis true, this Pageantry is of no use to the deceased, but it's an Honour to their Memory, and shows the Piety of the surviving Friend; besides, 'tis Magnificent, and the comfort of many a Lady, who makes the Thoughts of Death less frightful to her, when she but thinks of an expensive Funeral, white Flambeaux's, Chariots, Horses, Streamers, and a Train of Mourners. See! there are four and twenty that carry Banners before the Body; eight leading Coaches with six Horses; the Herse comes next. Can any thing be more adorn'd? Gay with Escutcheons, rich in Velvet and Feathers. Methinks 'tis no such mortifying Sight; the Coaches and Chariots that follow are numberless.

Astrea.

Astrea. Where are they conducting the Body?

Intell. About some two and twenty Leagues off. They wou'd imagine the departed cou'd not be at rest, lodg'd out of its appointed Sepulchre.

Astrea. As if the next Funeral-Pile, or uncover'd Earth, wou'd not as well serve to consume or receive despicable Clay! the most useless and affrighting Object, no longer a part of the World; what Nature abhors to look at, but with all convenient dispatch sweep from out both of their sight and memory.

Intell. Did Mankind confine themselves only to what was necessary, reasonable, or proper, there would indeed be no occasion for most part of the great expence they are at; the Oar might lie at at rest in its native Bed, Navigation wou'd be useless, Diamonds, and other precious Stones, secure in their Quarry; the Sea not ransack'd for Pearl, since, in the equal distribuion of Creation, every Country is sufficient to it self, for sustaining Life with Temperance, tho' not with Luxury.

Astrea. The Funeral is pass'd, and we are now at leisure to hear what you have to say of the deceas'd.

Intell. I must begin with her Husband. But, to give him you in his gay Cloaths, I think I had best present your Mightiness's with the Draught of an Essay, wrote by an obscure Poet, upon his Death. I'll quickly ransack my Satchel for it. You must know, Ladies, that most things so lately past, are, as it were, present to me. I know *Astrea*, upon the top of *Parnassus*, often gives the Prize to the most deserving, and therefore

is

is an undoubted Judge of good Writing; but because we don't pretend so much merit for this Piece, I'll only tell you, that a certain Poet, who had formerly wrote some things with success, but either shrunk in his Genius, or grown very lazy, procur'd another Brother of *Parnassus* to write this Elegy for him, and promis'd to divide the Profit. The Reward being considerable and sweet, he defrauded the poor Labourer of his Hire, who had been contented, for his advantage, to depart from the Reputation it might gain him; justly incens'd against the treachery of his Friend, he resolves to own and print this Piece in the next *Miscellanea*.

Astrea.

Beneath a dismal, unfrequented Shade,
Beneath a fading, melancholy Glade
Of Willow, and the murmuring Poplar made.
Two Nymphs, whose Form-Divine were lost in Care,
Widow'd of Joy, but wedded to Despair.
Soon as returning Light reviv'd the Earth,
With constant Horrour came to curse their Birth.
Each had a Lover lost, Melissa's *dy'd,*
The very day the Nymph was made a Bride!
Love's Altar dress'd for joy the Bed in view,
And Hymen's *wasting Taper downwards drew.*
Aminta *too had lost the lovly'st Swain,*
Then when her Breast glow'd with a mutual Flame.
Here, here, they met to mourn, not seek relief,
But to indulge, and to inlarge their Grief.
Melissa *first this Morn had reach'd the Grove,*
Exclaiming loud on unrewarded Love.
When late Aminta *join'd the mourning Fair,*
O, my dear Sister! partner in despair;

Wou'dst

Wou'dst thou new Griefs, new raging Sorrows hear,
Prepare thy Breast for Groans, thy Eyes for Tears!
Anguish refin'd, impossible to bear!
 Our little Woe scarcely deserves the Name,
But Sacharissa's fills the blast of Flame.
Thy Daphnis *was indeed the* Shepherd's Love,
And my Philander *grac'd the* Rural Grove.
But they, alas! were Swains of low Degree,
Only in Love *claiming* Priority.
But great Octavio, Sacharissa's *Lord,*
In whom high Birth, bright Fortune do accord!
Perpetual springing Wit, and ever-pleasing Youth,
The rapturous Heights of Love, and its enduring
  Truth.
A Form that caught the Eyes, and seiz'd the Heart;
His own untouch'd, as by some Magick Art,
But by th' enchanting Force of Sacharissa's *Dart.*
Prop to his Country, and to Liberty.
Yet leaving all the native Monarch free,
The Patriot, *and the* Subject, *poiz'd in just degree.*
Oh Glorianna! *mourn his early Fall,*
With Royal Tears adorn his Funeral!
  And let all Nature join th' Imperial Woe;
  Swell on, ye Flouds, ye Fountains overflow.

Melissa.

What! Great Octavio *snatch'd from Life away!*
Oh Tyrant Death! unbounded in thy Sway.
Speak on, Aminta, *tell the parting strife,*
Tell all the Mournings of a tender Wife.
That Task perform'd, that dismal Story done,
Add thou, a Mothers, for her only Son.
Suspend our own, their Sorrows be thy Scene;
Let whole Creation listen to the Theme.

         Attend

Attend ye Muses, aid this weeping Maid;
Nor with one Blast, ye Zephyrs fan the Glade.
Ye feather'd Quire, forbear a while your Song,
So sweet her Voice, ye cannot think her long:
Give Ear ye Eccho's, who in Caverns dwell,
Learn hence to speak, ye never spoke so well,
Octavio's Name's like animating Fire,
Apollo's scarce, can brighter Thoughts inspire:
And let whole Nature listen to thy Moan,
Subside all other Woes, subside our own.

Aminta.

Last Night, tempest'ous Boreas seem'd to keep,
His balful Revels on the roaring Deep;
Thunders augment the horrid rattling Din,
And the blue Fires disclose the dreadful Scene:
Tall Oaks, which many raging Gusts have born,
(Imperial still) from their broad Roots were torn:
The Wood-Nymphs quit with fear the falling Load,
And shrieking fly, to seek some new Aboad.
But I, whom Grief had wonted to Despair:
Explore the sweeping Winds, and wou'd the Tempest share,
Upon the naked Beach, by the white Lightnings glare.
Fearless I tread the Mazes of the Night,
And hunt out Objects terrible to sight.
For as the * *Roman Bards, 'tis sweet to see,*
To us who mourn, others as sad as we:
That they in part, support their Weight of Woes,
And Fate to us alone, directs not all its Blows.

---

* *Seneca, Virgil.*

Melissa.

Melissa.

Cease these Degressions, Nymph, *nor now declare,*
But of Octavio, *and his Love's Despair;*
The waiting Tears stand ready at thy Call,
The waiting Tears attend his early Fall.
    And let all Nature Join th' unequal'd Woe,
    Swell on ye Floods, ye Fountains over-flow.

Aminta.

Fantastick Boreas *rag'd himself to sleep,*
Lull'd on the Bosom of the ebbing Deep;
And struggling Light, beginning to regain
Alternate Sway, resum'd his chearful Reign.
Now Elves *and* Fairies, *quit the chosen Ground;*
No more with little Trips *beat fast the gaudy Round.*
The grumbling Thunder, solemnly retires,
Attended with Auxilliary Fires:
And all the dreadful Rant of Nature o'er,
Gives us to see the Objects we deplore.
    Join all the World in this excess of Woe,
    Swell on ye Floods, ye Fountains overflow.

Here, the departing Waves, in horrid roar,
Enriches, with their numerous Spoils, the Shoar.
Planks, Cordage, Sails, *are scatter'd all around,*
And breathless Bodies strow the conscious Ground:
Some are by rav'ning Fishes *piece-meal torn,*
For Cruelty's in every mortal Form.
Some grasp a Plank, *some to the* Mast *are ty'd,*
Thus by prolonging Fate, *they doubly dy'd.*
The various colour'd Shells, and yellow binding Sand,
No more appear, no more the shining Strand:

'Tis

'Tis all a Ship-wreck'd Scene of new-wrought Fate,
Dreadful to think, too dreadful to relate:
Polluted with the Touches of the Dead,
With Steps unnumber'd, hastily I fled,
Beyond the Mark, which the proud Sea confines,
Where great Octavio's Seat the Margin joins.
  But here all Nature weep th' exalted Woe,
  Swell on ye Floods. ye Fountains over-flow.

When warm Favonius, and the Spring invite,
With its young Bloom, to taste the fresh Delights
Of verdant Plains; the sweetly smelling Grove;
When Venus points out every Swain his Love,
Bright Sacharissa, and her Lord repair,
(Guiltless of Courts) to taste the fragrant Air:
To taste the Sweets they to each other give;
Blest in themselves, this part of Life they live:
For no Disquiets haunts the Rural Seat:
Ambition, Jealousie, the Tortures of the Great:
'Tis all Elysium, in this soft Retreat.
It was! But oh, no more! 'Tis past, 'tis gone:
Cold Death succeeds, and black Despair comes on!
  All Nature join, to weep the mighty Woe;
  Swell on ye Floods, ye Fountains over-flow.

This Palace so renown'd, for past Delight:
As near I drew, with Horror catch'd the sight.
The Lares hang their Heads, and inward groan;
The drooping Genii cry, their Lord is gone!
Virgins, who Garlands wove, his Head to crown,
Reverse the Work, and raving tear their own:
On Heaps of dismal Greens; ill-boding Yew,
Dark mournful Cypress, and the bitter Rue:
(Those Hyroglyphicks of their Woe) around,
A wither'd Plat of Grass, their Hair unbound,
With Garments torn, and scatter'd on the Ground:

Forlorn

Forlorn they lay, streaming their Eyes appear,
Directing to this Palace of Despair.
    Beyond, two human Forms in mourning Dress,
The motionless, dumb State of Death express.
Like Statues on each side the well-wrought Gate,
Guard the Ascent, to the sad Scene of Fate:
The Walls, which Antick Pictures *use t'adorn,*
In deepest Sables now their Master mourn.
Large Rooms of State, all black as low'ring Night,
Pale winking Lamps, glim'ring imperfect Light;
In Rank stand silent Shades, like those below,
But fix'd, not gliding, from this Scene of Woe.
Their down-cast Eyes, unheeding those who pass,
Eloquent Grief decypher'd on each Face.
    But, O! what change of Pain our Thoughts employ,
At the conclusive Scene of our past Joy?
Where great Octavio, *on the Bed of State,*
Gave us to think of dead Adonis *Fate.*
So Young, so Lov'd, so Mourn'd, so Dear, he fell,
And Sacharissa *sutes to* Venus *well:*
So full of Charms, so full of melting Grief,
So lost to Love, so hopeless of relief.
    All Nature weep, th'inimitable Woe,
    Swell on ye Floods, ye Fountains overflow.

  Hung round with deepest Night, the conscious Room,
Escutcheons, Streamers, and the waving Plume,
Proclaim the pompous Mourning of the Tomb.
Tall Lights, of whitest Wax, their Lustre gave,
For Ostentation follows to the Grave:
O splendid Woe! O vanity of State!
In Death's dark Realm, distinction 'twou'd create,
Where all alike are low, where all alike are great.
What means this awful Horror to our Eyes?
Within, within, the truest Mourning lies:

                                    Octavio's

Octavio's *Loss*, *struck the deciding Blow*;
There needs no heightning to supreamest Woe.
 Delia began to sing the Hero dead;
Delia, had in Apolo's *Court been bred:*
Nor Afra, *nor* Orinda *knew so well,*
Scarce Grecian Sapho, Delia *to exel:*
In Strains that tell the certainty of Fate,
And the uncertainty of Human State,
Imperfect tho' I am, I will her Song relate.

Delia.

Oh World! Oh Fortune! *vainly 'tis you charm,*
Against the Conqu'ror Death, *there's none can arm.*
Tear your bright Hair, ye Maids in Courts who shine,
And you blest Nymphs, *whom Rural Groves confine*;
In Consort wring your Hands, in Consort mourn;
Beat your fair Breasts, from thence gay Thoughts be torn.
Join in repeated Groans, in fragrant Sighs,
And quench with Tears your sparkling shine of Eyes.
See here! Alas! Look here what Death has done!
Rend your rich Robes, and put dark Cypress *on.*
Lament, lament the State of Human Woe:
Nor Birth, *nor* Youth, *can ward the cruel Blow.*
Look on Octavio, *once so good, so just,*
How early mingles he with common Dust:
From the Fair Book of Life expung'd betime,
Snatch'd in his Bloom of Years, whilst Love was in its prime.
Tho' Sacharissa's *most endearing Arms,*
Like sacred Amulets, *protects from Harms,*
Protects him from the force of any other Charms.
 Mourn all ye Sons and Daughters of the Bays,
Who now shall hear, who now reward your Lays?
For Profit ever mingled with his Praise.

Howl

Howl ye Distress'd, ye miserable Poor,
Cloath'd by his Goodness, fed from out his Store:
Let Sorrow now, what Wretchedness had done;
Ye perish'd all in his expiring Groan:
Unnumber'd were his Grants, like Ocean's Sand,
Ev'n Bounty took new Beauty from his Hand:
But———

O Annabel! Who can define thy Woes:
Alas! thou doubly feel'st the Mother-Throws,
Thro' all the Circle, thy fair Life has run,
Transporting Fondness blest this only Son:
To thee, more than his Birth, his Fame he ow'd,
Thy Graces in the Hero's Bosom glow'd.
What didst thou not, his Vertues to improve?
How early charm'd in Sacharissa's Love?
So Young, so Beauteous, the Beholders thought,
Cupid and Psyche to their Nuptials brought:
The Genial-Bed was fruitful——— There's thy Care,
Transfer thy Love, and raise Thee from Despair.
Guard those fair Blosoms from intruding Harms;
O! Early guard 'em from unlucky Storms:
View all their Father, in his blooming Race;
See thy dear Son re-lives in ev'ry Face.
Whilst———

Back, to the boundless Universe he rowls,
E'er this decides, the great dispute of Souls:
But his immortal Fame shall never waste;
Like still enduring Time, it must to Ages last.

Astrea. We that are us'd to the genuine Elegies of *Melpomene*, and other Performances of the Daughters of *Parnassus*, find but a faint Relish of the Muses in this Poem; however, since he has something of a *Genius*, we will be indulgent to the Attempt: He has accomplish'd his

H Hero;

Hero; I would know, whether he drew him as he was, or as he ought to have been.

Intel. First, Madam, the better to illustrate my Story, I beg your Attention for a second Performance of the same Poet, drawn in by the pretended Repentance, and reiterated Promises of his false Friend, who perhaps, (and that's no wonder) may deceive him the second time. 'Tis just warm from the Muse; finish'd but Yesterday, and newly communicated to me, to be distributed abroad.

Astrea.

Mourn'd by Aminta, *thus* Octavio *dy'd,*
A Nymph who had th' Extremes of Sorrow try'd;
A Cave she sought, far from the Realm of Light,
It seem'd the dark Aboad of Genuin Night;
Surrounded by a threatning gloomy Grove,
Where everlasting Ghosts incessant rove,
Pale Spectres, who had met their Fate by Love.
The Sun, nor penetrates at chearful Noon,
Nor at full Night, the glim'rings of the Moon.
No pleasing Bird, their warbling Throat employ,
Nor Nymph, nor Swain, e'er tasted here of Joy.
These fly the dreadful Shade, and haste away;
Those leave the Haunt, to Birds of dreadful prey;
The Regions native Horror they partake,
With Vulture Screams, and the dire Pinions shake,
They wound the Ear and double Darkness make.

Yet Friendship, *fearless, and alone can trace,*
The congregated Horrors of the Place.
Melissa, *braves the Terrors of the Grove,*
The Path seems rosie all, that leads to what we love.
Stretch'd on the Damps of that unwholesom Cave,
The Emblem of her faithful Lover's Grave.

By

By a dim Lamp's imperfect sickly Ray,
The poor Forlorn, Distress'd Aminta lay,
And mourn'd, and wept, and watch'd her Hours
  away.
When thus Melissa——

Melissa.

Thou seem'st a Niobe *of Grief, so petrid grown,*
That not one Sigh thy Breast, thy Voice a Moan,
Nor other sign of living Woe is shown.
But to re-animate thy sinking Frame,
If yet thy dying Fire can catch a Flame;
If vital Warmth's not quite extinguish'd there,
Or thy dear Eyes retain a latent Tear;
The Musick of thy Voice not fled away,
Or thy sweet Muse in its extreme decay.
But if they were, my Tale can force new Woe,
Bound thee from Earth, and every Grief bestow;
New Vigour add to thy expiring Life;
New Anguish to thy Soul, new anxious Strife;
As once thou mourn'st the Husband, now to weep
  the Wife.

Aminta.

Thy Voice indeed is sad, but deeply moves,
Suiting the Horror of our ruin'd Loves.
Of all those Woes, dispens'd by Hands divine,
Hast thou e'er heard a Tale to equal mine?
Can Angela *another Loss bemoan;*
Oh no! There is no second Grief, Octavio *gone.*

Melissa.

Yet I have Woes wou'd damp the Bridegroom's Joy,
And the gay Smiles of Conqu'rors destroy.

H 2

No new made Monarchs, eager of the Crown,
This Story told, wou'd put his Glories on.

Aminta.

Speak on my Friend, no more thy Grief refrain,
I live with Horror, and was form'd for Pain.
Thy brimful Eyes, much untold Sorrows show,
Give me the Cause; give me the Theme of Woe.

Melissa.

Too big for Words, and for Belief too great,
I scarce have strength the Story to repeat.
O! Canst thou guess, the worst ill Fate cou'd do,
That which can ev'n Octavio's Loss out-go!
Reflect on what's most terrible to Thought;
The widow'd World to Desolation brought.
Extinguish'd Beauty, Merit fled the Earth,
Youth, Goodness, ev'ry Virtue sally'd forth,
A rude rough Chaos, indigested worth;
Nought else remains; but, O! to sum up all,
We need but speak of Sacharissa's Fall.
She, she, is folded close in Death's cold Arms,
Death riots now in Sacharissa's Charms:
From her bright Eyes the Lightnings snatch'd away,
No more they bless the World, no more the Day.
Extinguish'd Lustre, Horror, Darkness, Night,
Succeed, alas! there most triumphant Light.
The fading Roses, slowly quit the Place,
A pale dead Hue, invades the native Face,
That Tyrant dispossesses every Grace.
The Ardor of her Sighs no longer warms,
No more her Smiles, no more her Sweetness charms.
In one sad Hour, how great a Change is made!
In one sad Hour, Ten thousand Beauties fade.

Aminta

Aminta.

This strikes indeed, it wounds with strong surprise,
But O to happy Realms, bright Sacharissa *flies.*
The Storm now past, and cruel Death o'recome,
New Joys arise from their united Tomb.
To blissful Worlds they fly, they rest from Care;
Admir'd and pointed out (by all) the happy Pair.

Melissa.

What shame to thee, to me, thus long to mourn,
With latent Tears, to hover o'er an Urn?
Had Love, or Grief, possess'd us as it ought,
We now had been beyond the pain of Thought.
Like Sacharissas, *had our Flame been strong,*
So short the Torment, and the Triumph long.
She! who had every Bribe that Bliss cou'd move,
Youth, Beauty, vast Possessions, smiling Love.
The Tribute of all Hearts, the Wish of Eyes,
Neglecting these, for her Octavio *dies.*
O lovely, faithful Wife! *O most sublime,*
Unequal'd Fair! the Muses Theme be thine.
All Pens, all Tongues, shall celebrate thy Fame;
And distant Regions learn to Bless thy Name.

Aminta.

This then's the Vision that I lately saw,
Charm'd by soft Sleep, which gives ev'n Sorrow Law.
Reclin'd, along that melancholy Stream,
I'll tell thee all; 'twas far beyond a Dream.
A Youth appear'd, divinely Bright and Fair;
His Eyes celestial Fire, Sun-beams his Hair!

A Silver Wand *did grace his lovely Hand,*
Which waving twice, he gave this sweet Command:
Come follow me, thou weeping, constant Maid,
And, for a while, be all thy Sorrows staid.
　　Away! thro' pleasing Worlds, all beautiful and new,
With softest ease, and swift as thought we flew.
Till resting on enamel'd flowry Ground,
Thus spake my Guide, cast-thou thy Eyes around:
See the kind Palms, *how fondly they improve,*
Their mutual Joys, clasp'd by the Arms they love.
Behold the wedded Myrtles, *and again behold,*
The spreading Ivy *does the* Elm *infold.*
The mated Turtles, *perch on ev'ry Bough.*
Mark how they Coe and Kiss, and seem to Vow.
By these fond am'rous Emblems that appear,
Can'st thou not guess whose Palace shou'd be near?
It must be Hymen's *sure, I weeping said,*
Hymen, *who all my tendrest Hopes betray'd.*
See there! forlorn he is, the Youth reply'd,
Mourning a lovly Fair, *that lately dy'd;*
A faithful Wife, bright Sacharissa, *who,*
Despising Life, flies to her Lord below.
See, see! his Saffron Robe is found,
In pieces rent, and scatter'd on the Ground.
Around the pensive God, the weeping Cupids *lay;*
Far he had thrown th' Hymenial *Torch away:*
Which now, but faintly glim'ring, seem'd t' expire,
But that the mourning Loves, *as faintly, fan'd the Fire.*
　　A River *next, my Guide, divides the Flood;*
On either side the crouded Waters stood.
Come view the Plains, he said, the happy Grove,
Where faithful Hearts swell with eternal Love.
We reach the shining Strand, the Golden Bow'rs,
Where Times no more; no counting Days, or Hours:　　　　　　　　　　No

No rouling Years, *that snatch our* Bloom *away,*
With change of Seasons, *bringing* Youth's *decay.*
Like the first Pair, in full Perfection form'd;
For ever Charming, *and for ever* Charm'd.
    Whilst thus intent, on all the glorious Throng,
A brighter Beauty, *sweep'd the Shades along.*
New-come she seem'd, new-landed on the Plain;
Caress'd and Crown'd by all the heavenly Train.
Some Garlands brought, and strew'd with Sweets her
    Hair;
The falling Sweets o're-press the welcome Fair:
Thro' Acclamations of celestial Voice,
They bear her to the Scene of all her Joys.
To her Octavio, *who her Heart had fill'd,*
For, oh! 'twas Sacharissa, *I beheld.*
    Whilst, with unbounded Raptures, they caress,
    A Radiant Youth, *thus sung their Happiness.*

The Praises of the Dead.

Strike the harmonious Lyre, *and sing aloud;*
Sing Sacharissa's *Glory to the Croud.*
Each Scene she finish'd with so nice a Care,
No Master-piece of Life was ever half so fair.
Most happy Father, *who has liv'd to see*
A Child, *of such unerring* Piety.
Bless'd Infants, *who from such a Mother came,*
You, fair Born Daughters, *imitate her* Fame;
As hers may yours, acquire a deathless Name.
Ye happy Sons, tread in the Path she made;
Keep but the Track, *your Laurels ne'r can fade.*
Honour, that Idol, never yet cou'd see
So fair, and yet so true, a Votary.
When Youth, Wealth, Beauty, *all invite to live;*
What the gay Court, *or gayer* Love, *coud give:*

That part divided, which enrich'd the whole,
Were Bribes too mean for Sacharissa's Soul.
Deaf to th' Enchantments of a tempting Age,
Deaf to those Blandisments which Youth engage:
Excluded from all Joy, to Grief a prey;
The eating Viper gnaw'd his fatal way;
Deep sunk in Woe, she scarce beheld the Light,
Never, O never, tasted of Delight.
Till Death, so often call'd for, came at last;
Death, when intreated, makes but slower haste.
Sullen and proud, he bids the Wretched stay,
But snatches the most prosp'rous in a day.
 These Storms o're-past, the happy Pair unite
Their Virtues, crown'd with uncontroul'd Delight.
Fix'd in the highest Orb, they brightest move;
The shining Gods such Happiness approve.
New Constellations they so grace the Sky,
Look up the World, and laud their Memory.

Astrea. I doubt this is but your Poet's Compliment; for, as lately as I came from thence, they knew nothing of the matter then.

Intell. That's no Business of his, he cares not whether ever they get there or no; I see his Flattery has not catch'd your Mightiness's applause nor approbation, and yet 'tis well enough, according to the rate of the present Writers. There are so few in this warlike, illiterate Age, that understand the true Beauties of Poetry, that the happy few that can distinguish themselves (in a just Indignation at its ignorance) are silent; the Critick is degenerated from his first Original; 'tis now only understood as speaking of a Person of Spleen and Ill-nature, who professes against being pleased at any thing but his own Compositions, or when he can find fault

with

with others; he never applauds, tho' in the right place, but often condemns in the wrong: And these (by Faction and Party) are Leading Men among the ignorant, who are fifty to one, the greater number. This silent Resentment, from the real Worthy, (those that can rescue declining Poetry) gives the greater liberty to the Poetaster to pester the Town, and overswarm it with their Bumbast. A certain Author says, " That he Tasts Verses like Melons, " if they have not something in their flavour " approaching to Perfection, he cannot relish " 'em. I'm afraid he must have resolv'd, had he liv'd now, not to have eat at all, or at least without the *Bon Goust*.

Virtue. My Lady *Intelligence* is wandred from her Subject, she has forgot the dead Lady, and her History.

Intell. But a short Digression, Ladies, 'tis natural to our Sex to Elope. You must know then, that the Lady St. *Amant*, the Poets *Sacharissa*, dy'd for Love; a Love so violent and indigestive, that she cou'd not throw it off at a less price than her Life.

Astrea. That is but what we found in the Essay: Can your Poets here below speak Truth?

Intell. Metaphorically, or by way of *Allegory*. The Lady St. *Amant* dy'd for Love indeed; but for whom? Not for *Monsieur Octavio!*

Astrea. On to the purpose; for we have great Affairs upon our Hands.

Intell. And I have yet very much to show and to inform you of, call'd to so eminent a Station: I shall endeavour to discharge my self as I ought of an Employment honourable and distinguishing.

Mon-

Monsieur St. L'Amant was Master of a very great Estate; so far the Poet's Character is right; he found the Wife his Mother bestow'd upon him much to his Mind, being neither nice nor enterprizing; he lov'd lazy Pleasures, and therefore never gave himself the Fatigue of Flattery and Dissimulation to the Ladies, without which you seldom prevail with them, unless it be by Dint of Money; and that he cou'd employ more to his Mind in the Revels of *Bacchus*, than the Rites of *Venus*; and that's one more Perfection agreeing with the Historian: But I should be at a Loss to carry the Parallel any further. As to his being a *Patriot*, I never heard of any thing he perform'd that way, dissenting but by a *No*; and encouraging that Party he would fain have it thought he was of, but by a *Yes*. His Pleasure was in his Appetite, I mean good Eating; eminent for the distinction of his Taste, and a nice order'd Table; Wine, and the hotter Liquors were the occasion of his Death; the Physicians vainly forbid him too liberal a use of 'em: He dy'd memorable for nothing, but introducing a Bosom-Friend of his to his Lady's Intimacy and Favour, and lessening his Children's Fortunes to enlarge her Dowry: 'Twas kind and obligingly done of him, he cou'd do no more, but die quickly out of the way, to leave her the richest Widow in all *Atalantis*.

A Donative so much to her advantage, gave her Parents the Alarm; her Mother, like a wise and prudent Woman, after the first Gust of her Sorrow was blown over, read her perpetual Lectures of Widows, that were undone and ruin'd by marrying of second Ventures; her Husband's Family were not at all pleas'd at the Distinction

Diſtinction he had made, in prejudice to the Children, and probably were then upon the watch, to find what they might have to object againſt her.

The young *Baron de Mezaray* was of a very ancient Family, but the too liberal Exceſſes of his Forefathers, had extremely impared the Eſtate, he could no more maintain it in its former Splendor; there were who love to concern themſelves in the Affairs of all Men, that wonder'd he did not ſeek to better his Circumſtances, by applying himſelf, either to the *Court* or *Army*; probably it was not his Principle, or he did not love the Fatigues of the *Camp* or *Cabinet*.

Monſieur St. l'Amant lov'd nothing ſo tenderly as he did the *Baron*; he would not by his good Will have breath'd a Day without him; he was the *Zeſt* to all his Pleaſures. *Bacchus*, (as well as he lov'd him) had not his true Flavour when he was wanting; and one wou'd think he cou'd have e'en ſhar'd with him the Delights of *Venus*, by ſo frequently forcing him upon his Lady: He would tell her, that if there were any thing ſhe could more oblige him in than other, 'twould be in tenderly reſpecting the *Baron*, who deſerved admiration more than all Mankind put together; that this degenerate Age had nothing elſe to boaſt of, had not Nature put him into the World; we muſt have been at a loſs to have gueſs'd at the perfection of our People of Virtue, that were born ſo many Ages before us; when the World was young in Vice, he was indeed a true Copy of 'em, their ſhining Qualities all center'd in him, his extraordinary Modeſty only kept him from univerſal Admiration, a Quality
in-born

in-born to the most worthy; that when he pleas'd, 'twas but making himself known to receive the first Dignities and Employments of the Empire, tho' the ill-natur'd will tell you, his greatest Merit, according to *Monsieur's Goust agreeable*, consisted in being a *bonne Companion*, in knowing when your *Craw-fish, Soups, Olios, Terren, Fricacies*, and other Elegancies of the Table, were in perfection; which were best for a Preparative, which for a Digestive, Spirit of *Clary*, Tincture of *Saffron, Barbadoes-Water, Persico, ou l'eau de vit, avec le Fleure d'Orange*. Madam *de St. l'Amant* had been marry'd so young, that Love had nothing to do in that Affair; he was not at all necessary to a Match made up by Friends; however she grew up with great Inclinations to comply in every thing with a Husband so obliging, therefore we must not think it at all strange, that she so readily obey'd him, in esteeming the *Baron*. He was by freedom of Conversation let into a thousand Intimacies, which gave him Opportunities of distinguishing himself by a more insinuating Behaviour, than was necessary to a Husband at ease, and in full possession of what ever a Wife can bestow. Love, that dangerous Enemy of our quiet, that sooner or later forces every Heart by Experience, to acknowledge him the Master, had a malicious desire to poyson that easie manner of Life, between *Monsieur* and *Madam St. l'Amant*, he trick'd up the *Baron* in all things that cou'd appear lovely to the Eyes of the Lady: Dress'd up his Air with killing Smiles; furnish'd his Eyes from his own Quiver; begg'd some of his beautiful *Mother*'s Sweetness, and her best Water for Complection; pilfer'd from every one of the *Graces*, to adorn his Favourite,

vourite, and e'en ſtole ſome of the *Ambroſia*, to diffuſe throughout his Perſon, ſo that nothing appear'd ſo charming as he to the Lady: I had forgot to tell you, that *Cupid*, tho' he be not very good-natur'd, in compaſſion to the reſt of the Sex, made theſe Perfections viſible to none but her; as to the ſuper Ornaments of the Mind, they were not neceſſary in this caſe. What have Lovers to do with Senſe and Judgment? Wiſdom was never ſo much as ever made mention of in their Court of Requeſts; brisk Repartees; ſome ſuperficial Sparklings of Wit; a well-turn'd Period; an agreeable manner of telling a Story, no matter whether the Story be good or bad; eternal Compliances; inceſſant Flattery; never-ending Praiſes; perfect Reſignation, and continual Importunities, are their Letters of Mart, and paſs better in Love's-Exchange, than fine Underſtanding.

Madam *St. l'Amant*, who was no Conjurer in unraveling Myſteries, tho' they were e'en thoſe of Nature, wonder'd what ſort of new Gueſt ſhe had entertain'd; ſhe neither eat nor ſlept, a ſort of languiſhing Melancholy made her Days and Nights uneaſie to her; *Spleen* and *Vapours* were then faſhionable Appellations for Diſtempers they cou'd ſtrickly give no other Name to; if a Lady wanted Money for the *Baſſet-Table*, and her Lord refus'd her, preſently ſhe was troubled with the *Vapours*; if a Set of Jewels to go to the Apartment, or Preſents for a private Favourite, ſtill 'twas the *Vapours*; if ſhe was forbid the freedom of a Hackney-Coach, with her Boſom-Friend the Mantua-maker, the *Vapours* were intollerably powerful, and nothing like a Jaunt *incognito* to allay 'em; in ſhort, poor *Vapours* was
forced

forced to father abundance of Inconveniencies. Madam *St. l'Amant* had recourse to 'em; she refug'd under the title of *Vapours*, a Distemper all new and perplexitive: *Signior Mompellier* the Women's Physitian, was order'd to sit in judgment upon my Lady's Indisposition; according to his way of rambling, finding it lay chiefly in the Fancy, he began to entertain her with something which he thought very diverting, his own Amours, and the Favours that had been bestow'd upon him. Madam *St. l'Amant* had indeed heard that was his way, but had never prov'd it before; she assum'd the severe Air of a Woman of Honour, shock'd at the extreme Liberty the Doctor took in his buffoon Relation: When he saw he had miss'd of his Aim, and cou'd not divert, he seriously advis'd her Husband to take care of her; she had the height of *Vapours*, which might degenerate into Lunacy; to prove this, he repeated those Stories which her melancholy Spleen had been proof against; and because she was not entertain'd with 'em, and did not burst out into a Laughter at his Jests, he concluded her mad; and yet this is the first rank'd Wit of the Age: But since I intend to carry you where your selves shall be Judges of his Conversation, I'll not forestal it by Description.

 Still the poor Lady languish'd under this nameless Melancholy; *Monsieur* was good-natured, and made himself troublesomly officious; but all his Kindness but increas'd her Malady; every thing he did was displeasing; she had even a Repugnancy in her Nature at speaking civilly to him; when he would touch her Hand, it redoubled her Distemper, but to kiss her Mouth was *Vapours*

[margin: Dr. Garth.]

wrought

wrought up to Frenzy. She wonder'd more than he did at this apparent Dislike; he began in good earnest to fear the Doctor was infallible, and that she would be mad; when he offer'd at carressing, she wou'd squeak out as if she were possess'd; Love for the *Baron* caus'd her (without her own knowledge) to hate her Husband; she receiv'd him with Frowns; answer'd him perversly, and from the purpose; hated to Eat or Sleep where he was, but when the *Baron* appear'd 'twas the Reverse; she smil'd whether she wou'd or no, mauger her self, her Eyes ran into a Dance of Joy; her Heart rebounded in her Breast, Spleen and *Vapours* were no more, her Conversation took a gay turn; the little affected Arts by which the Fair wou'd insinuate, became natural; she new-stampt her very Air and Words; all that the *Baron* said, all that the *Baron* did, was delightful to her; she cou'd sit at Table, nay ev'n eat, so he were but one of the Guest; she cou'd reconcile her self to Cards, provided he made one; nay more, her Husband became tollerable to her, in his company; there was nothing to be seen but Smiles of perpetual Joy, whilst the *Baron* was by; but when he departed all was Sun-set, or worse, rising Mists, and cloudy *Vapours*: Her Husband, without any Reflection to her prejudice) saw that nothing diverted her but the *Baron*, and therefore begg'd him as earnestly as if he were suing for the greatest good, to keep his Wife company till her Health was recover'd; he did not in the least wonder that she shou'd think well of him; he had endeavour'd all he could to raise a Friendship and Esteem in her; and because he himself was never so well pleas'd as when he was with him,

he

he easily believ'd another might have the same Sentiments, and be as well entertain'd with what he found so diverting.

The *Baron* was not so great a Novice in Love-Affairs, but he could guess himself the occasion of Madam's Distemper; whether he prided himself in the good Fortune, is not very material, or how great the Contest was between Friendship for his Friend, and Charity for the Lady, at last he concluded that 'twas height of Friendship to have Charity, for by that means he should preserve, and put out of pain a Creature that was dear to his Friend; but the difficulty lay not in his good Intentions, but the manner of assuaging the Griefs of the afflicted Fair One. She had been bred up in a perfect reserve to all the World but her Husband, the Offers of Love from another might probably shock her to a violent degree, and should she once take a Disgust, it might re-call and fix her wandring Heart to its first Object; he therefore concluded it best to redouble, if possible, his Diligence, and to let Chance determine the rest.

The Season was come for going into the Country, the Lady's want of Health seem'd to require it, but she cou'd not tell how to part with the *Baron*'s company; not that she suspected the Foulness of the Infection; she was pleas'd, without knowing what pleas'd her; the flushing Blood, obedient to the Dictates of her Love-sick Heart, wou'd immediately fly into her fair Face and Neck at his approach, a sort of shivering, an alternative of heat and cold would seize her, but still this was but the Lady's friendly Distemper, *Vapours*; but such *Vapours*, that was not in the power of *Sal-Volatile*, *Salmoniack*, nor *Spirit* of *Harts-horn* to cure; in vain did the Gentlemen of the Faculty fit in confultation; the *Baron* had more Vertue than all their Medicines; and becaufe good Nature and Friendfhip were his Talent, to oblige Monfieur, and ferve his Lady, he ftirr'd from her as little as he could; but the Husband, who lov'd nothing fo well as his Friend, and his Wife, always made a third; the Debauch went round in her company, tho' fhe would not fhare in it, which was her own fault, in not believing this Doctrine of her Mafters, *That the Bottle was a Cure for all Diftempers.*

Still was the *Fair* ignorant of the Evil that tormented her. The *Baron* one Day alone with her, fhe faid to him, What melancholy Hours, my Lord, are Monfieur St. *l'Amant*, and my felf, going to pafs in the Country, unlefs you can have the Goodnefs to go with us? I do not ufe to ask Favours of any one, but I find you fo neceffary to my Diverfion, from this dangerous Melancholy that has feiz'd me, in pity to my felf, I make you this Requeft. By this fine fet Speech, you may guefs at the Lady's Innocence; fhe was not accuftom'd to read Books of Gallantry; knew no more of Love than what fhe had got from *Opera's* and *Comedies*, where unlefs a Lady be in Love before, fhe feldom makes application; thofe of the Sex that have that happy Indifference, go to a *Play* but when 'tis cry'd up and becomes the fafhion, and then only becaufe the reft of the World goes; fhe'll go for Company, to fee if any Lady have finer Jewels than her felf, to expofe her own, and to obferve the Modes, *&c.*

She even fpoke to her Husband, to entreat the *Baron* to go along with 'em: He defired no more; he was over-joy'd at the Sympathy he found in his Wife's Inclinations; he bid her be eafie, the *Baron* fhou'd go with them; then he fell to teizing the *Beloved*, who did not want half that Courtfhip as he pretended, where could he be better regaled? Where could he live fo well as at *Monfieur St. l'Amant*? Befides, the fair Lady's Admiration and Pain for him, made him refolve to pleafe himfelf, and oblige her. They were no fooner got down, but the Lady fancied herfelf much better; the reafon was plain, the *Baron* was feldom from her, and her Intervals of Melancholy confequently fhorter; indeed, thofe Days that they went a hunting it went ill with her; then fhe had nothing to do but to have the *Vapours* in perfection; in fhort, fhe declared herfelf a mortal Enemy to that Diverfion, and oblig'd 'em to keep at home more than they would have done.

A young Relation of hers, named *Berintha*, to divert herfelf and others, came there upon a Vifit, with an intent to pafs away the Summer; fhe was very witty, entirely agreeable, full of *Amufement*, and *Coquet* enough: She would have thought it a great Injury to her Charms, if any *Cavaliere* fhould not feem to be fenfible of 'em; at firft fhe did not give herfelf thought enough to examine the different Interefts of the People fhe was with. She expected no great good (as to matter of admiration) from *Monfieur* St. *l Amant*, who had never been in Love in his Life, unlefs you'll call it Love to be a good and kind Husband to a Wife, that he had marry'd when he was a Child, and grew up with. Thofe are tender Friendfhips, free from the Difquiets, the Hopes and Fears for poffeffion; calm are their Defires; calm are their Joys;
they

they may be well term'd discharging ones Duty with a good grace, wearing your Fetters with no inclination to Freedom; but the fierce *Delights*, and *ravishing Sweets* of consenting *Love*, after *Toils, Assiduities, Despairs,* and *ardent Desires,* are all foreign to a *Hymen* imposed upon us before we have either Age or Leisure to desire it. But Parents think their Chidren can never be unhappy, if they do but take care of their Interest, which is the true reason that we so seldom see People of Condition, fortunate in their Marriages. The Men seek their Diversions abroad, and the Ladies often are not more innocent, at best their Husbands Inclinations elsewhere never fails to render them miserable.

Berintha having small Hopes of being adored by one that preferred *Bacchus* to *Venus,* thought she should have a melancholy time of it, if the *Baron* did not prove more sensible. Your true *Coquet* thinks all Pleasures insipid, that are not mingled with the Pretence of Love; I say the Pretence, for their varying Tempers never know what true Love means. What Pains will such a one give herself, to procure a little Flattery? How indefatigable will they be, to gain the Offer of a vain taudry Heart, which they are sure to despise, if once it becomes their real Conquest? But if a Man of Sense ever be so miserable, she is sure to make him suffer all that *Ostentation, Pride,* and Desire of having the World see her sovereign Power, can inflict.

Berintha, being *Coquet* in perfection, whenever she spoke to the *Baron,* she soften'd the Tone of her Voice, call'd Smiles to her Mouth, and Dimples to her Cheeks; assum'd a dying Sweetness in her Eyes; threw out the Bait with all the

Artifice of a skilful hand; not that she lov'd him, any other Man wou'd have serv'd her business as well; her *Pride* was this, to be admir'd: She mortally hated that Lady, whom she could not rob of her Gallant. Such a Solitude was afrighting to one of her Temper; if the *Baron* had immediately surrender'd, she had chang'd her first Designs of passing the Summer there, and gone to the *Hot-Baths*, where a much more numerous Assembly promis'd her much greater probability of Admiration.

The *Baron*, grateful to the Pains Madam *de St. l'Amant* felt for him, wou'd not give in to the Artifices of the *Coquet*, at least till he had suffer'd her to play all her Tricks over, and was come to the down-right advance, of telling him, that his Indifference displeas'd her, nay, (perhaps inflam'd by his Coldness, the Antiperistasis had really warm'd her) she reproach'd him one Day in the Garden, after so gallant a manner, that he knew not how to defend himself; she told him, 'twas highly unnatural, in a Man of his Age, to let a young Lady pass so neglected, she would not believe that these were Times for Gentlemen to leave their Hearts behind 'em; that shou'd a Beauty (as she did not doubt) have engross'd it whilst he was at *Angela*, he knew better, than not to have it now at Command, since new Places generally produced new Conquests, to People of his Merit.

Nothing could have been said more obliging; he was very near being catch'd with it, at another Time, and in another Place, he would not at all have hesitated; that fair Lady, or any other fair Lady might have commanded him, as far as she pleas'd, at least to the extent of his

Power,

Power, tho' he had ev'n ſtrain'd to oblige her. But he knew very well, that *Coquets* deſire nothing ſo much of the Conqueſt, as the Reputation of it. Twas impoſſible to have an Affair with any of that Stamp a Secret; they are the firſt themſelves in proclaiming the advantage they have over other Women. He ſhould loſe tender Madam *St. l'Amant*, her Virgin-Heart; her appropriated Kindneſs, for one that had not the leaſt part of her value; ſo that he did not know what to anſwer her. *Berintha* was as cunning as a Witch; by the perturbation of his Mind, which ſhow'd it ſelf upon his Face, and the ſilence he held; ſhe had her Eyes open'd in a Minute; ſhe recollected with an admirable ſwiftneſs of Thought, all Madam *St. l'Amant*'s Complaiſances to the *Baron*, and his Aſſiduities to her; ſhe no longer doubted but that was the Myſtery, and wonder'd that ſhe ſhould be ſo long unravelling of it; ſhe was ſure that Coldneſs could not be natural to him. Oh poor *Baron!* continu'd ſhe, with a loud Laugh, I pity you; I ſee how 'tis with you, you are afraid to make Madam *St. l'Amant* jealous.

Madam *St. l'Amant*, he anſwer'd, with a ſevere Frown, is not a Subject for us to trifle with, her Virtue is above being cenſur'd by the Standard of others; if your Thoughts and Inclinations be gay, you are not to judge of hers by your own. Nothing cou'd have been ſaid more diſobliging; it confirm'd *Berintha* in her Suſpicions, therefore to be reveng'd on them both, ſhe was reſolved not to throw up her Cards, till ſhe had ſufficiently perplex'd the Game. She feign'd to be of his Opinion; that what he ſaid he was in the right of, for Madam

St. l'Amant was a Woman of undoubted Honour; what she had spoke was only by way of Railery, to find (if possible) some Excuse, tho' never so improbable, for that excessive Coldness, wherewith he receiv'd the Favours, a young Lady, (not wholly disagreeable) bestow'd upon him.

The *Baron* fell into her Snare; he believ'd what she said, and to confirm her, spoke and did so many kind things, as would have pacified one less acquainted with the World; but she was too cunning, and knew whence they were deriv'd. She hated being oblig'd to another, for what she thought her own due, yet she feign'd to give in to what he said, but violently, (with a premediated Design) oppos'd him as he kiss'd and pull'd her. He proceeded neither with the Respects nor Transports of a Lover: *Berintha* was not to distinguish, at this time of Day, between the real and the pretended; she had so often acted her self, that she soon discovered the Counterfeit in him. They had left Madam *St. l'Amant* upon a Bed of repose, in a Banquetting-House, in the Garden, to try to get a little Sleep. *Berintha* did not think her self half enough tumbled, but with her little Graces and Affectations, she still provok'd the *Baron* to kiss and teize her, which she resisted as much as her strength would permit: Warm'd by the soft Play and Touches of a young willing *Coquet*, he follow'd her in good earnest, and pull'd her down by main force upon a Bed of Greens, in an Arbor where they were, till he had almost kiss'd and ruffled her to pieces.

Probably

Probably he had made greater advantages, if *Monsieur* St. *l'Amant* had not surpriz'd him. Oh, *Gud* Cosen, says the Lady, getting up from the Baron, who did then let her rise, was there ever such a Brute? He's ruder than a Bear! is this your modest Gentleman? I'll never trust my self with him again? Then brushing briskly by 'em, she ran down the Walk, and struck up another that led to the Banqueting-House, all discompos'd and ruffled as she was, and quite out of Breath with running, she flings open the Door in a pretended fright, and throws herself upon the Marble Floor, by Madam St. *Amant*'s Bed of Repose, who did not fail very earnestly to enquire the occasion of that disorder. It was a long time before she pretended to have power to speak, at last she told her, the Baron had undoubtedly ravish'd her, if her Husband had not come in and prevented him. What became of poor Madam St. *l'Amant* at this moment, this was the worst *Vapours* of all! her Blood ran to heart, and left her Face pale as the dying or dead. New-born *Jealousie* met with it in its passage, and, by a flush of Rage and Fire, return'd it back in perfect Scarlet: It cover'd her Neck and Breasts, as well as her Face, glow'd all over her Body, and rose to choak her Words, she cou'd not bring out the least Syllable. Lord, Cosen, cry'd cunning *Berintha*, (who had done all this to provoke her) are you out of your Senses? what's the matter with you? I'll lay my Life you are sick of a Distemper you don't know: 'A my Conscience you are Jealous, and love the Baron. Here the infallible Lady press'd the afflicted to speak to her, but she cou'd only burst out in a greater paſſion of Tears; and then 'twas all like to be well enough; no Woman ever dies of a Diſtemper of the Mind, when ſhe can once come to cry it out. *Berintha* us'd all poſſible arts to pacifie her, her Inſinuations were almoſt irreſiſtible. Madam St. *l' Amant* was all generous and ſincere, far from ſuſpecting artifice in others, ſhe never was herſelf acquainted with any. *Berintha* had nam'd to her that terrible Diſeaſe, which ſhe had ſo long felt, and yet cou'd give no name to. *Jealouſie* had diſcover'd it to be *Love*, becauſe he never appears in a place where Love is not. *Jealouſie* confirm'd it to be *Love*; becauſe in a moment ſhe paſs'd to an averſion for her Coſin, who before had been very well in her kindneſs. What ſhou'd ſhe do? That airy Creature was Miſtreſs of her Secret, and wou'd infallibly divert the Town with it; what cou'd ſhe do? She ſaw ſhe was in a moment going to loſe that long-valu'd Reputation and Eſteem that ſhe had been hitherto in poſſeſſion of; but what moſt amaz'd her, was, that ſhe cou'd be ſo many Months ignorant of her own Diſtemper. She hop'd it was ſtill a Secret to all the World but *Berintha*, that even the Baron himſelf was unacquainted with it, whoſe knowledge ſhe more dreaded than her Husbands; he had ever been ſo extreme reſpectful, that ſhe had reaſon to think him ignorant; for few Men but grow preſuming, when they believe themſelves deſirable.

Berintha favour'd her Modeſty, and gave her time to ſet her Heart and Mind in order; for as yet ſhe had not ſpoke one Word. The *Coquet* had what ſhe wanted, and did not care, upon ſecond Thoughts, to be made a Confident, for

fear

fear it might be some sort of a Tie upon her not to blaze abroad the Secret. Seeing her Cosin had left crying, and was fal'n into a profound *Resuery*, forgetting her late misfortune, as if she had not been like to be Ravish'd, nor no such thing had happen'd; she got up (singing a Tune in the new Opera) to adjust herself at a Glass; but when she saw what a Figure she was, how tumbled and disorder'd, she burst out in a loud Laughter, tho' not able to draw the Lady from her Cogitations. When she had compos'd her Dress, repeating the same Opera-Air, she went out of the Banqueting-House, and left her to herself.

The Baron, who had shifted off *Monsieur St. l'Amant*, under pretence of taking a little Sleep in that Arbor, to recover his amorous Fatigues, no sooner saw him return into the House, but he arose, and, by a round-about way, got to another part of the Banqueting-Room, wherein the two Ladies were. He listned and heard *Berintha* very busie upon his Chapter: This was exactly what he expected, but he did not know what to think, whether he shou'd be sad or joyful at her telling her Cosen that she was in love with the Baron, and Jealous of her: He heard the poor afflicted Lady's Passion of Tears, the *Coquets* endeavours to appease, and draw from her the confirmation (by Words as well as Actions) of that dangerous Secret; and, in short, all that pass'd till *Berintha* went out. He lean'd against a Tree, as if it were to weigh and determine with himself what to do, whether he shou'd leave the Lady to recover her Disorder, by time and reflection, or offer his mediation: He guess'd the worst of her Distemper (if she

really

really lov'd him as he believ'd) muſt be *Jealouſie*; therefore he thought it but Charity to eaſe her Mind in that particular. He fetch'd a little compaſs to bring him into the Walk which fronted the Door *Berintha* had left open, becauſe he would not have her think he had overheard 'em. So profound was her Contemplations, that ſhe ſaw him not, tho' her Face was that way, till the noiſe he made in entring rais'd her Eyes, which were heavy, and weigh'd down with weeping. He appear'd ſo lovely to her Imagination, and ſo reſpectful to her Sight, that ſhe had no inclination to receive him roughly. In the moſt inſinuating and paſſionate Terms, he beg'd (without interruption) a ſhort Audience of her; and tho', as he ſaid it was, what no Gentleman ought to do, to betray the advances that were made him by any of the fair Sex, yet he had ſo ardent a deſire to vindicate himſelf to her, that he would ſacrifice his very *Devoir* to compaſs it. Then he told of his whole Affair with *Berintha*. *Coquets* do not always appear ſuch to their own Sex, their free behaviour are generally attributed to Youth and Gaiety, which poſſibly may be innocent. This is what Madam St. *l'Amant* always believ'd of her Coſin; but when ſhe heard the Baron report of the advances ſhe had made him, and of her telling him that he durſt not take advantage of 'em, for fear of making her Jealous, the apparent deſign ſhe had to get him to tumble her in that manner, only that ſhe might the better draw the Secret from her, by her pretended diſcovery of the Baron's Rudeneſs. That Air of Truth with which he ſpoke, and her own powerful Inclinations to believe well of him, made her no longer

longer doubt any part of the Relation. He durſt not take notice to her, that he thought (by her Eyes) that ſhe had been crying, but contented to juſtifie himſelf; which, if there had been no *Jealouſie* in the caſe, he wou'd have thought himſelf oblig'd to do. No Man wou'd deſire to be found guilty of ſuch a breach of Manners, as to attempt to Raviſh a young Woman of Condition in a Relation's Houſe.

The greateſt part of Madam St. *l'Amant*'s uneaſineſs, vaniſh'd with her *Jealouſie*; her Heart aſſum'd its former Tranquility; if there can be any tranquility in a place where Love reſides; and yet undoubtedly there may be a calm, when compar'd to the tempeſtous Sea of *Jealouſie*. She beg'd him not to diſquiet himſelf for what ſuch an unthinking Creature as *Berintha* ſaid; ſhe thought ſhe ſerv'd him well enough to report what ſhe did of him, ſince he wou'd kiſs and teaſe her againſt her will; ſhe found it beſt to turn the Matter into Railery; but did not once repeat what had been ſaid of her ſelf, that was too tender a Point. They walk'd back to the Houſe in a perfect good Intelligence; *Berintha* met 'em with ſome Country Ladies that were come to Viſit: She ſwell'd almoſt to burſting to find her miſchief had no better effect, no longer doubting but ſhe was made the Sacrifice, and that the Baron was as happy as Madam St. *l'Amant* cou'd make him. The ill luck ſhe had at Cards that Evening, gave her a good pretence to vent her Spleen and Ill-nature. The Baron won, and did not fail (contrary to the exact Decorum of Good-manners) to inſult a little: *Berintha* cou'd not bear it; there were a

great

great many secret Reproaches thrown out, which were understood by none in the Company but Madam St. *l'Amant* and themselves.

Berintha saw the best of her Market was over at that place, and therefore thought it high time to remove to another; besides, she long'd to be ruining her Cosin's Reputation, and proclaiming her Amour with the Baron. The World is so uncharitable to Lovers, they never will believe that they see one another without Consequences, tho' nothing cou'd be more innocent than Madam St. *l'Amant*, nor respectful than the Baron. *Berintha* soon made it be thought otherwise. The first of these Ladies, warn'd by what she had found of her wicked Temper, had repented to her Heart those dangerous Proofs of Disquiets and Jealousie in the Banqueting-House; because her Tongue had been silent, she wou'd have had it thought, that she was only agitated by a prodigious Fit of the Vapors, so that she knew not what she did: *Berintha* was too cunning a Baggage to let this pass upon her, tho' she had too much Manners to contradict her Cosin. The Ladies parted with a world of indifferency on both sides: 'Twas worse between this and the Baron; he goes a Hunting, and stays at a Country-Gentleman's House two days before she went away, that he might be sure not to see her depart, because of being oblig'd to take his leave of her.

Assoon as *Berintha* was got to *Angela*, she laid about her very handsomly, in respect to her Cosin's Honour, and not only made a Confidence of her Affair with the Baron to all she met; but even told Madam St. *l'Amant*'s Mother (who was her

her near Relation, and enquired of her why she left her Daughter before the Season was over?) That for her part, she did not love to stay in a place where People grew uneasie; she cou'd not help it, if the Baron thought her younger and more agreeable than her Cosin; but that she thought again she was not over-prudent to publish her Resentment and Concern to all the World; neither did she find it was safe for her to stay in a place where her Honour had been attempted with such Impunity. These Reports were highly scandalous in the Ears of the old Lady, she did not fail to write a large Sheet of Paper to her Daughter, stuff'd full of Reproaches for her past, and Admonitions for a better future Behaviour. Neither did *Berintha*'s Malice stop here, so effectually she pursu'd it, that an old blunt Gentleman (highly scandaliz'd at what he heard) by her Agent's instigation, wrote to *Monsieur St. l'Amant*, whose Friend he was, to advise him to take care of the Baron and his Wife.

This fatal Letter found the Husband ill at ease, by the return of a Distemper which, young as he was, us'd to afflict him. He cou'd not believe what he read; the pain of his Body then became little, compar'd to that of his Mind; it seem'd to him as if he awak'd from a Sleep of Popies; he cou'd not but wonder how he shou'd thus long be blind, to what was so clearly seen by the World. His Lady and the Baron, had before employ'd their endeavours to make him return to *Angela*, for better Advice, but this Letter only determin'd him, he shou'd have an opportunity of getting rid of that dreadful Friend from under his Hospitable Roof.

The

The Baron did not fail to accompany 'em to their own Palace, where he took his leave at the Gate, with a Behaviour so tender and respectful, that St. *l'Amant* almost justify'd him, in his Thoughts. He kept this anguish close confin'd to his own Breast, not without a Million of times accusing himself, for so imprudently pressing his Wife to esteem the Baron, and yet he knew not how to condemn 'em, since herself had been acquainted with her own Distemper; she had more avoided the Lover, and sought her Husband, there was nothing omitted by her that an honest Woman cou'd do in the like extremity; she master'd herself as to those disgusts she formerly seem'd to receive from his Caresses, and declin'd being Entertain'd by the Baron; she prescrib'd herself a perfect Rule of Behaviour, from which she was resolv'd rather to die than depart; and endeavour'd to justifie herself to her Mother, by informing her of *Berintha*'s Malice.

Since the Baron knew nothing of all this, he was as assiduous as before, and the World, who knew he was perpetually there, did not discontinue their censure.

Monsieur St. *Amant*'s Distemper redoubled, he cou'd not confine himself to *Wine* and *Water*, or *Tissanes*, as the Physician wou'd have him, his Troubles of Mind seem'd rather to call upon him for higher Cordials, that he might drown their memory: One day, after a dreadful Fit, he caus'd his Lady to be call'd, and ask'd her, if he had ever fail'd in a tender Husband's Duty? She answer'd him in Tears, that he had not only exceeded all others, but even her own expectations and desert, however partial she might
be

be to her felf: He then ask'd her, (fomething abruptly) how fhe could excufe her felf for fo ill performing hers? at the fame time he gave her that Letter to read, which the old Friend had fent him into the Country: She threw herfelf upon her Knees, at his Bed-fide, and fell a weeping: He ask'd her whether fhe were really guilty? he cou'd forgive her if fhe would be ingenuous. Madam *St. l' Amant*, who was bred to hate a Lie, and held it unworthy of that generous Confidence her Husband had put in her, to abufe it, told him all fhe had fuffer'd, from the beginning to that prefent moment; *Berintha*'s Malice, her own Innocence and the *Baron*'s, who had never attempted any thing but what might have been heard and feen by all the World; there's fomething fo perfuafive in Truth, that he was convinced: She begg'd him to pity what he could not approve; it was not in her power to mafter the Paffion fhe had for the *Baron*, but it had been ever fo from giving him any Teftimonies of it. He told her, he did with all his Heart; and he forgave her, nay, even return'd her Thanks for fo well difcharging her Duty, when it was fo powerfully oppos'd by her Inclinations: He wifh'd that he had fpoke fooner of it to her, that he might fooner have receiv'd that fatisfaction, which he was now afraid came of the lateft to him; that he believ'd it had precipitated his Death, which he found coming very faft upon him; but to convince her, that his Efteem was ftill the fame for her, he would have his Will remaining as it was before this had happen'd, that he would ev'n have alter'd it, if it could poffibly have been made more for her advantage; but having

left

left her all he could leave her, tho' to the prejudice of their common Children; he begg'd her to be contented with being the richest Widow in all *Atalantis*, without ever bestowing her self or her Fortune upon the *Baron*; not but he eminently deserv'd every thing, but upon the Score, that it would confirm the bad World of those Reports the base *Berintha* had spread abroad. Madam *St. l'Amant* promis'd him more, never to marry again, tho' it were much to her Honour or Advantage. 'Tis possible he might not believe her in that point, because all Women assure their Husbands of as much. He seem'd only to accuse himself for so indiscreetly introducing a Man of the *Baron*'s Merit to his Wife, and dy'd soon after, an eminent Warning to all Husband's from falling into the like Inadvertency.

He was no sooner interr'd, and his Elegy publish'd, but all the Town gave her to the *Baron* for a Wife; they ev'n laugh'd to think how much out of Countenance the Poet would be, when his Mourning, Constant *Sacharissa*, should take the Comforts of a new Bridegroom. Thus they entertain'd themselves at her cost, and *Berintha* did not fail, in all Companies, to report the Business as good as done.

Poor Madam *St. l'Amant*, Heart-broke with inward Passion, struggling between *Love* and cruel *Decency*; full of Veneration and grateful Tenderness to her departed Husband; aw'd and terrified by her Mother's perpetual Remonstrances; rack'd at the remembrance of the *Baron*'s Charms, and the Promise she had made *Monsieur St. l'Amant*, forsook the Town, to retire to a small *Villa*, where she gave up her self to perpetual Melancholly; her Health was much impair'd by these

these Conflicts of the Mind. She would sometimes think that she was destin'd by Fate, to retrieve and draw the *Baron*'s low Fortune from obscurity, by her abundance; that he was rich enough in Merit to deserve all things. When he came to condole with her the loss of their common Friend, he allow'd much to Decency, and in several Visits spoke nothing of his own Pretensions, but at length, having found the time favourable, he began with an elegant Discourse, of what he had so tenderly suffer'd for her; he pleaded Merit from the Respectiveness of his Flame, and unwearied Silence, to hinder her from those Formalities that might retard his Happiness, he cut her short, by telling all that happen'd in the Banquetting-House, and the knowledge he had of that esteem she had honour'd him with, but appeal'd to her self, if from thence he ever assum'd any merit from it, so as to presume to declare it to her. The Lady, in return, told him, with the same Sincerity, the whole State of her Heart; *Monsieur St. l'Amant*'s Discourse; the Promise she had made him, and her Resolution to adhere to it: She begg'd him to see her no more, since it could not be significant to either, but hurtful to both; assur'd him, that as she did not marry *him*, she never would marry any other; but whatever was in her power to serve his Fortune, he might not only depend upon, but command.

Her Mother taking the Alarm from the *Baron*'s Visits, never left teizing her, till she fell down-right sick: She was continually remembring her what she ow'd her Children, and the memory of her Husband, to keep her from marrying a Beggar, as she call'd him; how poor and scandalous

dalous it would appear to the World; that she would rather follow her to her Grave, than see her in the Nuptial-Bed, with one, whose very acquaintance had been the Death of so dear a Husband, and the only Blot of her own Life. Unable to bear up under all these Disquiets, she was not long in giving the World a very singular Proof of Love and Constancy, tho' the Enemies of the Sex do not fail to interpret it thus, *Cross a Woman in her Will, and you take away her Life.*

Vir. And this has given occasion to the second Elegy. I think the Poet has been mistaken in his Theme; 'twou'd have been something very new, if instead of making her die for her Husband, he had taken the Story as it was, and shew'd her resolv'd upon any Extremeties, rather than be wanting in her Devoir.

Intel. There I must beg your Mightinesses Pardon, for, with submission, Madam, its much a newer thing to have a Lady die for Love and Grief for the loss of her Husband, than at any other thing under the Sun.

Astrea. Tho' what my Lady *Intelligence* has told us in this Story, be entertaining, yet I find nothing in it of use to my Prince, at least not till he be marry'd, unless it be, that he take care before-hand, to make his Wife in love with him, because she will else fall in love with somebody, and so far the Moral may hold good.

Vir. We are far advanced in our Journey: Behold that goodly Temple that stands open: Shall we not go in, and pay our Adoration to *Juno*, to whom it is dedicated?

Intel. The Fabrick is noble: Cast your Eyes upon the elevation, what a majestick height it bears,

bears, it seems to lose its Spire in the Clouds: Mark those curious Images! the Carving, the whole Architecture, is admirable: As you enter you shall pass thro' Columes of Marble-Pillars, numerous as the Hours in a revolving Year: Mark the beauty of the Windows; how various and lively are the Colours; how fanciful are the Works of Mortals! They also are numbred by the Days that *Phœbus* counts in his Solar Course, and to compleat the System, equivalent to the number of the Moons, are the Gates of this magnificent Structure; the Founder was order'd (in a Dream) by *Juno*, to erect this Temple to her Honour, which has a Promise annex'd to it, of enduring till the end of time, that Creation take a new Form, or be no more. The Foundation, (to make it more wonderful!) is laid in Water, which is perishable to all things, but this divine Fabrick; there is not above six Foot depth of Earth, all beneath is of the more liquid Element.

Astrea. Methinks I am not half so much satisfied with the Devotion offer'd in the Temple, as with the Temple it self: The High-Priest *B! of Sarum Burnett.* supine and drowzy, scarce attended to the Duty of the Place: He has a majestick Appearance; is clad in becoming Ornaments, but still he seem'd to be little at ease, drowzy, and rather fitted for a Bed of repose at home, than his Devotion here.

Intel. That is, because it was not now his time for declaiming to the People, then none more vigorous, fuller of motion, vehement in Speech and Gesture; he is admir'd and follow'd for his Oratory, but the Snares of Beauty, (against which he has not been able to defend himself) Pride, and some other Vices, have dared

K 2

to mingle with his Character; the respect I have for all that attend the service of the Altar, makes me chuse rather to conceal than publish their Defects.

Astrea. Methinks, little of Devotion mingled among the behaviour of the other Priests; the numerous Train cast their Eyes upon the Fair; they perform'd their Hymns as things they had by rote, without solemnity, as if the Heart, nay the Mind, had no part in it; in short, I am disgusted at the Coolness of their Behaviour; they seem rather to be paid for what they do, than to be pleas'd or affected, I will not say transported, as if the Service were only essential to their Body, not their Soul.

Vir. Night has overtaken us, it will be inconvenient traveling, till *Aurora* return, *Cynthia* is already mounted for her Journey, she is seated in her Car, behold her taking the Reins of Night, and administring to the World in the absence of her Brother. This lovely Walk of Trees, that leads to that House before us; this Arbor and Bench will serve us to repose, till we can re-assume our Travel.

Astrea. I see a Lady with a majestick Mien, beautiful, and her Motions gentile, coming towards us; there is a Cavalier with her, who seems earnest in perswading: They take the next Seat to us; we can at ease hear all that they discourse.

Bar. Why will you force me (my Lord) to give you so fatal a Proof of my Esteem, as must destroy all yours for me? Can nothing else prevail with you to leave me in repose? Must I demonstrate, as well as tell you, the impossibility there is of ever touching my Heart?

Count.

Count. Nothing less can precipitate me into that Despair, that is necessary for leaving you in repose. Quite bereave me, (as you have promis'd) of all hope, make me to see that you merit not to be belov'd, and this Ghost that incessantly haunts you, that gives you such occasion of complaint, may disappear, but till then, permit me to wander on, not utterly void of hope of one Day touching your Heart in my favour.

Bar. 'Tis impossible. I am my self devoted to Despair. Oh, my Lord! let it not be said, that one of so much Merit, as the Count of *Meilliers*, employ'd it only to make an unfortunate Woman more unfortunate.

Count. I renounce any such thought: But, charming *Baroness!* Why should my Love so prodigiously disturb you? Setting our Persons aside, (there I confess, it will be hard, in the whole World, to find an equivalent to yours) my Birth and Fortune may deserve you. In this languid Retirement, you give up your self a prey to black, melancholly, splenetick Vapours, and talk of Despair, which never yet knew how to approach a Lady so amiable as you.

Bar. Alas! How deceitful are Appearances? I must rid my self of your Love, tho' by it I lose your Friendship and Esteem; the Oath you have took to keep inviolably my Secret, will make me discover to you the only important Action of my Life: A Life wasted in Disgusts, and not so much as chequer'd with Pleasures, whilst I am by all thought happy, not deform'd, young, blest with the Smiles of Fortune, yet I find, and know my self a Wretch: Permit me the weakness of a few Tears, and then I will proceed in what you desire.

'Tis needless to report my Birth to you; you know the Reputation my Mother had for Gallantry; she liv'd divided from her Husband; the Baron of *Somes* was reputed her Favourite in the highest manner. He was then past the Flower of his Youth, declining; but handsom for his Age. The first thing I was taught to love, was the Flattery he bestow'd upon me; Flattery, the most pernicious Weed in the Garden of Education! my Mother betimes accustomed me to hear praises of my Beauty, she even bestow'd 'em upon me herself: There is nothing more poisonous for young Maids of Fashion, they are early (by it) taught to believe well of themselves, and contemptibly of others, easily impos'd on in the point of Self-merit, they are betray'd into a groundless Esteem and Desire to make themselves ador'd. How much to blame are Mothers, that heedlesly pass by the first tender Hours of their Children, without a true endeavour to bend 'em to Virtue? Mine manag'd not herself in that Point, she said and did things before me, that young tho' I was, I ought for ever to be ignorant of. I speak not this to accuse her Memory, or to excuse my self; to all others I shou'd defend her; but, my Lord, I wou'd have you believe, that I intend nothing but Truth in my Relation. The Baron ever carry'd himself more regularly in all his Visits, nothing came from him but what was Polite; if he had any criminal Conversation with my Mother, he took the utmost pains to conceal the least appearance of it from me; he was a Man of Letters, had an elevated Genius, refin'd by Courts, where he had perpetually pass'd his time: In short, why do I dwell so long

long upon his Character to you, that muſt needs have heard often of him, or at leaſt have admired him, in thoſe Pieces of his Compoſing that he has given to the World. He took upon him the Buſineſs of a Parent, gave me Inſtructions of Behaviour, Conduct, and, in ſhort, Rules to accompliſh a Maid of Faſhion. As I grew up, his eſteem grew with me, and he reſolv'd to divide me from my Mother, whoſe Education of me he did not approve, tho' he ſo much admired her. By his Intereſt at Court he procured me an advantageous Settlement about the Queen. Here it was that I diſplay'd in perfection, thoſe firſt Principles I had Imbib'd, the love of Flattery, and a greedy deſire of Admiration; I might have prov'd an accompliſh'd *Coquet*, had not Love touch'd my Heart in favour of the Prince of *Sira*. I ſaw him often at Court, his Employment about my Miſtreſs gave him audience when he pleas'd, but durſt not pretend to engage ſo elevated a Heart as his. My Fortune was to make, and tho' I had a little pretence to Beauty, yet theſe are ſcarce times (without a miracle) that Princes (who have as much occaſion for Money as other Men) take themſelves Wives of Inclination. About this time my Mother dy'd; and the Tears I ſhed for her, join'd to thoſe new Sentiments my Heart had entertain'd, brought me into an habitual Melancholy. I declin'd all Diverſions of a ſplendid Court, praiſe nor flattery no longer pleas'd me; I was no more a *Coquet*; ſo true it is, that a real Paſſion extinguiſhes in us that pernicious Humor. I ſaw the Prince often, but, alas! he ſaw not me; that is to ſay, he diſtinguiſh'd me not from the reſt; I durſt not tell him of my love,

love, because he had none for me. After the time of Mourning was expired, much to my surprize, the Baron of *Somes* addressed himself to me as a Husband; he made me an offer to settle his whole Fortune upon me, which was very considerable; by the course of Nature he cou'd not long survive, he was already past that Age that is generally allotted by Nature for the Life of Man, bow'd down by Distempers, and nothing cou'd seem more preposterous, than his desiring a Wife of my Youth. However he represented to me so many advantages to my Fortune, that I consented to it, to the admiration of the whole Court, who did not know the secret hopes I had, to make my self one day, by my Circumstances, worthy of the Prince of *Sira*.

After I was marry'd, my whole endeavours seem'd to be to please my Husband; I evaded giving him the least shadow of Jealousie; I went rarly to Court, and never without him; avoided the *Opera's*, and all publick Assemblies, confining my diversion among the Visits of those particular Friends that he did not dislike. I do not know but that my Conduct was generally approv'd of. I cou'd with the greater ease abandon Pleasures, of which I had no Taste, because my Heart only regretted the Prince, that Prince who I every day heard was engag'd with the first Favourite of the Princess of *Inverness*. I secretly sigh'd at her good fortune, nor cou'd the guiltiness of her Amour (for she was marry'd) hinder me from envying her being belov'd by the Prince. I did, I knew not what I did, I ran upon my destruction, by making a particular Friendship with her, where I had an opportunity

tunity often to behold that dangerous Prince. After once or twice, methought he receiv'd me with quite another Air; that Face which he had neglected whilst I was a Maid, and no less a price set upon it than Marriage, became his care and admiration now I was Marry'd. It was not long before he found an opportunity to tell me so. I never till then knew the true pleasure of Words! how insipid had my Life pass'd before? The whole extracted to a point, cou'd not have made the least part of that joy I felt by his enchanting Declaration. I had ever a native Sincerity, whether I did not enough endeavour to dissemble, or that my love was too powerful for Dissimulation. The Prince saw I was easily Charm'd, and perhaps seeretly condemn'd me for it, not allowing for his own superiour Merit, nor the first wound of a tender Heart, but this last he was then ignorant of. In short, he immediately (when he saw he was so well in my esteem) press'd me for the Effects of it, This he would not have so early presum'd to do, if he had not had an opinion of my Levity, by the apparent Transport with which I receiv'd his first confession of Love. I knew not how to be angry when he spoke, lest he shou'd speak no more; I contented my self calmly to refuse him, without forbiding him to hope that he might one day be succesful: he left nothing undone that was necessary to make a Lady's excuse, for yielding to the assiduities of a belov'd Lover; all was pleasing to me that he either said or did; our opportunities were few, and never alone 'twas that he requested; I had the courage to resist all his Efforts; I dreaded the consequence of such a meeting, till
tired

tired with that perpetual constraint I put upon my Inclinations, and weary'd by his Importunities, I promis'd him within two days, and we took our measures not to be disappointed nor discover'd; but the day after this concession, the Baron fell dangerously Ill; I never stirr'd from his Bed-side, gave him all that was necessary with my own Hands; he dy'd soon after, in a perfect good Opinion of me, and, as you know, left me in possession of a Fortune considerable enough to raise my pretensions, even to the Prince of *Sira...* The real Honour and Friendship I had for my Husband, even before he was such, my Duty (which the sweetness of his Behaviour, and extreme Kindness, had made easie, if not pleasant to me) gave me a true Concern for his loss; had not my Heart been prepossess'd for the Prince, I doubt not but I shou'd have been much more inconsolable. All the Court came (assoon as I was visible) to Condole my loss. I receiv'd 'em with a decent Sorrow, without any Salleys of that excessive Mourning so naturally affected by young Widows; and this gave the World no ill opinion either of my Sense or Sincerity. I was surpriz'd and touch'd that I found not the Prince among those who pretended to comfort me. Six Weeks, two Months pass'd, but no News of my Lover. I easily condemn'd my self for that fatal Promise I had made him, which might give him too bad an opinion of my Virtue, tho' I concluded with my self, that it wou'd have been proof against all his attempts. I had in my mind cast about how to regain his Esteem, by an Air of Virtue reassum'd; but his not coming broke all my Measures; I cou'd no longer bear to live in the uncertainty of his Sentiments,

timents, I writ him three Lines to intreat him to see me, at an Hour when he knew there wou'd be least Company with me. He came according to my desire, the Moments were favourable; we were alone and after the usual Compliments were past, I gently reproach'd him for leaving me so long in my Affliction, without attempting to alleviate it, tho' he knew that it was in his and no ones Power besides, to do it. I found his Pride had been a little piqued at my not meeting him according to my promise; but I immediately clear'd my self, by proving to him how ill the Baron was at that time. We were reconcil'd, and he renew'd his Pretensions to me, tho', had I not been wilfully blind, I must needs have concluded he cou'd not love me very much, who cou'd live so long and not tell me of it: However my Heart was for him, and Reason wou'd in vain have attempted to have made a Party against him. When he press'd for Favours, I insisted upon Marriage: He seem'd really fond of me, and I was resolv'd not to stoop to him upon lower Terms, now I had a Fortune to deserve him. He came over to mine, seeing he cou'd not gain me to his. There was no delays for a Passion so ardent as his seem'd to be. I had been but three Months a Widow, the time was indecent, what shou'd we do? A private Marriage, in an Age like this, wou'd not long have been such: I was afraid of being ridicul'd at Court, for one of those hasty Widows that secure themselves of a new Husband, before the old one is scarce cold. Oh how foolish were my Scruples! how much wiser had I been, to have risqued a little Tattle, than have lost my whole

Repose

Repose and my Honour together? The Prince was eager for what he call'd Happiness; my own desires pleaded for him, a cursed Medium was found to prevent the Discourse of the World, and undo me; we were solemnly Contracted by Words and Writing, before a Woman of my Bed-chamber, who was faithful to me; that done, I receiv'd him without scruple to my Arms; but long I cou'd not hold him there; a Disgust he both gave and receiv'd at Court, (of which it is not necessary I shou'd inform you) made him resolve to Travel. I was all in Confusion (succeeded by Despair) when he mentioned it to me as a thing resolved on. In short, amidst my Sorrows, Swoonings, Exclamations, unfeigned Tears, and bitter Anguish, he took his leave of me, with a promise to return before my years of Mourning were expired. Base and perfidious Husband! it was not so much from the Court, as me, that he ran away. Pierced to the Heart by his unkindness! Distracted by slighted Love and Despair! I retir'd to this solitary House, where Time and Reason, together with his Ingratitude, in never writing to me in years, has restor'd me a little to my Senses.

The only thing that disturb'd my Tranquility, was your Addresses; I saw you as a Neighbour and a Friend, you have Sense, your Conversation is Polite, I thought my self happy in the Friendship of a Person of your Merit; you put an end to my pleasure, by declaring your self my Lover; I was alarm'd at your Assiduities; you did more than was necessary to convince me of your Sincerity: I chose to use you nobly, as you had done me, to free my self from the censure of having

so

so ill a Taste, as to refuse a Person of such accomplish'd Merit. I have let you see all my Weakness; I have told you the important Secret of my Life, whilst all *Angela* is seeking in vain for Reasons, why (in my Bloom of Youth) I should retire from the Court, and Conversation, to bury my self here, in Melancholy and Obscurity: You are the only Person that is acquainted with the true Cause of an Action, which by most is condemn'd, and but by few applauded.

Count. Tho' you have told me too much, Madam, have you no more to tell me? or will you tell me no more? 'tis indeed enough to drive me into Despair, but not to compleat your Relation.

Bar. Alas! What can I say more? My own Misfortunes; my Tears; my Disquiets; my loss of Rest, and perpetual Exclaimings, are what I have contracted, for fear of wearying of you with 'em: Of the Prince I can give you no other Account, than what we have from the publick; he made the *Tour* of *Germany*, *Great-Britain*, *France*, and *Italy*, and our last Advices spoke him at *Brussels*, possibly upon his return for *Angela*. Oh Heav'ns! Why do I flatter my self with such pleasing Hopes? He that left it only to avoid me! me! who he hates to such a superlative degree, as to live a banish'd Man, an Exile voluntary, from his Country, rather than make happy by his presence, a Wife that adores him: A Wife, whose Heart was never sensible but for him; a tender Wife, who wastes her Bloom in perpetual Solitude, and Tears, regretting his absence.

Count.

Count. And is this all the Relation you think fit to give me of the Prince? How little sincere are you? or perhaps, indeed, you may be ignorant of your Misfortunes.

Bar. What mean you, my Lord? Do you believe I have left any thing material untold? O I perceive you! You know well the Jealousie of my Temper, and would alarm it; you have succeeded, at this moment the Furies are enter'd; my Breast is glowing with Doubts, Suspicions, Jealousies, and horrid Distrust; but since Uncertainty is the worst of Torments, I conjure you, (by all your former Kindness) to relate to me what you have heard of the Prince.

Count. Is it possible you can be ignorant of what Rumour has so confidently proclaim'd——— He is married———

Bar. O. Heavens!——— But go on: I wonder at nothing villanous in Mankind: My Solitude, and Resignation to the Gods, has taught me to receive all things with moderation; my Heart is in a moment becalm'd, my Passion sunk into an absolute Contempt, for a Prince so void of *Gratitude, Principles,* or *Religion.*

Count. I am pleas'd to see you receive as you ought, so terrible a Stroke; but you will more despise him, when you know who he has marry'd, and how sufficiently you are reveng'd: 'Tis a Lady without any Advantges, but Birth; past her Youth; never a Beauty; no Fortune, and had been long in vain endeavouring to make her self one, by her Address and Conversation, wherein consists all her Charms, tho' there is neither Judgment nor Depth found in it; a flashy Repartee, a Wit that permits it self to say every thing, must sometimes say something

to

to the purpose, and easily finds Applause amongst the young unthinking Men of Quality, who having in themselves no foundation, never look for it in others. She had in vain (for more than thirty Years together) sat every Night at the *Basset-Table*, at her Aunt's, (who is a Woman of Quality, that holds Assemblies for noble Foreigners, and others of the same Rank of her own Nation) without having the good Luck to engage any to her advantage, till the Prince of *Sira* came amongst them; there are who want to give themselves Reasons for all things, (not considering Men often act without it) and report that the Prince only design'd a Gallantry with her, but was over-reach'd by her, and her two Brothers, and forced to marry her; but I find no other ground for this Story, but the Lady's want of Youth and Fortune: He is excessively fond of her; they are upon their Voyage for *Atalantis*; notice is already given for his return, and 'tis only to your Solitude that I must attribute your Ignorance of an Affair, that has found matter of entertainment for the whole Court; the new Princess, it is said, caresses all of our Nation, whom she meets abroad, and by her Industry and Intelligence has furnish'd her self with the History of all our People of Condition; she pretends only to be show'd a Person, and then immediately to discourse him, with that Knowledge and Address, as if she had been born and bred in the same Family with him; this is all that I find wonderful in her Character, but whether this excessive Curiosity and Address be an Ingredient of Vertue, I leave to others to determine, who perhaps may place a

Woman's

Woman's Merit more in in her Wit and Tongue, than her Modesty and Silence.

Bar. Does the Traitor with Impunity dare to think he may live in a Place where he has so potently injur'd a Woman like me———? Help me, my Lord, I am undone with this last Shock: How necessary is a faithful Friend's Advice! Passion misguides me; that Calmness I boasted of is vanish'd; my Heart is upon the hurry; all things are in utmost Confusion and Disorder, within; I would keep my Glory, and yet be reveng'd, punish him, yet preserve my Reputation.

Count. Your best way will be to do nothing: You can pretend but to a Contract, which tho' prior, is not so binding as the Ceremony it self: He will undoubtedly oppose your Pretensions, to the prejudice of your Fame; for unless he can wound *that*, he must himself be wounded; the World that are not in Passion, when they are Judges of yours, will condemn you for to hastily believing what you desir'd, and for trusting a Man upon his Promise: There's something unaccountable, 'tis one of the *Arcana*'s of Nature, not yet found out, why our Sex cool and neglect yours, after possession, and never, if we can avoid it (and have our Senses about us) chuse our selves Wives from those who have most obliged us; 'tis, I confess, the grand Specifick of Ingratitude, but it seems so in-born in all, that I wonder there are still found Women that confide in our false Oaths and Promises, and that Mothers do not early, as they ought, warn their Virgin-Daughters from Love and Flattery, the Rocks upon which the most deserving are generally lost; Chastity is recommended as the

greatest

greateſt Ornament of your Sex, as Valour is of ours, becauſe of the difficulty there is in maintaining 'em, tho'. I do not think the Compariſon equal, becauſe Courage we ſee in-born to many, whilſt Chaſtity muſt be acquir'd, becauſe it moves directly againſt the prior Law of Nature, and has the whole Artillery of *Venus* to contend againſt.

I count you extremely happy in the midſt of your Misfortunes; that your Secret is unknown. What pity 'tis Inclinations ſo noble as yours, wanted the firſt Principle to ſupport 'em; that your Education did not enough arm you againſt the too haſty Impreſſions of Love: Of Love! 'till Gratitude, and true Merit in the Perſon that you ſhould be belov'd by, might make your Flame not only warrantable, but meritorious: But theſe Reflections are of the lateſt; I much more wonder, (conſidering your Infancy) that your Errors have been ſo few, than that you have had any. If you will be adviſed by me, continue in this Place, but abate of your Solitude; ſuffer your ſelf to taſte of the Diverſions that you may find in the Converſation of thoſe Neighbours who are ſeated round about you, and who have an unfeigned Reſpect and Admiration for you. Loſe your Cares in little Amuſements; put the Ax to the Root; uſe your own Endeavours (powerfully) to tear this corroding Anguiſh from your Heart; go to the innermoſt Receſſes of it; deteſt Perfidy and Ingratude in all its Forms, and then you will quickly deteſt the Prince; have all unlawful Paſſion in an utter abhorrence, ſo ſhall you ſoon extinguiſh that, which you feel for one who can no longer be yours, ſince he is by the moſt ſacred

L   Cere-

Ceremony made anothers; but, above all things, practice Moderation; learn Patience in Adverſity; think that the juſt Gods, who perpetually chequer the Lives of Mortals, left they ſhould loſe in Proſperity the remembrance of their Creation, has given you a gentle Stroke, to recall you to themſelves; fix there your Thoughts; transfer the warmth of your Paſſions to their great Originals; you cannot love too much; you cannot too much adore them, who are all Virtue, all Goodneſs, and will give you whatever is neceſſary for your Happineſs; they have already divided you from a Husband, with whom (his Principles being ſuch as they are) you could never have taſted of any true Happineſs.

Aſtrea. We cannot hear what Anſwer the *Baroneſs* gives to the *Count*; they are gone down the Walk; ſee they are entring the Houſe; her Tears and Sighs, I believe, are her only Language; methinks, for her ſake, I am incenſed againſt the Prince, and could with a very good Will revenge her Cauſe; there is ſomething of Ingenuous in her Relation; what pity 'tis ſhe was ſo injur'd; the *Count* muſt himſelf have worth, that can ſo worthily inſtruct and admoniſh her.

Intel. He has indeed, no more than the appearance of it; all this fine Advice tends only to his own Intereſt; he does not deſpair of getting the *Baroneſs* for his Wife, and can you blame him then for making her vertuous; her Fortune is convenient for him; a concealed Morgage eats up the Profits of his whole Eſtate; he will not be long in a Condition to ſupport his Title without a Dowry; this Lady is by much the richeſt in all the Province; ſhe will do his Buſineſs, if

he

he can accomplish her, and has let him into a dangerous Secret, if she be wife, she will never marry him after, left he upbraid her with it: See her Indiscretion, he will be provoked at her Refusal, as she will still refuse him, because she has an Aversion to his Person, and would rather chuse a favourite Domestick for her Master; and consequently he'll divulge her Secret at the expence of the World's Opinion, both of her Conduct and Honour.

Vir. Her seeming Ingenuity has made a Party for her in my Breast; I will do all that is possible to recover her to Virtue; I'll try if the Maxim be not false; That a Woman once departing from me, never returns, till old Age and Wrinkles have fitted her for nothing else. I will endeavour to warm her with my Precepts, and so render her as renown'd for her return to Virtue, as she is for Beauty.

Intel. The *Count* who declaims so well, keeps two Women for his debauch; he visits 'em by turns; who would believe it! but Hypocrisie is not the least reigning Vice among the Illustrious.

Astrea. I will have my Prince avoid it, as the poyson of all other Virtues; warn him against the Perfidy of the Prince of *Sira*; he has robb'd a Woman of her Honour upon a specious Pretence: He has not been afraid to play with Oaths; how criminal is this! A Man of true Honour would detest such a Practice. I will have my Prince renown'd for his Chastity; I will have him introduce the fashion amongst the Men; let the Reformation begin but there, and the World will be modest, if it were but held a Crime in the esteem of the Great, to

L 2   sollicite

follicite a Lady with unlawful Love, all would be vertuous. Women seldom are, and never ought to be the Agressors; if they were, and sure to be refus'd, with that scorn that they deserve, would it not retort a Blush to the Face of the most Impudent?

Vir. The Morning dawns upon us; let us return to our Travel: Conversation sweetly beguiles the Time, shortens the length of Way, and softens the Ruggedness —— See, my dear *Astrea*, what a multitude of People are assembled upon yonder Heath! Alas! they are seeing a Criminal executed; they must have a Fierceness in their Nature, that can be pleas'd with Objects so terrible! Not One in a Hundred of these People go for Edification, and true Mortification, but Pleasure! Methinks they should with Abjectness of Mind, reflect upon the wretched State of Mortals, that like a perpetual Flux subjects them to Evil. What barbarous Soul can find Diversion in such a Prospect! There's a Woman nail'd dead to the Gibbet; she seems a Person of Condition; dress'd in white, with the Veil of white Taffaty over her Face: Who can unriddle to us this Scene of Death? Methinks I want to be inform'd of what led to this Catastrophy. Mistress, you that seem all in Tears, returning from this doleful Execution, if you can make truce with your Sorrows, pray inform us Strangers of what you know concerning this Affair.

Country-Wom. With all my Heart. I have a little Habitation near at hand, if you please to walk in and repose your selves, you shall be obliged to the utmost of my Capacity.

The

The Lady who suffer'd was a Gentleman's Daughter of this Province; she permitted herself to be abus'd by a young Soldier of Fortune, (quarter'd near her Father's *Villa*) whom she fell in love with. These Soldiers are the perfect Bane of all Country-Gentlewomen; their fine Words, and their fine Cloaths, bear down all before 'em; they never go to the Temple to sacrifice, not they truly; that's the least of their Business; they mind *Ogling*, as they call it, of the Madams, instead of minding better things. Well! they single out one that seems best to their Fancy; their Rogue of a Landlord gives 'em, at their first coming, the History of all the People in the Parish, and then to work they go, shave and powder, and on goes the Blue, or the Scarlet-Coat, every Day; Cards and Balls are nothing to 'em; they'll squander away their Month's Pay in one Night, when they had better by half be in their Beds, forecasting how to pay their Debts; but no matter for that, they never trouble their Heads about it. 'Ads me! if I were a Gentlewoman's Father or Mother, and had Daughters, they should as soon eat the Fire, as come near one of those deluding *Red-Coats*. They can all sing, Forsooth, wanton Ditties is all they mind; you shall never hear any thing good come out of their Mouths, but Oaths: And then a great many of 'em (this was one of the Gang) can *toot, toot, toot*, it upon a Pipe; they have another Name for it, but the thing is the same; and this ravishes the young Gentlewoman's Ears; then they have Plays, and dying Love-Speeches at their Fingers-ends; these are generally, besides the cutting of a Caper, their whole Estate; if you look

look into their Portmanteau (except their Regimental Cloths, you ſhall find ſcarce any thing but a durty Plod-Morning-Gown, two or three Pair of Shooes, four old Shirts, and as many Neckcloths; fine they muſt be, forſooth, but worn (with often Waſhing) as thin as a Cobweb; for fall out what will, they muſt have a clean Shirt every day. Some of their beggarly Soldiers Trulls does nothing but Launder for 'em, they'r always at the Waſh-Tub, and, I believe, ſeldom enough paid for what they do.

Then they kiſs and complement the Country Milliners, to truſt 'em with Sword-knots, and clean Gloves, Ribons for their Sleeves, to hang ſtreaming down, and to dangle their Canes in; and thus ſet out, they go a ſutoring to ſome young Gentlewoman or another. But ſhe you ſaw, yours had ſixteen thouſand Crowns for her Portion, her Mother was dead; ſhe read Romances (Romances I think you call 'em) and Plays, and was counted to have a notable Wit as any, let the other be who ſhe wou'd, in a great way of her. Her Father's an old curmudgonly Cur, and wou'd never let her go to *Angela* our chief City, nor wou'd he give her any of her Portion till he dy'd, or ſhe marry'd to his liking; but yet he never look'd out for a Husband for her. Now my mind gives me, that if he had but let her go into fine Company (as other brave Ladies do) ſhe wou'd not have thought a ranting Officer ſuch *a God-a-mighty:* But he was too covetous for that, leaſt ſhe ſhou'd treat 'em again when he came to his Houſe. So ſhe was e'en aſham'd to go to theirs. The young Eſquire, her Brother, is as compleat a Man (tho' I ſay it) as any the Sun ever ſhon upon.

on. He was gone abroad into ſtrange Countries, to learn their Linguo, when this Rogue of red and blue Coat, courted her, or elſe he had never got his will of her; he wou'd have watch'd his Waters for him to ſome purpoſe, he's afraid of ne'r a Officer of 'em all. But, the more's the pity (poor Gentlewoman) 'twas not her luck. The Rogue wou'd not Marry her; becauſe he knew her Father wou'd not give her a Groat with him, but beſpoke her very fair. He us'd to be let in a Nights at the Back-gate in the Garden, and carry'd up to her Chamber. I know all their Intriegue (poor Soul) you cou'd not have lit upon one that cou'd tell you better. He ſo be-prais'd her, and invegled her, that, the ſhort and the long on't, in plain, downright Terms, he took her Maidenhead from her, and left her nothing in the room but a big Belly. Well, this paſs'd on, no Body perceiv'd it. Our Officer wanted to be gone, and go he did; their Company march'd away, but left I know not how many unborn Baſtards behind 'em. Joy go with 'em, I hope they'l never come here again. From the higheſt to the loweſt, a young Girl cou'd not go about her Buſineſs, but they kept a kiſſing and teaſing of her. I reckon the poor Soul that ſuffer'd cry'd her Belly-full, when her louſie *Hat* and *Feather*-Fellow march'd off. I know nothing of that, but, as I gueſs; only this I know, that the Eſquire came home juſt as ſhe was at her Time. He was hugely fond of his Siſter; ſhe fell into Labour when he was in the Room with her, but had provided no verſal Thing for the Child. She told her Brother ſhe was tormented with the Tooth-ach, and wanted to go to Bed. His Chamber was next to hers

hers, away he went, and to't she goes; Pain after Pain, Tear after Tear, Cry after Cry. The Esquire heard her, and wondred what was the matter; he came twice to the Door, but she wou'd not let him in, but said she was up in her Shift and almost Mad with her Teeth. Well, to Bed he goes, and after a few more Labour-pains, she is Deliver'd all-alone by her self of a brave Boy. Lest he shou'd cry, she tore out his Bowels in the Birth. 'Twas the Lord's Mercy she did not murther herself by it; but such have best luck, an honest Woman can scarce be brought to Bed without a Midwife. Well, up she wraps Child and Bowels, and altogether, in one of her Gowns, and to Bed she goes; in the Morning she rings for Mrs. *Alice* (that's her Chambermaid) and orders her to fetch a little Plague-Water, for she was very Ill, and horribly troubled with the Vapours: After a great many Good-morrows, and round-about Stories, she gives *Alice* an old Gown and Petticoat; to be short, makes her swear to be true, and not reveal her Trust, as she hop'd not to die in her Sins, and then tells her all about it, but conceal'd her part of the Murther, and beg'd her to carry the Corps upon the top of the House, and there lay it in a Leaden Gutter, that seldom or never was visited, till she was got well enough to help her to dig a Grave to bury it; for the Maid durst not do it alone. The Girl, with much fear and trembling, did as she was order'd. Some two or three days passed on, *Alice* was prick'd in Conscience, or, may be, like a right Chamber-maid, she long'd to tell all she knew; and so she reveals it to *Doll* the Dairy-maid, that was her Bed-fellow. These two Wenches, after this,

this, fancy'd, when they were a-Bed a-Nights, that a cold little Hand ftrok'd 'em over their Faces; they fo corrupted one another with thefe Figuaries, that at laft they believ'd, nay and fwore to it, that the Child Walk'd; who, if it had been alive, cou'd not yet have ftood. This Ghoft frighted 'em out of their Wits; they lov'd their Miftrefs, and was unwilling to difgrace her, for as yet they did not know of the Murther; but *Doll* had a Sweet-heart, one *Crifpin*, a Shoomaker, in our Town, as honeft a Fellow as ever liv'd; him fhe open'd her Mind to. The Fellow fmelt a Rat prefently, and was refolv'd to difcover it to the next Cadet or Judge. Away goes he, makes Oath of what *Doll* had told him. This Magiftrate mortally hated the young Lady's Father; a Warrant was granted, the Houfe fearched, and the Child found. She was try'd for her Life, and condemn'd for wilful Murther; but died very Penitent. She was a handfom Gentlewoman: I wifh all young Women may take warning by her fall,

The loquacious Country-woman had the thanks of her new Guefts for the pains fhe had taken to oblige 'em. She fet before 'em Curds new prefs'd, Cream frefh from the Cow, excellent brown Bread, and defired them to refrefh themfelves. The two Divinities, (who in all things were refolv'd to appear as Mortals) did not difdain her Bounty. She added to her Entertainment a Basket of Strawberries juft gathered, a Pitcher of Wine from her own Cowflips of the Meadow, and Butter fragrant from the Churn. Finding themfelves fo clean and heartily regal'd, they omitted nothing to exprefs their Gratitude.

After

After they were sufficiently refresh'd, they proceeded in their Journey to *Angela*, which lay not far before them. They were to cross a Meadow where a numerous *Congress* of Coaches presented themselves, Beauties resplendant, both by Art and Nature, *Cavaliers* dress'd *'en Campaign*, and well mounted, besides a swarm of Populace of both Sexes, a ridiculous Medly of Human-kind, fantastically Habited in Fashions of all Ages, and Airs of none: They seem'd to have forgot, or rather to be ignorant, of the King's dangerous Illness, for as yet the News of his Death was not publickly divulg'd. The occasion of that *Bell-Assembly* was a *Chariot-Race*. The Prize consisted in two Gold Goblets, and eight hundred Crowns in Gold. The fair *Marchioness du Cœur* was to bestow it. The Gentleman who inform'd the *Divinities*, was well-fashioned, talkative, and vain: He made 'em remark the number of Priests, that swarm at all Races, and are the formost in the Diversions of the Place: Some mounted upon lean lank Horses, others starch'd up (them of the better sort) in little Chariots, with an appropriated holy Air, cram'd with Women and Infants, Gazing and Betting, and more earnest than any of the Racers themselves. The Beau saw these stranger Ladies (for that time they were pleas'd to be visible) gracefully Charming, he had too great a *tendre* for the Sex not to oblige them with all things in his power; he gave himself Airs of Scandal, as well as Gallantry, and affected to appear knowing in all the Intriegues of the Place; he show'd them a Prince of the Empire at ease in a Coach and six Horses, he was one of the Racers, but his Servant was to run. Those days

days are long since past, when the Royal Charioteer thought it Glory, in Person to gain the Goal before his Competitor: Then the Prize was Renown and Applause, not Gold and Jewels. The Gentleman made 'em observe the close and morose Countenance of the Prince; he assur'd them that the Prize would be his, for that was the way now: He had brib'd the Racers to yield to his Charioteers. My Lady *Marchioness* her self must lose to him, tho' she thinks herself safe in her Politicks, because has also brib'd, but not so high as the Prince. True indeed, another young Prince startles their assurance of *D. Richmond.* Success, he puts in for the Prize, but will run himself, and there's no bribing in that Case: But the Marchioness has a remedy even for that; see he's at her Coach-side, and she entertains him with all the affability imaginable; she has a Battle of *Ratifia* with her; mark what a pint Glass they give; Oh, brave Prince, 'twill bring you to the Goal indeed! If his Head does not swim with this, and the violence of the Course, my Lady Marquess will be much disappointed; but the other Prince will be more, who has paid better for it. He loves Money above all things, unless it be Chastizing his Domesticks; in a Word, he is a Man of a proud, sullen, yet cholorick and avaricious Temper; no Body will be pleas'd if the Prize falls to him, and yet he cannot possibly fail of it. They are already started, and are to have three Heats. Charming young Hero! the Prince himself, by the favour of *Ratifia*, has gain'd it; he is Conqueror for the first time; but see, the second Bout his Eyes dazzle, he has mistook his Ground, and runs of the other side of the Post. This is the

Mar-

(156)

Marchioness's Cunning, but she shall not be the better for it; the moross Prince has got the Prize, as I have foretold, and there are but very few upon the Place that are pleas'd at his Victory.

Astrea. Pray, Sir, who is that Lady Marquiss? Her Lord seems to be old; she has all the Appearance of Joy and Ease upon her Face, and something that is sprightly and agreeable.

Gent. The Marquiss himself is one of the most artificial Men of the Age; he loves nothing the plain way, all must be Intrigue and Management where he is concern'd; he has made himself eminent upon that Score, yet far greater are the Party that wonder at his Cunning, than those that approve or esteem his Capacity. His first Lady was a Woman of real Worth and Honour, rich in all the Graces of the Mind, as well as bless'd with those of Fortune, yet he could never affect her, and when this Lady, with her large Dowry, fell into his possession, there were none that knew him, and beheld her Youth and Innocence, but condol'd with her in their Hearts, for those melancholy Hours she was then going to pass; but it has happen'd quite otherwise, my Lord Marquis wanted an Heir to her Possessions and his own, nor did he much matter which way he came by it; whether he distrusted himself upon that Head, as the Report runs; but he gave her so many Opportunities; taught her the Relish of Gallantry, and, in short, made her so entirely Mistress of her Conduct, that it would have been wonderful indeed, if she had miss'd the Censure of the World, in that Miscellania of Company that she kept; her Favourite-Woman had an Affair with an Officer of the

the Court, 'tis believed she drew in her Lady, that she might not have any thing to object against her. The young Cavalier *Bellair* fell passionately in love with the Marquess, as who can resist her, that has the Honour of tasting her easie and agreeable Conversation, then her Person has inexpressible Charms; her Face, without boasting of what you call a regular Beauty, has something so gay, so sweet, so gentile and agreeable, that one cannot defend one's Heart against her; she breaths the Air of nothing but *Love, Pleasure,* and *Diversion,* the more criminal Vices, *Scandal, Revenge, Hatred, Cruelty, Pride,* with that mixture of *haughty* and *sullen,* are put so far away from her, that she knows not what they mean; then she is bountiful as *Ceres,* generous as the Deity, when he inrich'd one Man with so valuable a World as this; in short, all that know her, can't but forgive, (let them be never so severe) her little Excursions of Love and Gallantry.

The *Gentleman* having ended his Relation, they would have took their Leaves of him in an obliging manner, but he was too gallant to part with 'em so; all the Arguments they could use would not hinder him from following them, till by virtue of their Divinity, having made themselves invisible, they left him to wonder at their disappearing.

Intelligence, who neither bore *him,* nor the *Country-Woman* any great good Will, for usurping upon her Province, and forcing her to a long and painful Silence, drew away the Ladies to attend the Shrieks and Cries that came from a little House, at the end of a neighbouring Village, the Door was open, and a vast Crowd about

about it. The fight was pleasant enough, an old thin raw-bon'd Priest, in his Sacerdotal-Habit, combating his Wife, who buffetted him again, and seem'd to be the Agressor: He had not only lost his Hat and Perruke in the Scuffle, but his Face look'd all over besmear'd with something, no body could tell what, but at last it was known to be a piping Hot Apple-Pye, out of the Oven, which she had scalded him with, in a very handsome manner, but was so kind to throw a Pound of Butter immediately after, to cool him again; his righteous Spirit, raised by the smart of the burning, catch'd hold of her Top-knot, to demolish that Fabr$_{\mathrm{ick}}$; it was fastned so close to her Head, that he pull'd and pull'd in vain: She shriek'd out as he pull'd, and well she might, for he had tore a piece of her Ear from her Head, which made the Blood run down, and was easier to come off than the Head-Geer, which was so interwove with Pins, Top-knots, *false* and *true Curls*, that it stood impenetrable like a Rock buffetted by the Waves. *Astrea* assum'd a Visibility to part the Combatants, which none but her self and her Companions endeavoured at amongst the great Crowd of People. They knew her too well, and were delighted to see the Scuffle. As soon as they were parted, the *Priestess* flounced out of the House, call'd for her Coachman, and bid him put in his Horses, for away would she go, (in that very Condition) to sue for *Justice*, if there were any *Justice* in the Nation; the poor Fellow durst not but obey her, tho' he lov'd his Master ten times better.

Intelligence was very forward to inform her self about the Combat, the good old Gentleman had

had Water brought him to wash off the baked Mask from his Face. The Gazers dismiss'd from the Gate, (and then after recovering a little vital Air) he begg'd *Astrea* and her Companions to repose themselves, and have pity upon a poor Man, who for his Sins was match'd to a She-Devil incarnate; you see what she is for Person, my good Friends, and new Acquaintance, said the Priest, nothing was ever so homely; her Face is made in part like a Black-a-moor, flat-nos'd, blubber-lipp'd; there's no sign of Life in her Complexion, it savours all of Mortality; she looks as if she had been buried a Twelvemonth; neither her Cheeks nor Lips can claim any distinction, they all are of an earthy hue; her Teeth rotten, and sweet as the Grave, or Charnel-house, and yet the Devil was in me; I marry'd for Love: Lord bless us! Love of what? not her good Conditions, I'm sure: But I am an old Man, as you see, and she's a *Wit*, that took me, tho' I understood never a Word of what she *writes*, or *says*: Deliver me from a poetical Wife, and all honest Men for my sake! She rumbles in Verses of *Atomes*, Artick and Antartick, of *Gods*, and strange things, foreign to all fashionable Understanding; because she was Ingenious, I thought she'd have been a Help-meet to my Memory, being something decay'd, but she hates her Duty to me, and to the Gods, and never goes to the Temple above twice a Year, and then she falls into counterfeit Fits; the Bottle of *Hartshorn*'s sent for, and her self carry'd in a languishing posture home; her Tongue is at perpetual War; her Discourse one continu'd Reproach, derogating from mine and my Childrens Honour; if there be any body pre-

sent

sent then she's sure to be most virulent; if I happen to bear it with heroick Patience, she is defeated and undone, falls into Fits, beats her self to be reveng'd on me. She has often kick'd all the Bed-cloaths off, and her own Linnen, till she has been stark naked, when the Under-Priest, the Coachman, and Boy, have been holding of her down, yet I've good reason to think all this but a Sham, I mean her Fits, for if you'll let her alone, she'll quickly come to her self; but any body that compassionates her, (as People are apt to do till they know her) she'll hold 'em tack from one Frolick to another, for four long Hours, and then, to compleat all, as if nothing had ail'd her, she'll start up of a sudden, and fall a boxing of me couragiously, or her Chamber-Maid, or both; when she has had her Revenge, she's at ease; but if by chance she finds my Mind unguarded (against the bitter Assaults of her Tongue) and that I do fall into a Passion, as it is not possible always for me to forbear, then she's pleas'd; then she's delighted; and finds her Joy in my Torments; is this any thing but the Temper of a Devil? The Day before I'm to sacrifice, she's sure to perplex me all Night long, on purpose to discompose, and put my Mind out of Frame; I've often attempted, upon such Occasions, to lie in another Bed, but that won't do, I should be too much at my Ease, and that would be her Hell: Up she comes roaring, and stamps her Foot impetuously and incessantly against the Door, till 'tis broke open. She's as strong in her Freaks as a *Granadier*; then she falls a howling and sobbing; tells me she can't sleep without me, and either forces me to rise to her Bed, or comes to Bed to me,

and

and is sure to keep me awake all Night long with her Scolding, as that's all her End and Design; there's no Intervals; no Truce to be had with her: She has frighted away all my Children, won't suffer one of 'em in the House; had once like to have choak'd my Daughter, that's a Woman grown, by flying upon her, with her two Hands about her Throat, she had stopt her Windpipe, till the poor Girl's Tongue hung out of her Mouth, and her Face was grown black, and had certainly kill'd her in a few Minutes more, if I had not come in and prevented her. What safety (think you) can my Life be in with such a Fury? and yet I know not what's the Remedy; she won't go from me, if I were to give her all that I have, (tho' she's sordidly covetous) because she dares not torment any body else as she does me; and yet I keep her a Coach, and four Servants, have a plentiful Income and an Estate of my own, and she had little or no Fortune; I was bewitch'd to marry her: Then she's in love with all the handsome Fellows she sees, but her Face, I believe, protects her Chastity, for none sure was ever yet so couragious to assault it. She vents her Passion in Love-Verses and Dialogues of *Clarinda* and *Daphnis*; a pitiful Lawyer's-Clerk was a long time her *Alexis*, and there was Love-Letters and Verses printed, with rattling Epithets, bumbast Descriptions, romantick Flights, and, in short, nothing of Nature in 'em, yet these must be printed, with an Epistle to her adored *Moneses*, who I've understood since, was a foolish Apothecary, that us'd to recover her from her Fits, without the help of *Galen*, or *Hippocrates*; then for her Morals, a Lady whom she had invited to stay

M at

at our House that Summer, assum'd the reasonable Freedom to advise her against Passion and Anger, she took it so ill at her hands, that to be reveng'd, she made her self a voluntary Evidence in a Law-Suit against her, of all the Discourse they had had together in freedom, and by adding a great deal of false to the true, made her lose her Cause. I had been abroad to Day about business, and had miss'd my Dinner; coming home, I ask'd for something to eat; she had took care; (after dining plentifully her self) that there should be nothing left for me; one of the Maids whisper'd me, that there was a large Apple-Pie in the Oven to be kept hot for the Gentlewoman's Supper, but I was to know nothing of it. Being pretty sharp set, I went to the Oven, as by instinct, out I drew the Pie, got a Plate of Butter, and fell to buttering of it in happy Security, as I thought, because she had retir'd to her Closet, pleas'd with putting the Victuals out of the way, that I should have nothing to eat; the Devil would not let her rest long without tormenting of poor me; down she comes, and before I was aware, snatches the Pie, and by a dextrous whirl of her Hand, sends it full in my Face and Eyes, the Plate of Butter follow'd, then the Tankard full of Drink, and, in short, whatever came to hand; enrag'd at the Pain I felt, my usual Moderation forsook me; I leap'd briskly at her Top-knots, she squal'd, which allarm'd the Neighbours, and your selves to behold this comical Combat: 'Tws Nuts to those Rogues, my Neighbours, who would not have parted us, tho' we had kill'd our selves upon the Spot: But for you, my good Friends, I am much oblig'd to your Endeavours,

Endeavours, but I see small Hopes of redressing these Grievances, that lie heavy upon me; were I of another Profession than I am, by a just Indignation, I would assert the Authority of a Husband, but our Talent is expected to be Meek under Persecution; Long-suffering; particular Scandal often reflects upon the general; my Brethren may be aspers'd for my sake, so that I content my self to sit down under this Chastisement, coming from the Hand of Heaven, as a Punishment for my Sins, in marrying a Wife not above half so young as my self, when I had Children grown up to keep my House, and administer comfortably to my Necessities.

Here the two Divinities, by stroking with their Hands, and applying a proper Antidote, expelled the Fire that had swell'd the poor Priest's Face and Eyes, in a terrible manner: He return'd 'em a thousand Thanks for their Civility: They took their Leaves very courteously, often regretting the Miseries he seem'd to suffer with such a Fury of a Wife.

Intel. You are now, Ladies, very near *Angela*, but just at hand is the *Prado*, a Place eminent *Hyde Park* for what's either Illustrious or Conspicuous; here the Rich, and the Fair, adorned in their most distinguishing Habits, come to take the Dust, under pretence of Air. If a Lady be new marry'd, and longs to show her Equipage, no Place so proper as the *Prado*; a Beauty just come to Town, that has a mind to be a Toast, exposes her self first upon the *Prado*; the Gamester, after a lucky Run, from no Shoes, and a Coat out at Elbows, steps into a large well-built Coach with Pillars and Arches, glorious Horses,

Horses, and Trappings, with rich Liveries, and where's the Place so proper for admiration as the *Prado?* The Aldermen's Wives come to learn Fashions, and make the Court envy the lustre of their Jewels at the *Prado*; young amorous *Beaus*, that have a mind to ogle the airy vain *Coquet*, whisk to the *Prado*; a Town-Husband would have but an ill Life (these fashionable Times) if he grudg'd his Wife a Chariot for the *Prado*; nay, the very Country-Gentlewoman, (humble in Town, and proud in the Country) when she has got her Husband in the mind, to let her come to *Angela*, thinks she had as good stay at home, if she be not able to have her only Pair of Horses drag her thro' the dirty Roads, in order to carry her to the *Prado*, with her Country-built Coach, and her rustical Airs, to divert the rest of the Company; nay, the very Coachmen here are so refin'd, they shall ridicule a Brother, come from the Country, and find fault with his driving, because it mayn't be exactly *à la mode de Prado*; both the Men and Women, who are not able themselves to keep Coaches, make their Court with indefatigable Industry to those who have, flattering all their *Haughtiness, Affectation, ill Nature,* and *Vanities,* calling their very *Vices Vertues,* to purchase by these egregious Follies, a back-place in their Coach, that they may spark it in the *Prado*. Not long ago an honest Gentleman, (whose Father being alive kept back the greatest part of the Estate) suffer'd his handsome Wife, to compound with her Gallant, (who had given her a Settlement for Life) upon such and such Terms, provided he toss'd in a Jewel for her Neck, and a Chariot for the *Prado*; and therefore, Ladies, if you have

Curiosity,

Curiosity, it must be impossible you should not desire to see the Cavalcade of the *Prado*.

Astrea. My Lady *Intelligence* judges of us by her self, that we likewise find Diversion among the most company; tho' I cannot fore-see any great use this will be to my design, yet being an Establishment since I left the World, I am contented to follow you to your admirable *Prado*.

Intel. See there the Prince *Adario*, conspicuous for his Equipage, but much more for his having his Princess in the same Coach with him: She come down deep to his *French Valet de Chambers* for this Favour: My Lady *Vertue*, she is certainly of your Court, and the greatest Ornament of that of *Angela*'s; is not her Person graceful, her Air sweet and modest; would not one believe her Charms are sufficient to conquer a thousand Hearts? yet they make no impression upon that only One she desires to touch; her Birth is most illustrious, descended from a Race of Heroes, neither has Scandal, (which scarce spares your very Ladyships) tainted her Character, but when they object, they tell us she loves Cards too well, which was a Diversion she probably took up, to amuse her trouble of Mind from her Lord's repeated Inconstancy: How great and how little is that Man? something so very high, and yet so very low in his Character, even his Generosity is a Virtue too much extended, and borders so intimately upon Extravagancy; that one knows not how to divide 'em, then the Merit of his Courage is so allay'd by his want of Conduct, that in praising one, it always puts us in mind how much we ought to blame the other; so ambitious in his Principle,

(166)

Principles; so humble in his Converse; so managed by his Favourites, and so mistaken in his unworthy Choice of 'em; in his Amours only there's no Contradiction, there 'tis all of a piece, Vice without any allay; he has corrupted more Women than a Grand-Seignor; his Pleasure consists in Variety; he leaves nothing undone to compass his Ends, and because Money makes the best dispatch, he is lavish of that to profuseness; the Traders in *Amour* no sooner see a handsome young Girl come to Town; a Citizen marry'd to a pretty Wife; a beautiful Daughter expos'd to the Frowns of Fortune by the death of her Parents, but they run with their Intelligence to his Highness; the *French-Valets* introduce 'em, one is very well rewarded, and the other, by these Services, keep themselves in favour; yet has he this of Magnificent in his Temper, he turns none of his Women to starve when he has done with 'em; there are several, (that sometimes shine in the *Prado*) to whom he has given large Cantons of his Estate; his now favourite Mistress is a Woman of exalted Birth; he purchas'd her of her Mother, (and that was most abominable) by a considerable Sum to her self, and a Settlement of Two thousand Crowns a Year upon her Daughter; the reverend Matron did not blush to sell the Prince's Favour to all that would purchase; (a wretched Principle) she was not asham'd to take sixty Pieces of a poor Poet, (all the Profit that his Brains had ever been able to present him) to make him only a *Subaltern*; the *French-Valets* rejoic'd at her death, because she was very like, during her Daughter's Reign, to run away with their Profit, the Bribes having all found the way

to

to her. When the Prince went to his *Vice-Royalty* in the *Indies*, the Princess, his Wife, was forced to give an incredible Sum to those rascally Fellows, or she had been left behind; yet had she the new Mortification, to find her Lord so wholly neglectful of her, and of all Business, as to shut up himself whole Days, to write long tedious repeated Assurances of Love to his then reigning Mistress; neither was he ever easie till she arriv'd, but those Transports are pretty well abated of their first violence; he has return'd long since to his darling love of Variety; 'tis pity no kind Hand is found to rescue him from this continu'd Vice, to paint on his Lady's suffering Merit, that, if possible, he may, tho' late, do justice to it. He's now no longer in his Youth; 'tis time these Follies shou'd pass away, but I doubt there's small hopes of it, whilst he is in those Hands, that manage him; but by the continuation of his Frailties, and will not, in all probability, so much to their own prejudice, awaken him from that Lethargy he appears so many Years to have been buried in: He's positively good-natur'd, all the Errors of his Life seem not to proceed so much from himself, as his Flatterers, who have cherish'd and encourag'd 'em in him; had his Choice first light upon Men of Honour, and true Principles, how eminent might he now have been? neither is it yet too late, if he strive to redeem his Character, it will appear, as if those ill Habits had been rather acquir'd than natural to him.

Be pleas'd to look into the Coach that follows next the Prince, there sits the proudest Woman in *Atlantis* (if you can tell for what except

(168)

[margin: D. of M—u / Dutch.? of / Montague / Widow to / D. of Albemarle]

except her Sister, who ran Mad for Pride. A certain Grandee had no other method of gaining her, but by bribing her Women, and carrying the Lady to a Mount, whence they had the prospect of Men making Bricks in the neighbouring Fields. He assur'd her those were his Slaves, the People he held in Captivity, for he was the King of *Egypt*. This tumbled the Lady and all her Wealth into his Arms, she wanted to be a Queen, but having once possessed himself of that, he shut her up of her own side for a Lunatick; holding a large Estate by her Life, it's thought (by most People) he won't find it convenient for her to die, so long as he lives.

This Sister of hers, that just pass'd us, carries her pretty Daughters to the Opera-Market and *Prado*, for Husbands; her own has out-liv'd five Brothers of his to come to the Estate, and there's yet one remaining that hopes he shall be the seventh that survives the sixth. The Lady herself, tho' never handsom or distinguishable, (for any thing but Pride) believes so well of herself, she scarce does any one below her the favour to rise when they come in. There seems nothing in her so commendable, as her value for that fourth Person which was with them in the Coach. The Lady once belong'd to the Court, but marrying into the Country, she made it her business to devote herself to the Muses, and has writ a great many pretty things: These Verses of the Progress of Life, have met with abundance of Applause, and therefore I recommend 'em to your Excellencies perusal.

The

The Progress of LIFE.

I.

How gaily is at first begun
  Our lives uncertain Race,
Whilst that sprightly morning Sun,
With which we first set out to run,
  Enlightens all the place?

II.

How smiling the World's Prospect lies!
  How tempting to look thro'!
Parnassus to the Poet's Eyes,
Nor Beauty with a sweet surprize,
  Does more inviting show.

III.

How promising's the Book of Fate,
  'Till thro'ly understood!
Whilst partial Hopes such Lots create,
That does the youthful Fancy cheat,
  With all that's great and good.

IV.

How soft the first Idea's move,
  That wander in our Mind!
How full the Joy, how fair the Love,
That does that early Season move!
  Like Flow'rs the Western Wind.

V.

Our Sighs are then but vernal Air,
  But April drops our Tears;
Which swiftly passing, all grows fair,
Whilst Beauty compensates our Care,
  And Youth each Vapour clears.

VI.

But oh! too soon, alas, we climb,
  Scarce feeling we ascend
The gentle rising Hill of Time;
From whence with grief we see that prime,
  And all in sweetness end.

VII.

The die once cast, our Fortune known,
  Fond expectation past,
The Thorns that former Years have sown,
To crops of late Repentance grown,
  Thro' which we toil at last.

VIII.

Then every Care's a driving harm,
  That helps to bear us down;
Which fading Smiles no more can charm,
But every Tear's a Winter's Storm,
  And every Look a Frown.

IX.

Till with succeeding Ills oppress'd,
  For Joys we hop'd to find

By

By Age so rumpl'd and undress'd,
We gladly sink us down to rest,
Leave following Crouds behind.

Astrea. The Lady speaks very feelingly, we need look no further than this, to know she's her self past that agreeable Age she so much regrets. However I'm very well pleas'd with the Thought that runs thro'; if she had contracted something of the second and third Stanza, it had not been the worse. I presume she's one of the happy few, that write out of Pleasure, and not Necessity: By that means its her own fault, if she publish any thing but what's good; for it's next to impossible to write much and write well.

Intell. See that beautiful Gentleman at Loll in the next Chariot, born from as beautiful a Mother! he has made a dreadful Havock among the Ladies, I can name you three (all of Rank) that have had dangerous Compliances with him; and yet an indisted Girl, with four hundred thousand Crowns, has resistted his Charms, and the Grandeur he cou'd raise her to; to bestow her self, (as 'tis thought she will) upon a Person who has more of his Vices, and less of Quality and Estate.

How likes your Excellencies that goodly Lady that rolls on next in course? Has not she Fat enough to have prevented any Wife in *Angela* from running mad, thro' Jealousie of her Lord and her? The Wife came in one Day very inopportunely, to visit at a Woman of Condition, where she had the misfortune to surprize her Husband, and the Person before us, in very convincing Circumstances; the poor Lady fell
into

into such an ill Habit of Mind, that she could never recover her Peace, but led the *Count*, so very disagreeable a Life, so outragious and *jealous*, that unable to bear the continuance, and hopeless to reform her, they are parted, and she has the Mortification of lamenting alone her too warm Resentments, which all prudent Women will dissemble, if they do but consider that Husbands have often been reclaimed by gentle Methods, never by rough, unless they depend upon their Wives Fortune for the best part of their own; and that, I must confess, varies the Case; yet notwithstanding her known Gallantries, an honest Gentleman has lately ventur'd to make a Wife of her.

[*margin note:* Gen.ˡˡ Hervey]

Look what a grave Seignior comes next, he was once in the Government, and the Head of a Party, but he too much neglected both, to admire a singing Creature at the *Opera*, whom no body else could admire, and yet he gave her Four thousand *Chequins* for her Favour, and the like Sum repeated to keep it secret; but as there are few things such in the Prince's Court to whom I belong, you may depend upon Dame *Intelligence*, for what you hear.

[*margin note:* E. of A— Nottingham]

See that gay Lady, that laughs aloud, and lolls upon her Companion; her Eyes by Intervals thrown abroad in search of Gazers; eager to be admir'd; she has lately presented her Husband with a considerable addition to her Fortune, tho' she had a large one before; a Relation has been so kind to die, and leave her the power of such a Compliment, which is no more than is necessary to soften her ill Conduct; at this very minute she receives a *Billet* from the Orange-Wench, under the pretence of buying that

[*margin note:* M.ʳˢ Hammond]

that Basket of Cherries; *Coquet* as she is, 'twont be easie to her, unless the whole *Prado* know she is admir'd; at the next round we shall find her reading on't, that the World may see how well things go with her; the Husband of this airy Lady is as great a Libertine as her self; he has always distinguish'd himself by his Humility, and good Nature, in caressing despicable poor Creatures, abandon'd by all things but the Extremes of Vice; these he can with pleasure revel away his Time, and large Estate upon, tho' he be reported to have Understanding; the Lady had an Affair with one of the young Sons of the Sea-green-Deity; handsome, and of an eminent Extraction; Lady *Bertha*, his Sister, was intimate with *Clarissa*, so's the Lady named that we were speaking of; they wou'd often wonder together at the Caprice of the Men; how *Clarissa*'s Husband neglecting her, could doat as he did upon the last and lowest of Womenkind; she scorn'd however to revenge these Abuses upon her self, and so to be a sufferer both ways; she knew better than to take up with the solitary Reliefs of Prayers and Tears, there were other Comforts better fitted to her Genius; she would not vainly waste her Youth in Retirement, expecting a Reformation that might never happen, but Dresses, Rambles, Plays, Intrigues, is managed by her Woman, and a Mantua-maker is her chief Favourite. Lady *Bertha*'s lovely Brother pursu'd his good Fortune, and was even put into *Clarissa*'s Bed; in his Sister's Night-Dress; I believe Lady *Virtue*, they did not consult your Excellence, so much as Convenience, when the fashionable Establishment was made of separate Beds. *Clarissa* us'd to have whole Nights to her
self,

self, and therefore did not so much distrust her ill Fortune, that she should be disturb'd now; but as she was throwing off her Cloaths, to fly to Lady *Bertha*'s Bosom, her Husband comes into the Room, to pass the Night with her; she runs to the Door to stop him, fawns and smiles, throws her Arms about his Neck, and with a Kiss, whisper'd in his Ear, that Lady *Bertha* was gone into his Bed, very ill of the Head-ake, and he should take heed how he made a noise to disturb her. *Monsieur* lov'd the Ladies too well to be indifferent on that Chapter; he could not hear so handsome a one was laid in his place, but he resolv'd he would be paid for his Concession, therefore he tells *Clarissa*, a Kiss he must and would have of Lady *Bertha*, and half a Dozen good Huggs, or she must not expect to lie there. *Clarissa* begg'd he would return to his own Apartment; Lady *Bertha* would never forgive her, she did not use to be kiss'd and tumbled; that was all one, she must begin now then, what did she do in his Bed? The Plot thicken'd, guess at their Confusion: As to the Hero in Pinners, I suppose he scorn'd to tremble, unless it were for the sake of his Mistress; however, he left the matter to the Woman, who are always readily assisted by Fortune, when their ill Conduct precipitates 'em into Dangers; he only hid himself in the Pillows, and pull'd the Bed-cloaths over him, lest his Chin should not be quite so soft as his Sister's; the Husband threw himself upon her, (as he imagin'd) hugg'd and embrac'd her as she lay cover'd up, endeavour'd to get at her Face, pull'd the Bed-cloaths with all his might; *Clarissa* him, but both in vain, till he rose of himself, and swore Lady

Bertha

Bertha was the strongest Woman ever he met with in his Life; begg'd but one Kiss, and he would be gone; *French Madeinoiselle* cry'd Lady *Bertha* would never come again; she was certainly provok'd, and would speak to none of 'em, whilst he was in the Room. *Clarissa* gave her self violent Airs; and ask'd him if he would never have done being a Brute, did he know no distinction? Was a Woman of Quality, (who did her the honour to pass a Night with her) to be us'd in that manner? Fie upon him! he might be asham'd of himself for ever: Thus she taunted the kind Husband to his own side, but not without threatning how many Kisses he would have in the Morning, when her Head was better; and begging *Clarissa* not to let her go, till he had made her pay sufficiently for robbing him of his place; but the Lady durst not stand the Encounter, when he came there to drink his Chocolate by her Bed-side, as he thought, he found the Bird flown: *Mademoiselle Frippery*, the *Suivante* told him, Lady *Bertha* was so very angry at his Rudeness, and so afraid of him, that she could not sleep all Night long, lest he should come in, by virtue of his Master-Key, to disturb her; which made her Head ake ten times worse than it did before, and sent her away, at Five in the Morning, to her own House, to recover the Fatigue she had suffer'd that Night for want of sleep.

'Your *Divinities* having naturally a regard to the Ingenious, be pleas'd to direct your Eyes towards that Pair of Beaus in the next Chariot; the Equipage belongs to him that sits of the left-hand, by boasting of an intimate Friendship with the other, he has got himself enroll'd enroll'd among, and in the Catalogue of Wits, not forgetting a very neceſſary Ingredient; a good Eſtate; as large as you ſee him, his Father and Grandfather are both profeſs'd Sparks, and ſpruce up in Cherry, and other gaudy colour'd ſilk Stockings; he talks of *Rochefoucault*, *Fontenelle*, *la Bruyere*, as his intimate Acquaintance, and ev'n gives the latter the preference; when I can't but find what ſeems moſt eminent in him, is but borrow'd from the other two. If a Man of Eſtate has a mind to be thought to have a Genius, he has but to fall in labour of ſome little Trifle, a *Prologue*, *Epilogue*, *Song*, or *Flouriſh* to *Cælia*, and be generous, to the next Poet he can (get his Friend) to adviſe to dedicate to him, and preſently he's *Virgil* and *Mecenas* too; the Gentleman looks indiſpoſed at preſent, his native Fire quench'd in unnatural *Tiſſane*, elſe nothing ſo gay and ſo coquet, pardon the Expreſſion, it may not be thought ſo proper to the Sex; but they of late ſeem to put in for an equal Claim; he angles not without a Strain of Affectation for Hearts; catches at Applauſe; ſoftens his Eyes and Voice, gives Snuff to the Ladies upon his Knees, that his fair Perſon may appear to advantage, with that graceful and ſubmiſſive Turn; his buſineſs, ('till of late) has rather been to make Love than take it; but a certain Military's Wife has had more Darts for him than is neceſſary; he was too nice to divide her even with her Husband; far from ſuſpecting Partnerſhip with another, and therefore took her to ſubſiſt upon his Fortune, which was laviſh'd with the prodigality of a new and true Lover; he had a troubleſome Place of profit in the Government, a thing quite out of his

his Road; he lov'd writing, indeed, but not that fort; it engrofs'd too much of the Time he could not fpare from his fair Miftrefs, and the Mufes, but to quit it with the better Grace, he took the laudable and fingular pretence, of being difgufted, becaufe a Friend of his, who procur'd it him, was difcharg'd from an Office upon which his, in fome meafure depended, tho' the truth is, himfelf had made fuch Difcoveries againft the ill Management of the Minifter, that it was but vain for him to hope to keep it after.

They tell you that his Miftrefs, not contented with all the Love that handfome Perfon of his could beftow, went in fearch of other Adventures, the confequence of which, is fending him to the *Doctors* for *Tiffane*. They fay he loves her even to a forgivenefs of that, and all other Faults. I can but fmile to think, whilft the height of the Love-fick-Fever lafts, the Women have their turn of revenging the Injuries that are done to others of their Sex. A Perfon, whilft fhe is belov'd, can commit no Crimes, for as *Rochefoucault, As long as we love we can forgive.*

That Friend of his on the right, is a near Favourite of the *Mufes*, he has touch'd the *Drama* with truer Art than any of his Contemporaries; comes nearer Nature and the Ancients, unlefs in his laft Performance, which indeed met with moft Applaufe, however leaft deferving; but he feem'd to know what he did, decending from himfelf, to write to the *many*, whereas before he wrote to the *few*: I find a wonderful deal of good Senfe in that Gentleman; he has

(178)

Wit, without the Pride and Affectation, that generally accompanies, and always corrupts it. His *Myra* is as well celebrated as *Ovid's Corina*, and as well known. How happy is he in the favour of that lovely Relation? She too deserves Applause, (besides her Beauty) for her *Gratitude* and *Sensibility*, to so deserving an *Admirer*. There are few Ladies, when they once give in to the Sweet of an irregular Passion, care to confine themselves, even to him that first endear'd it to 'em; not so, the charming *Myra*, she loves the Pleasure but in regard to the Lover, not the Lover for the sake of the Pleasure.

Would you believe that Weather-beaten Equipage, of two Years standing, belongs to the richest Prince in *Atalantis?* nay, almost as rich as all the Princes put together, with as narrow a Soul; nothing seems to me to be a truer Emblem of it, than the Entrance into his own Palace, the large magnificent Gate is entirely made up, there's no Passage that way; you go in by a small Postern, or Back-Door, an exact Resemblance of that narrow Channel by which Generosity is convey'd to his Heart; a certain Poet had occasion to name him in a Panegyrick, not doubting of a very good Reward, presented one of 'em to his Highness: He order'd two Pieces for a sorry Gratuity, but before it could be receiv'd, the Poet was oblig'd to leave a Receipt with the Steward, for so much in Silver, Gold not happening to be in the *Treasury* at that time. -I would fain know if there's to be found upon the *File* at any other *Princes* in *Europe*, a Certificate of that Nature?

That

That opulent Heiress, his Daughter, makes the *Prince* smile, whom I serve; she will give her occasion, in a little time, to make use of her thousand Ears, and her thousand Tongues.

Behold the Reverse of what last pass'd us; see that magnificent, young and graceful *Prince*, the *Duke de Beaumond*, his Horses are, in their kind, almost as well cast as himself, and all from his own Breed: He claims a Descent from a long Race of Kings, and an untainted Loyderiv'd from his glorious Predecessors: He is young you see, just step'd upon the Stage of the World; his Inclinations are adequate to his Birth; he will show what it is to be a Prince, that is, what a Prince ought to be, Magnificent, Humane, Sedate, free from all those Vices that ruffle the Calm of Youth, and cost the best part of their Time to reform from, if ever they reform; he's an encourager of the real Ingenious, not fond of Applause, nor yet with Pride and Sullenness rejecting it from those who know where to give it; he will imitate his illustrious Grand-father in his practice of all the *Virtues*. Oh *Astrea!* We must lead you to his *Palace*, where both your Divinities will be satisfied, will be charm'd, to find so perfect a Resemblance of your selves.

Does your Excellencies behold who fills that large handsome Coach? People that seem to be very merry, and infinitely at ease, but many a Heart-ake has gone to the forming of that Equipage; a notorious Gamester, who for his Excellency in that Faculty, has a Mock-Title given him; he's call'd *Monsieur le Chevalier*, by those Fools he has cheated out of their real Estates; no body

(180)

lives greater than he does; luxurious Dinners; *Quails, Hortolans, Terrene, Pheasant's-Eggs, China-Birds-Nests, Hermitage, Champaign*; whatever is to be bought or procur'd. The Jolly Woman on the left-hand passes for his Wife, tho' the Lady, I have the honour to serve, not only whispers, but speaks aloud, notwithstanding her Demureness; her appearing in all Places of Credit; haunting the publick; visiting, and being visited, she has a lawful Husband alive. Observe but the Widow on the right-hand; because he loves Niceties, he has got her to live in the House with 'em; she's a Lady of the best Intelligence in the World; she knows what's done at all the Assemblies; who goes to the *Chocolate-House* for Letters; whence they come; what Answers are return'd; who wins at the Races; who loses at *Hazzard* and *Basset*; when such a Lady granted the Favour; how long before 'tis probable that such a one may be brought to do the same; she's very near being one of the youngest Grand-mothers in *Atalantis*, and yet she's older than she looks for; that artificial Face of hers is still the same, for how can that be said to wear out, that's made new, or renew'd every Morning? She's handsome by Nature, but loves Money too well; her Admirers are infinite, has been the fashion these twelve Years, and that's a long time in this varying Age, especially when we consider *Le Grand Maistre du Hostel-Royale* furnishes great part of her Expence, and upholds her Chariot for the *Prado*, where this *faux Prude* set at gaze, scorns to own the least Acquaintance in publick, nor will return a civil Salute to those, whose lesser Vices are not crown'd as eminently with Fortune's Favours as her

her own, tho' she make no scruple in private at Cards, to manage 'em out of their Money. As to the *Chevaliere*, by Whim and Custom so call'd, he rose, (if it may be call'd rising) from the very Dregs of the People, a Waiter at a *Bowling-Green*, from the most abject Slavery, to the greatest Profusion of Wealth and Pleasure; had either of your Divinities assisted his Ascent, it would have been Glorious, but in his practice he has nothing to do with *Justice*, or any other of the *Virtues*: *Fortune* only is pleas'd to show how preposterously she can work, to make the gaudy Gamester shine in the *Circle*, whose original Place was among his Livery-Companions, at the Gate, she makes 'em acceptable to, and Companions of the greatest; those eminent both for Quality and Beauty, hug these Scoundrels to their Bosom, set 'em glaring in the Face of Day, for the well-managing a Die; but if a Man be but once Master of Money, this complaisant Age never scruples how they came by it.

Vir. Who is that alone in yonder Chariot? his Equipage is handsome, but his Person needs no setting-off, he appears much a Gentleman, his Eyes are continually in the next Coach, which is adorned with a wonderful gay Lady: She either sings well, or fancies she does, for I've observ'd, that still as she came round, she was humming an Air; sure she was at the Chariot-Race; he seems to steal his Glances, and be upon the reserve.

Intel. I must take leave to answer your Mightiness, (without power) by a Leer, and a malicious Smile, because I am infinitely pleas'd at your Query, it borders so much upon my beloved Diversion, Scandal, and lets me into a

very

very ample Theme: 'Tis the *Chevaliere Bellair*, of an ancient Family, and a confiderable Eftate; yet fond of Honour; he has lifted himfelf un-der *Bellona*, and moft part of the Year expofes himfelf (that fine Perfon of his) to the Fa-tigues of the Campaign, the reft of his Time he devotes wholly to the Lady you fee in that Coach; at firft, he was as happy as Love and Opportunity, with the help of the favourite, Mantua-maker, (for thofe People are now migh-tily the fafhion) could make him, but the Lady foon grew inconftant, and has left him to wait whole Days together at the *Chocolate-Houfe*, in expectation of the happy Moment for her calling of him, according to her Promife, whilft fhe drown'd in the loofer Revels of Wine, and new Love, forgets that he is upon Duty, impatient, and fretting at her Delay: One of his Rivals is a Perfon of Poetical Dignity, he firft made her a Mufe, and fhe in return made him a For-tune; hisBounty was imaginary, hers fubftantial; a beautiful Youth of Quality, whom I have already fhown you in the *Prado*, is another, but ftill the *Chevaliere* is the ftanding Difh, and may very well go down, when in the Country, where her Huf-band is going to confine her, their *Villa's* are not far diftant from each other: Her Lord has, what he wanted, an Heir, to deprive the next Succeffor, whom he mortally hates, and thinks it, high time, by banifhment, to put an end to her publick Indifcretions.

The *Prado* empties apace; 'tis almoft Night; the King's Deceafe has put all things out of Frame; at another time you fhould have feen twenty times the number of Coaches. View that beautiful black Lady, fhe has the killingft Eyes in in the World, she first brought the bright Olive-Beauty in request, but weary with her own native Charms, she chang'd her Complexion, and turn'd Fair; the Town would not be impos'd upon, they could not so suddenly lose their Memory, they would attribute to Art what the Lady endeavour'd to pass upon 'em for Nature; to her it is that we owe the first Assembly and Invention of giving Musick in the *King's-Gardens*. A certain Minister, renown'd for Wit, and call'd a Poet by all the Poets, (for fathering one Copy of Verses, by whom ever wrote) the *Mecenas* of the Age, an honour acquir'd with little Expence, where few or none are found to contest it with him, they scorn to be guilty of that unfashionable Vice, Generosity to the Ingenious: He was in love with this Lady, and wanting opportunity to declare his Passion, bethought himself of giving the Royal-Musick, and best Voices, in a manner, where the whole Court would not fail to come, because they were sure to find only themselves, the Cits being either ignorant of the Assembly, or excluded; it fortunately answer'd his Expectations, after the Musick was over, the Lady was seen to walk with him down a close Walk, where some that belong to my Prince's Court, do not stick to report, she gave him the Promise of a more fortunate Rendezvous.

See that dapper squat Gentleman, with a tolerable Face, poring on a Book, and feigning to read, tho' it be too dark to see: He would willingly be thought a Wit; not one of the Writers, but brisk at Repartee, by large Promises, he has often bubbled the common Women out of what they had to bestow, but is now with his own consent sufficiently bubbl'd himself:

himself: *Laurentia,* a young *Courtezan,* who owes her Birth to the free-born Joys of Love, has had the good fortune to captivate him in such a manner, that he renounces the whole Sex for her sake, and 'tis thought he may be such a Fool as to marry her, which is more than ever her Mother could persuade her Father to do for her, tho' she be a Woman of an intrieguing Brain, but having profited by her own Mistakes; she instructs her Daughter in the Art of Management; this seems to me a sort of lengthning of Life, or of living one's time over again; at this rate a *Courtezan,* (the Daughter of a *Courtezan*) must be much too cunning for any Man in the World: She joins her Mother's Experience, to her own Youth and Charms, and so set out, might pretend to out-wit the Devil himself, if he once appear'd in the shape of a Gallant.

Laurentia's Mother affecting Quality-Airs, in all what she says or does, drew in a pretty Boy to marry her Girl, while they were very young, the Boy had Friends at Court, that might have provided very well for him, but this unlucky Marriage put 'em out of Hopes; they sent him among the *Marines*; in a little time he grew in so great Dislike of what he had done, but was either kill'd, or else he dy'd, so soon after, that she was left a young Widow, and a moot Point whether not a Virgin; so the Mother would have had it believ'd, by all that were not likely to make Experience of the contrary, their Circumstances were very low, something to better 'em; she could not refuse the privilege of her House to a declining *Coquet,* who was her intimate Friend, and had made her many Presents. This Lady, after a long Run of Love and Gallantry,

lantry; having rather increas'd than diminish'd the Fortune her Father left her, found a young Gentleman Fool enough to marry her, tho' he had a pretty Estate in hopes, depending on a pretended Uncle, or a real Father, one would have thought it was an Obligation to her, to prove a good Wife, but like the *Cat*, metamorphos'd into a *Lady*, she must run at the *Mice*, tho' she were sure to lose her Preferment by it, and be turn'd into a *Cat* again; so Cards and Gallantry were not things so easily renounced, but because she had something more to manage than before she was marry'd, she met her Lover *incognito* at this House, 'till at last *Laurentia*'s Mother, by her Artifice, and extolling her Daughter's Charms, drew the *Chevaliere* to consider 'em; he became false to his old Mistress, and as 'tis suppos'd, paid his price for his new. Then was the Girl seen in a Gold-watch, that had scarce before a Shoe to her Foot; thus was she introduc'd, till from one degree to another, she arose to the honour of pleasing this Gentleman, who has One of the best Estates, beneath the Nobility in *Angela*.

He parted with a very considerable Employment for ready Money, to put his Mistress into repair; from a narrow Compass, and poor Education, she is risen to the height of Expence and Delicacy, nothing almost is nice enough to please either her Mother, or her self; the *old Ones* discourse trolls all upon *Virtue*; that her Daughter would sooner die than do an ill thing; she can answer for her Daughter's Honour: I wonder some *Macilente* (when he hears her thus exclaim) does not ask, whence then are deriv'd these fine Lodgings, Wax-Lights, Card-Assemblies,

(186)

blies, nice Eating, and rich Cloaths? we live no longer in an Age when *Fairy Kings* and *Queens* bring Riches to Mortals: People are seldom seen to change into such Extremes, without a visible *Wherefore.* The Spark, I think, does not pretend to dissemble, or else-whence comes those passionate Raptures? that he'll never love another Woman, *Laurentia* will never suffer another Man; they have made a reciprocal Vow, not to kiss, touch, or scarce to come near any of the Sex but themselves; hence I suppose it is that that we find him reading in the *Prado,* for fear he should be thought to take a pleasure in looking at any Woman but his Mistress.

That disagreeable Woman, that whisks away next, is always dirty, when she's set out with Jewels; she loves Cards better than any thing but Money, and for the sake of Money she loves Cards. Being first upon the Place appointed, the Day that she was going, (within the Year) to bestow her self in second Marriage, she told the Gentleman, she hop'd 'twas lucky, for so it happen'd with her other Husband; who fortunately dy'd first, and left her very rich: One would have thought this Compliment would have disorder'd the Bridegroom; but he wanted nothing of her but her Money, and therefore made her this Repartee; the Omen was not less auspicious to him, for exactly so it happen'd with his other Wife, who more fortunately for him, dy'd first, and left him the possibility and honour of becoming her Husband.

She lets a Brother of hers want Bread, in a common Prison; 'tis true he has lost to Gamesters an incredible Sum of Money, and a very great Estate; but still, let one's Relations be
never

never so abandon'd, I think, they ought to receive bare Subsistance from so near a one as a Sister, especially when it is so much in ones power, as it is in hers.

O let me ease my Spleen! I shall burst with Laughter; these are prosperous Times for Vice; d'ye see that black Beau, (stuck up in a pert Chariot,) thick-set, his Eyes lost in his Head, hanging Eye-brows, broad Face, and tallow Complexion, I long to inform my self if it be his own, he cannot yet sure pretend to that: He's call'd *Monsieur Le Ingrate*; he shapes his Manners to his Name, and is exquisitely so in all he does; has an inexhaustible Fund of Dissimulation, and does not bely the Country he was born in, which is fam'd for Falshood and Insincerity; has a world of Wit, and gentile Repartee; he's a Poet too, and was very favourably receiv'd by the Town, especially in his first Performance, where, if you'll take my Opinion, he exhausted most of his Stock; for what he has since produc'd, seem but faint Copies of that agreeable Original, tho' he's a most incorrect Writer, he pleases in spight of the Faults we see, and own; whether Application might not burnish the Defect, or if those very Defects were brightned, whether the genuine Spirit would not fly off, are Queries not so easily resolv'd?

M. Steel.
Sr Richard
Wales

I remember him almost t'other Day, but a wretched common Trooper; he had the luck to write a small Poem, and dedicates it to a Person whom he never saw, a Lord that's since dead, who had a sparkling Genius, much of Humanity; lov'd the Muses, and was a very good Soldier; he encourag'd his Performance,

Lord Cutts.

took

took him into his Family, and gave him a Standard in his Regiment; the gentile Company that he was let into, affifted by his own Genius, wip'd off the Ruft of Education; he began to polifh his Manners, to refine his Converfation, and in fhort, to fit himfelf for fomething better than what he had been us'd; his Morals were loofe; his Principles nothing but pretence, and a firm Refolution of making his Fortune, at what rate foever, but becaufe he was far from being at eafe that way, he cover'd all by a moft profound Diffimulation, not in his Practice, but in his Words, not in his Actions, but his Pen, where he affected to be extreme religious, at the fame time when he had two different *Creatures* lying-in of bafe Children by him. The Perfon who had done fo much for him, not doing more, he thought all that he had done for him was below his Defert; he wanted to rife fafter than he did; there was a Perfon who pretended to the great Work, and he was fo vain as to believe the illiterate Fellow could produce the *Philofopher's-Stone*, and would give it him; the Quack found him a Bubble to his Mind, one that had Wit and was fanguine enough to cheat himfelf, and fave him abundance of Words and Trouble in the purfuit: Well, a Houfe is taken, and furnifh'd, and Furnaces built, and to work they go; the young Soldier's little ready Money immediately flies off, his Credit is next ftaked, which foon likewife vanifhes into Smoke: The Operator tells him, 'twas not from fuch fmall Sums as thofe he muft expect perfection, what he had had hitherto was infignificant, or minute, as one Grain of Sand, compar'd to the Sea-fhore, in value of what he might affure himfelf of in the noble Purfuit of
Nature;

Nature; that he would carry him to wait upon a Gentleman very ingenious, who had spent more than ten times that Sum, in the Hands of the ignorant, yet convinc'd of the Foundation, was ready to Join with him for the Expence to go on with a new Attempt; accordingly *Monsieur* is introduced to One, who was indeed a Friend to the Quack, but did not absólutely confide in his Skill, tho' he still believ'd there was such a thing as the *Philosopher's-Stone*; yet hearing how illiterate this pretended Operator was, he could not imagine he had attained that Secret in Nature, which was never yet purchas'd, if ever purchas'd at all, but with great Charge and Experience: This Gentleman had an airy Wife, who pretended to be a sort of a Director in the Laws of Poetry, believ'd her self to be a very good Judge of the Excellencies and Defects of Writing; she was mightily taken with *Monsieur*'s Conversation, pray'd him often to favour her that way; being inform'd of the narrowness of his Circumstances, she gave him credit to her Midwife, for assistance to one of his Damsels, that had sworn an unborn Child to him; the Woman was maintain'd till her lying-in was over, and the Infant taken off his Hands, *par la sage Femme*, for such and such Considerations upon Paper; he had no Money to give, that was before-hand evaporated into Smoke: Still the Furnace burnt on, his Credit was stretch'd to the utmost; Demands came quick upon him, and became clamorous; he had neglected his Lord's Business, and even left his House, to give himself up to the vain Pursuits of Chymistry: The Lady who had taken a Friendship for him, upon the Score of his Wit, made it her business to inform her self

from

from her Husband, of the probability of their fuccefs; he gave her but cold Comfort in the Cafe, and even went fo far as to tell her, he believ'd that Fellow knew nothing of the matter, tho' there was a great City-Hall taken, and Furnaces order'd to be built, that they might have room enough to tranfmute abundantly: The Operator had perfwaded the young Chymift to fell his Commiffion, which he was very bufie about, and even repin'd that he met not a Purchafer as foon as he defir'd, for he thought every Hour's delay kept him from his imaginary Kingdom; but it was to be fear'd, when he had put the Money into the Doctor's Hands, to be laid out in *Mercury*, and other Drugs, that were to be tranfmuted into *Sol*, (as fmall a Sum as it was) he would give him the Slip, and go out of the Nation with it: The Lady was good natur'd, and detefted the Cheat; fhe begg'd her Husband that he would give her leave to difcover it: He advis'd her againft it, it might do 'em both a mifchief; but fhe infifted fo much upon it, that he bid her to do what fhe would; the Lady was then in Childbed, among a merry up-fitting of the Goffips, *Monfieur* made one his Genius fparkled amongft the Ladies, he made Love to 'em all in their turn, whifper'd foft things to this, ogled t'other, kifs'd the Hand of that, went upon his Knees to a fourth, and fo infinitely pleas'd 'em, that they all cry'd he was the Life of the Company; the fick Lady was gone to repofe her felf upon her Bed, and fent for *Monfieur* to come to her alone, for fhe had fomething to fay to him; vain of his Merit, he did not doubt but fhe was going to make him a paffionate Declaration of
Love,

Love, and how sensible she was of his Charms; he even fancy'd she withdrew, because possibly she was uneasie at those Professions of Gallantry he had been making to others; he approach'd the Bed-side with all the Softness and Submission in his Air, and Eyes, all the Tenderness he well knew how to assume; the Lady desir'd him to take a Chair, and afford her an uninterrupted audience in what she was going to say; this confirmed him in his Opinion, and he was even weighing with himself, whether he should be kind or cruel; for the Lady was no Beauty, but lay all languishing in the becoming Dress of a Woman in her Circumstances. She entertain'd him very differently from what he expected; in short, she discover'd the Cheat, and advis'd him to take care of himself, and to withdraw from that Labyrinth he was involv'd in, as well as he could; he was undone if she sold his Commission, all the World would laugh him to scorn, and he would hardly find a Friend to help him to another: A Thunderbolt falling at the Foot of a frightful Traveller, could not more have confounded him than this did our Chymist: What! all his Furnaces blown-up in a moment, all evaporated into Smoke and Air; he could never believe it, the Plumes (all elate and haughty as he appear'd before) sunk upon his Crest; who would have believed there could have been such a shrinking of the Soul? such a contractedness of Genius; such a poorness of Spirit; so abject a Fall from so tow'ring height; he was not able, in half an Hour's time, to speak one Word; his Address was departed, he knew not what to say, only begg'd leave to retire. 'Twas necessary that he must go thro' the Chamber, where

where the Ladies were, to go to the Stairs; he pull'd his Hat over his Eyes, without seeing 'em, and away he went. The Lady was satisfied with doing the friendly and honest part, let him receive it how he would; the *Coquets* fell upon her with violence, and ask'd her what she had done to *Monsieur*, what she had said to him had certainly bewitch'd him; never was such an Alteration, for they had easily seen his change of Countenance and Air; she defended her self as well as she could, and they were forced to conclude the Entertainment without him.

The young Chymist was so base, (as he afterwards told the Lady) to believe this only an Artifice of her Husband, to keep the learned Doctor to himself, and deprive him of his share of Philosophical Riches, in this Thought he mortally hated the Discoverer, but his Eyes being open'd, and his Sight clear'd, he quickly saw the Fallacy as plain as the Sun at Noon; be was already undone, or very near it; they had contracted abundance of Debts; the Doctor was a sort of an insolvent Person, the Creditors knew that, and did not trouble their Heads about him. *Monsieur* was forc'd to abscond, all he could preserve from the Chymical-Shipwrack, was his Commission: This Lady engag'd her Husband to serve him in his Troubles, and sent him perpetual Advices when any thing was like to happen to him; she prevented him several times from being persecuted by the implacable Midwife; he us'd to term her his *Guardian-Angel*, and every thing that was Generous and Human.

But Fortune did more for him in his Adversity, than would have lain in her way in Prosperity,

rity, she threw him to seek for refuge in a House, where was a Lady with very large Possessions, he marry'd her; she settl'd all upon him, and dy'd soon after. He re-married to an Heiress who will be very considerable after her Mothers decease, has got a place in the Government, and now as you see, sparks it in the *Prado*.

The Lady who had serv'd him, lost her Husband, and fell into a great deal of Trouble; after she had long suffer'd, she attempted his Gratitude by the demand of a small Favour, which he gave her assurances of serving her in; the demand was not above ten Pieces, to carry her from all her Troubles to a safe Sanctuary, to her Friends, a considerable distance in the Country; they were willing to receive her if she came, but not to furnish her with Mony for the Journy: He kept her a long time (more than a Year) in suspense, and then refus'd her in two Lines, by pretence of incapacity; nay, refus'd a second time to oblige her with but two Pieces upon an extraordinary Exigency, to help her out of some new Trouble she was involv'd with.

It is not only to her, but to all that have ever serv'd him he has shew'd himself so ingrateful; the very Midwife was forc'd to sue him; in short he pays nor obliges no Body, but when he can't help it.

Astrea. I think you have dwelt much too long upon so bad a Subject, we may find perpetual instances of Ingratitude, but very few Specificks against it. A Man, whose Principles are corrupted by Hypocrisie and Covetousness, can never be either good or grateful; it is a great misfortune to the Generous; they judge others by themselves, and are never undeceiv'd till at their own

own coſt, and when it is too late to remedy it.

Intel. There's a demure Lady in that Coach, and of Quality too, who had a comical Adventure happen'd to her ſome Nights ago; her Gallant ſhe has choſe is neither Young, nor Rich, nor Sweet, nor Handſom! all ſhe cou'd find to induce her muſt be his Impudence, and the reputation he has of pleaſing the Lady that favours him; beſides, he's a Drunkard, and in his ſleep tells all that he does, and acts over again the buſineſs of the Day. This old Stallion of the Senate-Houſe, had a Note ſent him by the Lady that her Husband was gone into the Country, and wou'd not return that Night, conſequently ſhe invited him to paſs it away with her; he ſent her word he wou'd not fail to obey her Commands, but ſtay'd too long at the Bottle after Supper, believing the Doſe wou'd heighten his Spirits; when he came to the Lady it was two Hours beyond the time ſhe had appointed him, Gay, and fluſter'd with Drinking. He's one of thoſe that intend ever to be Young tho' in deſpight of time, let his Looks contradict his Tongue never ſo much; this laſt depends upon him, and that will always be youthful. Whilſt he was pacifying the Lady's Choler, juſtly rais'd againſt him, for baulking her of two Hours Diverſion, her Husband with Authority knocks at the Door, the Lovers were in the dreſſing-Room over the Bed-Chamber, ſhe begg'd the Senator to ſtay there in the dark; her Husband us'd to fall aſleep as ſoon as ſhe was in Bed, and then ſhe wou'd come up to him, for 'twas impoſſible to get out now, whilſt their People were about, orders the Woman to blow out the Candles, and

and down fhe goes into the Bed-Chamber. Th Husband was return'd fooner than he defign'd, and very weary, fo to Bed they went: She waited but the found of his Nofe to rife and go to her Lover, who by this time, being in the dark, and the fumes of the Wine beginning to work, was fallen afleep himfelf. He put his Hands upon his Cane, and refting his Forehead upon his Hands, refolv'd to take a little Nap; there was a Couch and eafie Chair in the Room, but he wou'd not indulge himfelf there, left he fhou'd fleep too long, and the Lady finding him in that pofture might be fcandaliz'd at his fecond neglect. In his fleep he fell into a fit of talking, and acting over again what he had been doing at the Tavern whence he came; it feem'd (according to cuftom) he had been quarrelling with the Drawers, who knew him fo well, till he had call'd and knock'd twenty times, they never car'd to come to him. Being thus agitated in his fleep, he baul'd as loud as he cou'd, *Ricardo*, *Tomafio*, *Willielmus*, and knock'd with all his might with his Cane over the Husband's Head, never waking himfelf with all that Action; the Lady immediately hear'd him, and was frighted out of her Wits, fhe cou'd not think what he fhou'd knock for, in that dangerous place, unlefs he were a dying. Nothing, no not even giving up the Ghoft, fhou'd have forc'd him to make a Noife there; whilft fhe was making thefe Reflections, he redoubles his Efforts, he dreamt himfelf very angry at the Fellows for not coming, and knocks and calls again; this quite awaken'd the Husband, who had heard the firft attempt imperfectly, he ftarts up in the Bed feels for his Night-gown to rife, and fee what was the matter. Thieves were in poſſeſſion of the Houſe, and were knocking down the things over head. His Lady cling'd to him, not in a pretended but a real fright, and begs of him for the *Lud*'s ſake not to expoſe himſelf; they wou'd ſhoot him dead upon the ſpot, for they were apparently Maſters of the Houſe (juſt at that inſtant the knocking and bauling was repeated) they were calling of their Rogues together, and they ſhou'd be all kill'd. At the ſame time ſhe rung her Bell for her Woman, who was gone down Stairs for ſomething; when ſhe was come into the Chamber the Senator renew'd his Battery over-head, which was information enough to the Chamber-maid how things went; ſhe pretended to let fall the Candle in her fright, the Husband animated with the ſight of the Light (notwithſtanding his Wife's Efforts) was got half out of Bed; the Woman pretends to be bereav'd of her Senſes with fear, runs out and double locks the Door after her, goes to the noiſy Gallant, wakes him, and tells him the Miſchief he has done; there needed not many Arguments to induce him to withdraw, which he was ſo lucky to do, before the Houſe roſe; the Woman had the preſence of Mind, to throw open the dreſſing-Room Window which anſwer'd upon a Garden, and conveying away her Lady's dreſſing-Plate, and ſome ſmall Jewels that were left upon the Toilet, ran and call'd the Footmen, and other Servants, telling 'em there were Thieves in the Houſe; mean time her Maſter made a terrible battery to burſt open the Chamber-door; the Lady rung the Bell inceſſantly, the Family came together, the Houſe was ſearch'd, but no Thief; the things miſs'd, and the Window

dow found open. It was not doubted but at the hazard of their Neck, bing disturb'd, they were gone that way; the Lady had opportunity to sell or bestow, as she pleas'd, her Set of Plate and Jewels, for her Husband presented her with new: However, she tells her Woman, it ought to be a warning how People make choice of a *Debauchee* for their Lovers, for if all were like hers, they can neither keep Counsel awake nor asleep.

The next departing Coach brings us the famous last Years Toast (a modern Title for a reigning Beauty) her Health was drunk by the Name of the *Blossom:* She had pass'd all her Life before in her own Country, without any such reputation of Charms, they even distinguish'd her not at all; but after the prodigious *eclat* she had made here, Heav'ns! how they there throng'd to admire her; they could scarce believe they had ever seen her before, or any thing so beautiful; accus'd their own blindness! Sure they were infatuated! and a thousand such Exclamations; so true it is, that we often borrow from others, even to our very opinion of Things and Persons.

I see but two Coaches remaining; the last is a History, and therefore to be told at leisure.

If your Divinities please to remove a little out of the Dust they have rais'd; the Moon begins to dance upon the Water in the Canal, we will repose our selves near the Bank, and then I'll tell you, That the last Coach but one holds a young Lady, whose Mother had something particular in her Fortune. Her Husband was a *Chevalier*, but under some Circumstances that had impair'd his Estate: He resolv'd to absent him-

himself till time had redeem'd the Misfortune; his Lady knew little of the Matter, or so pretended: She had a young Son and a Daughter by him. The *Chevalier* had made a slight Acquaintance with a Gentleman of so considerable an Estate, that few (who are not Noble) had better, and even many of them not so good. He takes his Wife and two Children with him some sixty odd Miles into the Country to this Gentleman, under pretence of making him a Visit: The Gentleman, whose Name was *Ramires*, entertain'd him according to his Temper, not only with Hospitality, but Generosity; his Soul was large, he lov'd Expence, and to live up to that mighty Fortune he possess'd. After a while, the *Chevalier* takes his leave of him, and begs that his Wife and Children may remain there till his return, which you may be sure he told 'em shou'd not be long. His Lady was not handsom, but had a prodigious deal of Wit and Management. Some think she was let into the Secret by her Husband, or at least cou'd not but guess at their indifferent Circumstances: She apply'd her self with all possible Artifice to gain *Ramires*'s Esteem, knowing that a Friend of his Capacity could do her no harm. As much a Country-Gentleman as he was, he lov'd Magnificence, and a well-order'd Table. The Lady *Laurentina*, that is her Name, had a very good Genius for that, and every thing else; she knew one certain Maxim, That to be well receiv'd, it is indubitably necessary, to make our selves useful to those we wou'd recommend our selves to; no matter whether to their Business, or their Pleasure, so we be but useful. *Ramires* wou'd often say, He had never known the Elegangancies of Life, if he had not known *Laurentina*; without her he had been ignorant of the true use of an Estate, and dead to all the Charms of Wit and Conversation: She it was that had put new Spirit into him, had refin'd him, from a Brute into a Man: In short, she had put something into him that he was unacquainted with before; that little Devil of Love was got into his Breast, from whence the Lady took care it should not be frighted. Mean time they heard nothing from the *Chevalier*, nor *Ramires* did not desire she shou'd; tho' amidst all his Passion, he cou'd not help wondring, what he meant by leaving his Lady and Children so many Months in a place intirely strange to them, and almost so to the *Chevalier*; but he was mistaken in him, he knew what he did; in the small time of his Acquaintance he had study'd him throughly; generous and open Tempers are much easier seen to the bottom than others; the *Chevalier* knew the Charms of his Wife's Conversation wou'd quickly compensate, in *Ramires*'s Esteem, for the Charge of their Subsistence; which was a Trifle he despis'd in comparison to the Company he lik'd, even when Love was not in the Case. The Lady pretends (and it might perhaps be really true) that she knew not what to think of it; however, as she had always been obedient to her Husband, she was willing to expect his return in that very place, because he had commanded her not to stir till he came to fetch her. In short, one Year, two Years, and several Years past on, but no News of the *Chevalier*; still she was entertain'd with as much, or more Respect than at first: Care was taken that the best Masters should be had to educate her Children,

who

who were both very handsom, you saw the Daughter, and I can assure you nothing is more agreeable than her Son. *Ramires* paid her a most profound Respect; she manag'd the whole Family with the same Air and Authority as if it were her own; the best Apartment was hers; the Servants plac'd or displac'd as she pleas'd; her own and Childrens Expence (even to their very Cloaths) defray'd out of the Estate: *Ramires* never was so easie, as when he saw her so; neither cou'd there be any thing that he heard was the Mode, either for Dress or Living, but what he caus'd to be presented to her and *Mamoisel Margerita* her Daughter. *Ramires* was a young Man, all his Friends prest him to marry for an Heir to preserve his Name; he told 'em, he was very much at ease for that, an Estate seldom wanted an Heir: He caus'd his Sister's Son to be brought to his House, and made him take his Education with *Laurentina*'s Children; they were now grown up to an Age, wherein the Inclinations begin to distinguish themselves. *Laurentina* had so well pack'd the Cards that she was almost sure of the Game. *Ramires*, at her instigation, order'd his Nephew young *Rinaldo*, to make his Court to *Mamoisel Margerita*, and endeavour to please her; the Youth was one of those, that without being very ill-natur'd, had nothing benign in his Temper: He was come from a Mother who detested Lady *Laurentina* and all her Works; they look'd with utmost prejudice upon her, blackned her Reputation, tho' all her Behaviour, if she were criminal, was so well manag'd, that not one of the Servants, tho' all Servants are Spies, cou'd ever discover it. Young *Rinaldo* had no very strong Head;

pre-

prejudic'd by his Mother and Uncles, he hated *Margerita* and my Lady, not confidering *Laurentina* wou'd not have confented to the Marriage under lefs advantageous Circumftances, than his being declar'd *Ramires* Heir, but that he look'd upon himfelf as defign'd for, without being oblig'd to marry *Mamaifel Margerita*: The furly Youth oppos'd her in all her little Defires; thwarted her at their Exercife, whether in Dancing, Singing (for fhe had a very pretty Voice) or any other Diverfion, there was nothing but perpetual Complaints of *Rinaldo*'s rudenefs to *Margerita*; his Uncle reprimanded him in vain, his perverfenefs was difpleafing to him till he fent him off to the Academy to perfect his Studies, and prepare himfelf for fomething lefs than being his Heir.

Mean time certain News arriv'd, not from himfelf, but others, that the *Chevalier* was well and in the *Indies*; elfe it is not doubted, but *Ramires* had perfuaded Lady *Laurentina* to marry him; but that being no longer practicable, his Friends rais'd fuch a clamour againft her, that he faw wou'd infallibly ruin her Honour; he muft refolve to marry, or part with her out of his Houfe, where fhe could no longer ftay with Reputation, but under the umbrage of a Wife: her Choice directed him to a Lady of a very paffive Temper, eafie, provided fhe had no trouble given her, fhe was fure to give others none: Her Dowry was forty thoufand Crowns, which tho' inconfiderable to what a Man of *Ramires* Eftate might expect, yet it was counted a great deal for a Wife to beftow upon a Husband, whofe Heart was in poffeffion of another. They were marry'd, and Lady *Laurentina* continu'd her former

mer Empire; the Bride was as complaifant to her as the Bridegroom, becaufe fhe was naturally good, and the other only artificial: But *Ramires* did not fo eafily relifh this new change of Life; all his Eftate could not make him happy, fince he had not his former freedom to talk whole days apart with *Laurentina:* He fell into a languifhing Diftemper, of which he dy'd about fix Months after he was marry'd.

He fo far refented *Rinaldo*'s Contempt of *Mamoifel Margerita*, that he ftruck him out of his Will, leaving only a fmall Legacy in comparifon, and call'd his Brother's Son to the Eftate, tho' he had at firft defign'd it for his Sifter's) a new Name being to be affum'd by the Poffeffor (that of the Family) it was of no importance what they were before. When they came to examin the Cafh, they could not find how forty thoufand Crowns cou'd have been confum'd in fix Months, befides his own large Income, and no Debts paid; they cou'd account for none of it, neither as to Plate or Jewels, and not above two thoufand Crowns was found in Specie, fo that it is not at all doubted but he gave the whole to Lady *Laurentina*. Her Husband is not yet return'd; fhe lives in a very handfom manner, and which is wonderful, *Rinaldo* (come back from the *Academy*) fell paffionately in love (as much as his Soul cou'd love) with *Mamoifel Margarita*; thofe that pretend to divine, feem to think, that it will one day be a Match, tho' it does not appear to be either of their Interefts, unlefs the Lady draw out fome of her conceal'd Bags, if fhe have any; but fhe'll fcarce do that while fhe lives, or till her Husband return, left fhe confirm the opinion, that *Ramires* Lady's Fortune was empty'd into her Lap. *Ri-*

Rinaldo is perpetually with *Margerita*: Her Charms drew some time ago the Vows of a young Gentleman, Nephew to the Favourite; they hop'd he wou'd marry her, but that is not yet done, and therefore not probable, if they stay for the consent of those who will never be brought to give it.

Astrea. The Moral that may be drawn from this Story is, that the two Sexes ought never to meet in such dangerous Intimacies, where the Consequence is forbidden: Perpetual Conversation with the Ingenious, Habitude, Friendships, Tenderness, easily rise to love; to defend themselves against such Arms, they must have supernatural Aids; 'tis not to be purchased from below, under the forfeit of their Instincts. The Punishment fell as it ought, upon him, who could make the Holy Tie of Marriage subservient to his unlawful Passion. We may also see in *Rinaldo* how deprav'd is Human Nature; when it was his Duty to love, he hated *Margerita*; when he knows not well how to attain, he loves her. But pray my Lady *Intelligence* proceed, the Moon aids us to view a beautiful, tho' limited Prospect; 'tis better passing a Night in your Conversation, than otherwise; nothing can be better understood than what you say in your Discourse; I see the World without going into it, and hear so much, that I do not desire to see it.

Intell. Yet will your *Excellence* be much better inform'd from your own Observation. I pretend to morrow to have the honour of conducting you to the *Imperial Palace*; there you shall behold our graceful *Empress*, whose Heart is intirely Upright, were she but to judge all
things

by her own Eyes and Ears, all things wou'd be adminiſtred with the ſame Impartiality and Juſtice, as if your ſelf held the Balance. But, alas! What defence is there againſt the Corruption of Favourites, and the by-Intereſts of Miniſters? 'Tis impoſſible a Prince can come to the knowledge of things but by Repreſentation; and they are always repreſented according to the Senſe of the Repreſentator; either Avarice, Revenge, or Favour, are their Motive, and yet, how is it poſſible to prevent it? A Prince knows not how to diſtinguiſh by the out, and are ſeldom let into the inſide; all appears fair to 'em, if he be a good Man; who ſo forward as the Atheiſt in affecting Piety, the Debauchee becomes regular, the Covetous and Revengful, generous and calm; the moſt Cholerick knows nothing elſe but Smiles: not that they have in reality exchang'd their Vices, but the appearance of 'em. There are few honeſt Men found at Court; they care not to furniſh at the expence of their Sincerity, wherewith to maintain the Poſt of a Favourite; none ſerve there but in proſpect of making, advancing or preſerving their Fortunes. 'Twou'd be very hard to deny a Prince the Prerogative of every little Breaſt; the Joys of Friendſhip to a generous Mind, the greateſt Sweets of Power, is in doing good; and how natural is it to begin with what moſt affects us? Therefore, till there can be found upright Miniſters, and diſ-intereſted Favourites, Grievances there will be, and (ſince the Price runs ſo high) I fear hard to be redreſs'd, or not till the laſt general Conflagration.

From the Empreſs's ſide, you muſt be pleas'd to paſs to the *Favourites*, where if it is to be a pub-

publick Day, you will find her very intimate with a Woman that has a beautiful Appearance, adorned with every thing that's Splendid and Ravishing! sweetness in her Eyes! invitation in her Looks! She is call'd by all, that but superficially behold her, *Virtue*; she deceives People at the first view, but then with a very little acquaintance, we find 'tis only *Virtue pretended*; but of late she is become the Idol of the Court, *the Favourite* (tho' their acquaintance be not of a long standing neither) has introduc'd her. She has borrow'd from her Highness here an exact imitation, tho' with a little examination we find something in her Air very constrain'd; uneasie till the appearance she have assum'd be dismiss'd, and she return to her native Vice, which is ever in the Cabinet, at their *Couchee*, and in familiar Conversation. Her assistance is only requir'd upon extraordinary occasions at Council-Audiences, times of great Festivals or visiting Days, and then her two fashionable Maids of Honour are perpetually prompting her, for fear she shou'd be out in her part. These are Beauties very much admir'd, nam'd *Artifice* and *Flattery*. The Mother of the Maids is call'd *Hipocrisie*, and is very busie in keeping all under her Charge in exact *decorum*. They have the *Lares* and *Houshold-Gods* in *Angela*, as in Old *Rome*, the *Favourites* is the *God* of *Riches*, set upon a shining Altar within an *Alcove*, but she lets none have the Key of it but her self; there are found kneeling upon the Steps three Figures, inscrib'd, *Corruption*, *Bribery*, and *Just Rewards*; the two first perpetually furnishes Diamond-Rings, Chequins of Gold, and Bank Bills; the other insignificant Presents, which are hardly accepted, Ribbons, Gloves,

Gloves, Cordial-Waters, rich Wines, and Rarities for his Mightiness's Table; but these he looks down upon with Contempt, ev'n Plate and Jewels are but coldly receiv'd, as knowing they are valu'd by the giver at the prime Cost, but when they are sold will not come up to above two thirds, therefore ready Gold is the only thing current in his Empire. Behind and at a little distance, seem a long train of Merchants and Artificers with Bills in one Hand, and Rewards in the other, to pay for the Signing of those Bills; curious Clocks, repeating Watches, Jewels, Silver Stuffs; fine pieces of Linnen and Lace. On each side of the Altar are crouds of Petitioners suing for Places, either in the Army, Navy, Government, or Houshold, with their Bribes dispos'd in very regular and decent Order, but not any are found so weak as to pretend to Preferment in that Court without one.

Having seen what's most remarkable in the *Favorites* apartment, I pretend to conduct you to a handsome hospitable Lady that keeps a Bank, and Cards, for all idle and avaricious People, either to fling away or improve their Mony, as their Humours are different, and all extraordinary; I won't forestal your Entertainment, which I may be positive is new to your *Eminence*, for I dare to swear, *Astrea* was never yet at a Basset-Table.

Whilst the Lady is busie at her diversion in one part of the Room, you may glance your Eyes and Ears and find her Lord no less employ'd at his; he pretends to brightness of Understanding, to determin *De Bell Lettrès*, who writes insufferable; which intolerably; pardon the

the Tautalogy, 'tis his own Phrase, which with a mediocrity, but none excellently, except it be the Cabal, of which the Lord *Giraldo* has the Honour to be an eminent Member: They produc'd, indeed, one taking Comedy, and let an inferior Person try for the reputation of it, tho' the Town was not so complaisant to give it him. The next that came out, was too studied, it smelt of the Anvil, 'twas neither Tragedy nor Comedy, tho' so call'd, thro' the whole it cou'd not force a Smile; yet cou'd he magisterially, from his Throne of Criticism, condemn and look down with Contempt, upon all that did not think as well of it as the Fathers who begot it. The Lord *Giraldo* is indeed a Man of Wit and pleasant Conversation, and wou'd much more deserve Praise, were he less Partial; he takes too many things upon Trust, and often condemns a Book for the Author, as if either Genius or Expression were always the same, they that generally creep may sometimes soar; at least it seems to me to be an Injustice to believe the contrary, till they have prov'd it: a later Author has produc'd two very diverting Volumes, and promises us two more; I doubt not but if he had carefully conceal'd his Name, they wou'd have been applauded from the Lord *Giraldo*'s Quarter, but having a prejudice to the Man, they condemn the Work, and without reading, cry they wou'd not give two *Chequins* for whole Reams of his Writing, tho' it be never so correct. If you ask any one their Opinion of such a Poem, Play or Book, they immediately answer, 'tis cry'd down at the Lord *Giraldo*'s; they don't like it at the Lord *Giraldo*'s; what shou'd you see it? what shou'd you buy it for?

'tis

'tis condemn'd at the Lord *Giraldo*'s: Not that this so much quoted Lord *Giraldo*, can be suppos'd to spare so much time from the Publick, and the Duties of his Charge, to read all those Books whose Reputation he destroys; but his *Levee* is too open to little under-Criticks, even to the very Women-Wits, who saves him the labour, and gives the detail according to their Prejudice, or mistaken narrow Understanding; and then his Lordship does them the Honour to report it as his Sense, tho' in a thing he knows nothing of; and at that rate how shou'd the Author avoid being cry'd down at the Lord *Giraldo*'s?

When you have sufficiently diverted your self there, for I can't pretend your Excellency, if you wanted it, wou'd gain much Instruction from that Quarter, I'll lead you to the *Council-Board*, and the *Senate-House*; it wou'd take up a great deal of time to report you the several Histories of each particular Member, that of the Nobles and others, but I shall have care to omit nothing that has happen'd extraordinary, together with their Foundation, Institution, real and pretended Interests: The Arts of Government, which are here elegantly display'd to the Sight of a nice Observator; Reasons why a place of no seeming Profit shou'd have so much Mony expended in the pursuit of it; by what means they find their Account in this Lottery of Fortune, where (as 'tis now manag'd by the Wise) none but Fools draw the Blanks.

You shall see the *Arsenal*, the *Stores*, and management of those that preside over the *Marine* Affairs, the abuses and unheeded detection thereof; from thence I'll conduct you to the Army,

into

into the very Tents of their General; report to you how much he has done, and how much might have been done; fhew you the Interefts and Inclination of the Officer, the wretchednefs of the Soldier, and the debauchery of the whole; their inceffant Endeavours to prolong the War, their Arts to prevent or retard a Peace, which will level the Power of fome, and annihilate the exorbitant Expence of the whole.

For a change of Scene, it may not be amifs to take the Tour of the *Opera* and *Theatre*, you'll find the fame Injuftice in their little Commonwealth as in greater: The favourite Poet (in concert with the Mafter) has of courfe the reading of all new Pieces brought to him for his approbation, which he is fure never to give, to what feems more meritorious than his own, left he fhould put their Reputations upon a level. Hence the poor Poet is forc'd with infinite Patience and Humility (tho' he be deem'd in the beginning), to dance attendance for two or three Years together; they refer him to one, then to another, fo to a third, till they have run the whole round with him, and then difmifs him with an, *It won't do*, when they have already plunder'd it of all that was either new or well exprefs'd, to drefs up their own Colle&tions; you may judge there's no appearing for him, if they wou'd permit it, when his Market has been fo foreftal'd.

The very Women are not incourag'd and paid according to the merit of their Performance (certainly their value confifts in well Speaking and true Action, in a juft imitation of Nature, a capacity of varying and reprefenting the Paffions; and thofe other Excellencies appropriated

(210)

to the Character of a true Comedian) but the whim and liking of the Superiour advances his own Favourite to the Profits that are due to others; for if she have the luck but to please him, no matter what becomes of the Audience; he pays those for Speaking who never knew how to Speak, even to the imitation of a *Parrot*. If this had not been obvious, they wou'd never have suffer'd, by their Injustice, the admirable *Bracillia* to leave 'em, who in some things cou'd be only excel'd by the incomparable *Berenice*, in most but by her self, and in all, was the usefullest, as well as the most agreeable Women, of the Stage.

If you shou'd have any further inclinations to Gallantry, we will make the *Tour* of the *Tuilleries*, where Vice and Vanity appear in their own Kingdom! I wonder the Women of condition do not leave to walk there, since it is become so profess'd a Market for the Bad! it will raise at once your Pity and Indignation, to see so many very handsome, young, well-fashion'd Women, abandon'd to Destruction: They come to be bought after the most detestable manner, for an Hour or a Day, or as the Customer pleases; and when once their Folly and Poverty has reduc'd 'em to such an ebb, they are pollution to all that touch 'em, not only in regard to their Health and Body, or loss of Chastity (which is not strictly numbred among the Virtues) but their Souls become a sink of Abomination, a harbour for Lying, Revenge, Jilting, Deceit, Slander, Theft; Mony is their Deity, Interest their Heaven; in their acquaintance is the destruction of all Principles, the bane of Conversation, and something of more Wickedness

ness than is to be found in any other Specie of the Creation!

But that the City may not complain *Astrea* does not visit there, we will lead her to the *Bourse*, to see at once the magnificence of their Building, and the deceit of the Merchant, the whole mystery of Artifice and Trade, the immensness of their Riches, and the means by which they have acquir'd 'em, the opulency of the whole, and the parcimony of the particular, some great Ones excepted; where are to be found the Vices of the Court with a worse Air, and more Ostentation, the Citizen's ambitious Wife, giving those Laws in her Drawing-Room she has taken from above, with a lame imitation of that Splendor, Luxury, Cards, and Gallantry, which seems appropriated to the Great, and but forcibly ravish'd, and never can appear natural to these.

You may likewise have a view of the City-*Physician*, who neglecting the favourable Inclinations of *Esculapius*, runs mad after *Apollo*, who as carefully avoids him, forbidding the smallest of his Rays to glance that way, and even warn his *Daphne* from bestowing a branch of her Laurel upon one who so little understands his own Interest or Talent; had he contented himself indeed with Writing, not much, but well, or only given a Specimen of what he cou'd do, in his Episode of the Creation, we had lamented the future silence of an admirable Poet; but to prescribe in Verse, to Eat, Drink, Sleep, Walk and Ride, has Jaded his Muse, and sent him back to *Galen* and *Hippocrates*, sufficiently humbl'd, one wou'd think, and convinc'd of his Error, when he preferr'd the airy praise of *Parnassus* to the substantial Fame of being a good Physician.

Dr. Garth. Not so his Brother, *Signior Mompelier*, who wrote not much, but well, he seems to understand the difficulty to maintain an acquir'd Reputation, and is therefore wiser than to hazard the losing of it by a new Attempt.

These Degressions have carry'd me from my first Subject, I shall conclude 'em with but advancing one Curiosity more, and that seems to be where *Astrea* is principally concern'd, the Courts of Justice: What would you say, to see as I have done, two People (eminent for Dignity and Fortune) contending Years together, *[D. Montague / E. of Bath. / Granville.]* for an Estate, to which neither of 'em have a right: One pretends to a Will, another to a Deed, when, in truth, the lawful Heir dies a Prisoner, tho' under the specious pretence of assisting him; the Suit is prosecuted to the height, till both Parties pretty well tir'd, lay down their Animosities, and conclude the Peace, by dividing the Estate between themselves, leaving the Heir, and his Children, to seek their Bread where they can get it.

What would *Astrea* have said, to have seen in one Gause, and at one Tryal, seventy Witnesses go away perjur'd, most of them so well manag'd, as to believe themselves in the right? Would she not have exclaimed at the Impudence, as well as the Injustice of Mortals? And yet the Redress they pretend to give us for the Grievances of the inferior Courts of Justice, is in its Nature the highest Grievance. We have an Appeal from written Statutes, and known Laws, made by the wisest of our Legislators, prov'd and confirm'd by the Senate and Sovereign; but what is the Appeal? why truly to one Man's Opinion, whether influenc'd by Prejudice, Revenge,

venge, Avarice, Love, Ambition, or any of those Paſſions, that byaſs the Breaſt of Mortals; and this is call'd the *Perfection of Juſtice*; there have been but few, very few, that have born this great Office uprightly. A certain *Chevalier* ſeem'd [Sr. H. Johnson] to underſtand Mankind perfectly well, when he refus'd to ſue for a great Eſtate that was detain'd from him, whilſt the *Grand-Preſident*, that [Sr. R. Wright] then was, officiated; he knew he mortally hated him, and could not enough confide in his Principles, to ſecure himſelf from being oppreſſed by his Reſentment and Power; therefore he let the Cauſe ſleep till he was remov'd, and a new one put in his room, by which means he is poſſeſſed of the Eſtate, and the late *Preſident* bears yet his Animoſity unſated.

The laſt Coach that we beheld in the *Prado*, belongs to the ſecond Wife of one that was *Grand-Preſident* in the Reign of *Segiſmund* the Second. [Charles 2] I will acquaint you with ſome Paſſages of his Life, before he enter'd upon that exalted Dignity.

Volpone, the elder, was poſſeſs'd of a large [Sr. W. Cowper] Eſtate; he had two Sons, *Hernando Volpone*, who [Ld. Cowper] was afterwards *Grand-Preſident*, and *Moſco* the [Spenſer Cowper] younger. *Volpone* was of the Party oppoſite to the Court; an old *Debauchee*, given to irregular Pleaſures, not ſuch as the Laws of Nature ſeem to dictate: After marrying *Hernando* to a Wife he hated, and *Moſco* to one that had been his own Miſtreſs, he dy'd ſuddenly in the midſt of his Exceſſes; whether it were that he were ſo covetous, or could not ſpare ſo much from his own Expences: He did not beſtow a liberal Education upon his Son, but bred him to the practice of the *Law*, in that manner that is the leaſt

least generous, and most corrupt, but *Hernando* had natural Parts, that surmounted all those Inconveniences, together with a good paternal Estate, that his Father could not hinder him of; all the great Successes he has met with, is due to the brightness of his own Genius, he ow'd much more to his natural, than acquir'd Parts; his Memory was good, so was his Luck; to these were join'd a great deal of Wit; a volubility of Tongue; ready Sentiments, and a most plausible Address; Religion in pretence, none in reality; he held it lawful for a Man to attain by any Methods, either Pleasure or Riches; he was violent in the pursuit of both; quitting his Interest for nothing but Pleasure, and his Pleasure, for nothing but Interest.

A Man compos'd of such Elements, wanted nothing but to be known to be advanced, but because he was yet too young to possess those Employments and Dignities he aspired to, he suppress'd his tow'ring Thoughts, and was contented to plod on, in the necessary Tracts that all must follow, who aim to be one Day considerable by the Gown.

There was an *Orphan* left to his care, her Fortune not large, but her Person very agreeable: *Hernando* was amorous; he hated his Wife, tho' he liv'd civilly with her, and had the Art of dissembling so natural, that it cost him nothing to appear a good Husband. *Louisa* was the Name of his beautiful Ward; she was brought-up in the House with his Lady, who had a great kindness for her. *Hernando* had none of those terrible Conflicts, I before described in the Case of the Duke, and *Mademoiselle Charlot*; he was not acquainted with those violent Airs of Honour,

nour, nor scarce in his narrow Education convers'd with any who travell'd that Road; however their precise Party, held it a violent Scandal for a marry'd Man to corrupt a young Woman, especially under his *Ward*, therefore care was to be taken that it should not be known, and then it would be as it were undone. Her Mind had taken a natural bent to Orizons and Devotion; his Lady encourag'd the good Spirit in her, and laid the Foundation of a Virtue not easily shaken, tho' *Hernando* was indefatigable in his Pursuits, yet he would rather have had it in *Ambition* than *Love*; he did not care how easie he came by his Pleasure, nor how dearly he paid for 'em, as appear'd afterwards by a Taint he receiv'd, the usual Present that lewd Women bestow upon such, who do themselves the injury to converse with 'em.

Mademoiselle Louisa found nothing so obliging as her Guardian, what ever she requested was granted; what ever she but seem'd to wish, she enjoy'd, but was at a loss how to begin with her, if by a formal Declaration, it was teaching her to deny. My Lady had instructed her in all that was necessary to make a young Maid set a value upon her Chastity; she seem'd to bear an incorruptible Desire of preserving hers; their daily Conversation, nay Diversions, roll'd upon nothing that was loose or amorous; all Appearances were against him, and yet, in spight of Appearances, he resolv'd to proceed, and undermine that seemingly invincible Chastity; it would be a sort of Triumph over his Wife, whom he hated, as well as over *Louisa*, whom he lov'd, but how to attempt her first was the Point; he saw nothing of an amorous Constitution;

tion; nothing of the native *Coquet*, all was regular, all was cool and innocent; how much to blame was he to make her otherways? Are there such violent Desires that Reason cannot suppress? Is Love such an irresistable Tyrant? Will he trample upon all Obstacles? Are the most sacred Ties of no obligation in his Sense? O no! for if it were but *true Love*, 'twould seek the good of the Person belov'd; but *Hernando* was in his Temper a Friend to none but himself; amorous, and convers'd every Day with a young handsome Woman, which was impossible for him to do, without desiring of her. The little Freedoms that were permitted, inflam'd him; he could not pass near her without trembling; when he did but touch her Hand, his Blood flush'd in his Face; sometimes he would ravish a Kiss, in the way of play, but then he was lost in pleasure; he took all occasions for those pretty Liberties; her Bed-side was not refus'd him when he us'd to view her there in a Morning; he would fix his sparkling wishing Eyes, cross his Arms, and sigh in such a tender manner, that *Louisa* must have been very ignorant, not to have discern'd a Mystery in such a Behaviour; he would alway affect to sit near her, to take the Place she had quitted; to touch what she had but touch'd, and when his Lady was not present, her Glove, her Handkerchief, was Extacy to him; yet with nothing of a fulsome Address; he had a native becoming Gallantry. *Louisa* thought her self oblig'd by these Distinctions; they even created a sort of Gratitude, that warm'd it self to Tenderness; She was pleas'd to see, to hear him; his Company seem'd more diverting than others; she knew no harm in it, she thought no harm. At

"At that time there was a young Gentleman [Mr Sambrooke] from the Country, a Relation of *Hernando*'s, Lady that fell in love with *Mademoiselle Louiſſa*; his Circumſtances were advantageous for her, and his Perſon very agreeable. Mr. *Wilmot* begg'd the honour to wait upon his Couſin, and the young Lady to the *Opera*. *Hernando*'s Blood flaſh'd in his Face; he immediately gueſs'd that Mr. *Wilmot* was engag'd; he thought it now high time to declare himſelf; he had fool'd too long; there was an audacious Lover, by the Rites of Marriage, going to pretend to take her from his very Table; he confeſs'd 'twas advantageous to her; he was his Lady's Relation; ſhe lov'd *Louiſa*, and would not fail to preſs it to oblige both; nay *Louiſa* her ſelf might approve of him, he was handſome, he was young, he was amorous: She was innocent and unengag'd; nothing oppos'd *Wilmot*'s ſeeming Happineſs; but all things ſeem'd to be againſt his; theſe things revolv'd in an inſtant thro' his Mind: He ſaw 'em riſe to the *Opera*, with a concern he was not able to ſupport. *Wilmot*, by the Laws of Civility, was to lead the Lady *Volpone*, to put her firſt in the Coach, *Louiſa* was preparing to follow; *Hernando* catch'd her in ſuch a Tranſport, that was highly favourable to his Eyes and Air, he never look'd ſo handſome as then: No *Mademoiſelle*, ſays he, *Wilmot* ſhall never touch this Hand whilſt I am alive; they were too near to ſay more. *Hernando* agreeably ſurpriz'd his Lady, when he ſtept into the Coach to 'em, and ſaid he would go to the *Opera*. 'Twas known he had appointed buſineſs of mighty conſequence, that would ſuffer by being delay'd, like a good Wife, ſhe did not fail to repreſent it to him,

him, for fear he should have forgot it, that was all one; no business could come in ballance with *Louisa*; he saw that must be the time to defend her Heart from the first Impressions of a young assiduous Lover. He sat over-against her in the Coach, and without knowing what he did, press'd her Knees with his, till he pained her; she wonder'd at the Excess, because 'twas what he was not us'd to; but she durst not complain, for fear of his Lady. The Story of the *Opera* chanc'd to be of a Woman that had marry'd a second Husband, her first yet alive, tho' unknown to her; after seven Years absence he returns, the second Night after their new *Hymen*; discovers himself to her; she knows and owns him; falls into extreme Despair at the Misfortune; runs mad; and in her Lunacy stabs her self: The Play was wrought up with all the natural Artifice of a good Poet, *Louisa*, who did not often see such Representations, became extremely mov'd at this: Her young Breasts heav'd with Sorrow; the Tears fill'd her Eyes, and she betray'd her Sense of their Misfortune with a Tenderness that *Hernando* did not think had been in her; he was infinitely pleas'd, and employ'd a world of pains to applaud, instead of ridiculing, as his Lady did, that sensibility of Soul; when they came away, he took care that her Hand should fall to his share. As they were going home, he sat over against her, in the same manner as before. At Supper, the Play was their Subject: His Wife was reasoning about the Accident of the double Marriage, and said it was necessary the Poet should dispatch her out of the way, for loaded with such a Misfortune, 'twas impossible she should live without being infamous, and

con-

consequently detesting her self. *Hernando* was not of the same Opinion, and upon that Head, in his eloquent manner, introduc'd a learned Discourse of the lawfulness of double Marriages; indeed, he own'd that in all Ages, Women had been appropriated, that for the benefit and distinction of Children, with other necessary Occurrences, Polygamy had been justly deny'd the Sex, since the coldness of their Constitution, the length of time they carry'd their Children, and other Incidents seem'd to declare against them; but for a Man who possess'd an uninterrupted Capacity of propagating the Specie, and must necessarily find all the Inconveniencies above-mention'd, in any one Wife; the Law of Nature, as well as the Custom of many Nations, and most Religions, seem'd to declare for him; the ancient *Jews*, who pretend to receive the Law from an only God, not only indulg'd plurality of Wives, but an unlimitted use of Concubinage; the Children were bred up together without distinction, as being all the Sons of one Father, nay their *Land of Promise* was divided by equal Portions among a Mans (whom they call *Jacob*) twelve Sons, tho' some of 'em were born of his two Concubines, and the rest not from one Wife, but two, living at one time in and of the same Family. The *Turks*, and all the People of the World, but the *Europeans*, still preserved the privilege; that it was to be own'd, their Manners in all things were less adulterated than ours; their Veracity, Morality, and Habit of living less corrupted; that in pretending to reform from their Abuses, *Europe* had only refin'd their Vices; Pleasures that were forbidden had a better *Gusto*, and tho' they had

ty'd

ty'd themselves out of Policy to one Wife, to make particular Families great, and maintain diſtinction; yet there was ſcarce a Man (but himſelf) that had Capacity to uphold his Pleaſures abroad, but went in ſearch of 'em; that, true, he condemn'd a promiſcuous purſuit, becauſe it was irrational and polluted, but if one or more Women, whether marry'd or not, were appropriated to one Man, they were ſo far from tranſgreſſing, that they but fulfill'd the Law of Nature; it was agreeable to the practice of great *Jupiter* himſelf, and therefore could only in a political, not religious Senſe, be accounted infamous; that the loſs of the World's Eſteem was very well recompenc'd, by the true and valuable Joys of Love; that a young Lady ought never to oppoſe thoſe good Inclinations ſhe might find in her ſelf towards a marry'd Man, becauſe ſhe was gratifying at one time, both her Paſſion and her Duty.

You may be ſure this Harangue did not reliſh very well in his Lady's Ear, but it was not for her he intended it. *Hernando* appeal'd to Mr. *Wilmot*, if he had ſaid any thing but what was rational; he, who did not know the other's Deſign, and like a right Man, was for upholding the Sex's Charter, did not fail to applaud it; tho' it were but an ill Mode of making his Court to a Lady he pretended to marry. *Louiſa* very well obſerv'd it, in being his Wife, ſhe found ſhe muſt prepare her ſelf for the Mortification of one or more Rivals, and that he would plead Cuſtom, and bring Preſidents for it; this diſguſted her extremely of that ſide; ſhe preſum'd thet no unmarried Man ought to advance ſuch Doctrine, before a Woman he lov'd;

'twas

'Twas only to be look'd upon as the Husband's refuge, when he was so unfortunate to meet with a Wife he did not like; and how firm soever was the Foundation, should not be built upon but in Extremity.

Next Morning *Hernando* beg'd the favour of his Lady, that she wou'd take *Louisa* down with her to their *Villa*, near six Leagues from *Angela*, and endeavour to divert themselves, as well as they cou'd, for two or three days, at which time he would be sure to wait upon them; this was to send her out of *Wilmot*'s way; he cou'd not rest while he thought another pretended to her. Their departure was so sudden, that the Lover had not time to interest his Relation in his Cause; he wou'd ev'n have follow'd em, but *Hernando* gave him such a cold reception, and told him, his Wife, fatigu'd with the Hurry of the Town, retir'd to avoid Company, and wou'd very well spare the extraordinary Complement, that he resolv'd to delay it till their return.

Mean time, *Hernando* weigh'd with himself how he shou'd declare himself: Paper is never out of Countenance, and tho' he did not use often to blush, yet the natural Timidity of a Lover, taught him to despond when he was near his Mistress: He knew many things were lost, not because Men cannot attain to 'em, but because they don't attempt 'em. He did not well know whether a Letter wou'd escape his Wife's hands, and fall into *Louisa*'s; nay, ev'n whether *Louisa* wou'd not her self expose it; he thought the hazard was too great, and therefore resolv'd to depart that very Night, within two Hours of Twelve, when he was expected of none. He had a Master-key that open'd all Doors and

Gates

Gates; he took no Servant with him, but mounting his Horse, he flew away with the speed of a Lover, little at ease till he be with his Beloved: A *Surtout* and riding Periwig, sufficiently disguis'd him; he alighted at the Garden back-Gate; the Moon was at the full, and lent him more light than he had occasion for. 'Twas then past Midnight; he knew *Louisa*'s Chamber was on the Ground-floor; two large folding-Windows open'd into the Garden, which the extreme Heat of the Weather might possibly cause her to keep open: He believ'd the whole Family was (if not asleep, at least) in Bed; his Lady's side was on the other part of the House; avoiding the Gravel, for fear the Noise shou'd discover him: He fetch'd a compass by the grassy Walks, to come to *Louisa*'s Chamber; where he found the lovely Maid, in a melancholy Posture, leaning with her Arms upon the Window, and gazing at the Moon: His Heart beat violently at the sight; he was afraid of showing himself, lest he shou'd frighten her, and in her surprise she shou'd cry out; neither was he sure her Attendant, was dismiss'd, for the Lights were still burning; but Boldness being ever a Friend to Love, he advanc'd, and calling softly *Madmoisel Louisa*, charming *Louisa*, are you alone? The Tone of his Voice was sweet and particularly softned; *Louisa* only started, but did not cry out: She ask'd him in a Minute, having presently known him, When did you come? How long have you been here? Have you any body with you? Dear *Madmoisel*, he interrupted: No, she said, all the House is in Bed; I've just sent away my Maid, am all undrest, even to my very Night-gown; not being
dis-

difpos'd to go to Bed, nor in the leaft fleepy, I thought it was cruelty to keep her up; but I'll call her to bring Lights to let you in, and wait upon you up to my Lady's Chamber: Hold, hold, *Madmoifel*, and with that he gave but one jump into the Room, and then another to catch her in his Arms: She fell a trembling, and ready to fink as he held her, being taken with a Paffion of Fear and Surprize; fhe fear'd, but fhe knew not what: *Hernando*, with all the fubmiffion of a Lover, taught by Nature more than Education, fell upon his Knees clofe to the Chair where he had plac'd her; dear *Madmoifel*, I muft beg you to recover your Diforder; what are you apprehenfive of? Are you afraid of fo fubmiffive a Lover? He ftop'd here to fee how fhe would receive the Declaration, but her trembling and fright continuing, he faw fhe was juft going to have a fit of Swooning; he had heard in thofe Cafes, that the beft Remedy was to lay her at her length; fo that taking her without refiftance, in his Arms, he carry'd her to the Bed, and flipping off her Night-gown, with as much Modefty as the Circumftance would permit, he threw the Bed open, laid her in, and cover'd her up very handfomly, then caft himfelf down upon the Bed-cloaths, his Face to hers, where he could not refift the Pleafure of paying himfelf in Kiffes for his pains; this, and what was done before, recall'd the young Beauty; fhe remov'd him gently with her hand, and turning that way, Oh Sir, fays fhe, what are you about? Do you mean to ruin me? I mean to love you, Madam, to adore you, to die for you, I mean to marry you, if you will make me fo happy: Dreams, anfwer'd the Lady, are not you marry'd ry'd already? Oh, Madam, if you did but love me with but a grain of that Paſſion I have for you, it would be more than a Dream, 'twould be reality; but that is my Misfortune, all I ask of you at preſent is, that you will diſmiſs your Fears, for upon my Faith and Honour, I engage you ſhall have no occaſion for 'em; all wild as I am, with extremity of Love and eager Deſires, you ſhall command me as you pleaſe; I will not ſo much as pretend to the liberty of a Kiſs without your leave; let me have but one of your fair Hands, that I may proteſt upon it my never-dying Paſſion; I have long and deſperately lov'd you; I believe, ſmother'd by Pain, I ſhould have dy'd rather than have reveal'd it to you, if that Country-Booby's Pretenſion had not alarm'd me, and gave me Courage to ſpeak. For you only I am come hither alone; for you only I ſhall return ſolitary and dying with Grief, at leaving my better part behind; 'tis too dangerous a Secret to be ſhar'd with any but our ſelves, upon the Road I would have given my Life for this fair, this ſilent, happy Opportunity; don't make it of no effect by groundleſs Fears; reaſſure your ſelf, *Madmoiſel*; baniſh, Madam, that treacherous Enemy to Love; Oh that you would but permit me to give you only a Taſt of what I feel; that you would once but admit of ſo much Curioſity in my Favour, to prove but a glimmering of that Delight, that mutual Lovers beſtow upon one another. Here he ſought her Lips, and preſt 'em ſo tenderly, and ſo reſpectively, that he could not fail of inſinuating, by that dangerous Contact, ſomething new and tender into the Breaſt of the unexperienc'd Virgin; he purſu'd her ſo artfully, that ſhe

she consented he should stay there till Morning; and before they parted, promis'd to hear him again upon the Article of Marriage. She confess'd, she preferr'd him to all Mankind; she wish'd he were single, she should never like another so well, but her Honour and Chastity were above her Life: The Battery was renew'd against that piece of Fortification; he told her, 'Twas only a Dream, a Notion, that scarce any Lady who had been so happy to love, had any more of it than the Pretence; good Management and Conduct were Honour and Vertue too; he was pleading for nothing criminal; she was un-ingaged, un-marry'd, and had a despotick Power in favour of any one she had a mind to make happy; then he urg'd Arguments innumerable, all to the same purpose as the Night before, to perswade her to the lawfulness of Poligamy, he found that must be the Mine that was to blow up her Chastity: She listned, she enquir'd, and where she doubted, made Objections, which with his Sophistry he immediately answer'd; till at length he almost convinc'd her, that the Law of Nature was prior, and ought to take place; one was ordain'd by the Gods, the other instituted by Man, and therefore the first was undoubtedly to be preferr'd: He begg'd she would permit him to see her in the same manner every Night; there was no danger of a Discovery; he wou'd pretend the great Heat made him desire to lie alone, and have his Bed made in a low Room in the other Wing, answering to the Garden, as that did, by which means he might get out of his own Window, and come into hers.

Q When

When once a young Maid pretends to put her felf upon the fame Foot with a Lover at Argument, fhe is fure to be caft: *Louifa* had no very ftrong Head; his fuperficial Reafons might quickly take place, efpecially when they were feconded by Inclination: Unknown to her felf fhe lov'd him, elfe all his Attempts would have been infignificant; he fhow'd her fhe was a Woman at liberty, had her own Fortune at command, and his with Advantage: What could fhe expect in another Husband that was not to be found in him? Why truly the Opinion of the World; but that not being a part of her Duty, might very well be exchang'd for thofe incomparable Delights, that are feldom or never found in mercenary Marriage; fince fhe already lov'd him, fhe could contract none with any other Man, that would not be fo; therefore all they were to fence againft was, left it fhould be difcover'd: It was not neceffary fhe fhould lofe Efteem, as long as fhe could preferve it; but in thefe repeated dangerous nightly Converfations, Love had arm'd her with Fortitude, fhe was become bold, as to Opinion, contented within her felf, that fhe did nothing againft the Laws of God and Nature, which he had taught her, it was her Duty to fulfil.

Having, with a world of pains, fix'd this immoveable Principle in her Breaft, fhe confented to marry him; fhe could admit of *Poligamy*, but would not hear a word of *Concubinage*; whether the difference be fo material I leave to the *Cafuifts*; but the difficulty was, how they fhould be marry'd unknown. *Mofca* (*Hernando*'s Brother, much about the fame pitch in Devotion, and or: He was call'd to Council. *Hernando* told him, he could not carefs his Wife, the Rites of Love were naufeous to him; and fince it was a folly to pafs away that idle time of Life without Pleafures, he had fought it with eafe and fafety in *Louifa*'s foft Bofom: But becaufe fhe would not condefcend to make him happy without a Prieft, he did not know how to procure one that would be fecret. *Mofco* anfwer'd, that he fuppos'd all that he pretended to by marrying the Girl, was to pleafe her; and fince that might as well be done by a falfe, as a true Prieft, their beft way was, to let him procure the Habit, and officiate to their Content: By that means *Hernando* fhould fcreen himfelf from her Perfecutions, when he was grown weary of her; as that would be no wonder, to his knowledge, for he was fick at heart of young *Zara*, *Mrs Stout the Quaker* and did not know how in the World to get rid of her. This was applauded as a notable Expedient; he gain'd the Lady by it; and fhould fhe ever take a fancy to put in her Claim, 'twas impoffible for her to find the Prieft, and therefore 'twould be in vain to pretend it: They only demurr'd, left fhe fhould know him, maugre his Difguife, or fufpect the Tone of his Voice: As to that, they did not doubt but the Drefs, together with another colour'd Wig, would make him quite another thing; his Voice fhould be alter'd with a Bullet, or Plum-ftones in his Mouth, and fpeaking *a la Francoife*, he might very well pafs for a *Refugee*, a People that are to be found in swarms thro' all Parts of *Europe*, especially the *Islands*.

Hernando would not have it deferr'd; he caused her to come to *Angela*, upon a slight Pretence: His Lady remain'd in the Country, they durst not share their Secret with any other, few of the Servants being in Town, and those that were, sent out of the way. After Supper, this pretended Priest comes upon a visit to *Hernando*; he took care there shou'd be but little Light in the Room, the Ceremony being only to quiet the Ladies Conscience (who thought she did no ill, so thoroughly had he wrought upon her) there was no Witness requir'd; so marry'd they were; the false Priest receiv'd his Fee, made his Legg, and brusht into a Coach that waited for him.

The new marry'd (I mean the Bridegroom) was very impatient to go to Bed, the Lady as Dutiful as Obliging, did not let him wait long; when the Servants were dispos'd to their rest, he was introduc'd into her Chamber, where he pass'd the guilty Night, I suppose, to both their satisfactions.

The next Day they return'd into the Country, but *Hermando* was too much in Love to pass a Night without the Joys of his young Wife, the Invention of the Window still held good; but what shou'd they do when the Season call'd 'em to *Angela?* when they shou'd be forc'd to abandon that dear *Villa*, a thousand blest Opportunities presented themselves, which they cou'd not find elsewhere; they lost none of 'em; the conscious Walks and Gardens all witness'd to their Passion. *Louisa* cou'd not enough Love a Husband

so

so very amiable; she devoted all her Thoughts and Wishes, her whole Days and Nights to him; the same unaccountable thing that cools the Swain, more warms the Nymph: Enjoyment (the death of Love in all Mankind) gives Birth to new Fondess, and doating Extasies in the Women; they begin later, with-held by Modesty, and by a very ill tim'd Oeconomy, take up their Fondness exactly where their Lover leaves it.

This was sufficiently prov'd by the young Zara, a very pretty Girl, whose Mother liv'd in the same *Villa* with *Hernando*, but so great a Bigot, that *Zara* had seen nothing but their own forbidding Crew of Sectaries: Her self was born with genteel Inclinations, and had something *jantie* in her Mien and Conversation; they did nothing but teize her for not conforming her self enough to their Manners. Her Fortune was considerable for one of her rank; she had eight thousand Crowns in her own Hands, which was more than three times as much to Ladies that dress and live in the World. Her Father was dead, and she went often to *Hernando's* and his Brothers to converse, which were the principal People of the *Villa*. *Mosco*, who never saw a Woman he cou'd not have bestow'd some of his Favours upon, let her be handsome, or indifferent, was mightily taken with pretty *Zara*; he had not the command of Mony as his elder Brother had; all things mov'd in a much narrower Sphere than at *Hernando's*, his Lady had been his Father's Mistress, and his Mother never forgave him his Marriage with her, it wou'd be no dis-

disadvantage to him to have the command of *Zara*'s: The young Creature took a fatal Passion for him, which was not in her Power to conceal, not even from his Wife. If she were at the Table at dinner with her, and he return'd unexpectedly, her Surprize and Joy were usually so great, that all the World might read in her Face the disorders of her Soul. The Lady did not love her the less for it; she believ'd her sick of a Distemper she cou'd not help; and did not imagine it wou'd arise to any guilty Commerce between her and her Husband. Mean time she put all her little Matters in *Mosco*'s Hand; he it was that dispos'd of her Fortune, and made what wasts or improvements he saw good; when she had affairs at *Angela*; if he were there, she took up her constant residence at his House; perpetually put her self in the Road where she might meet him: He saw this *Empressment*, and was not at all displeas'd with it; his Soul was almost as Amorous, and his Person almost as handsome as his Brothers: I've already told you their Principals were the same, tho' perhaps quite so much may not be said of his Address and Natural Parts; however he had a great deal of Wit and Attempt; understood very well his Business, but had not the good Fortune to be born an elder Brother.

By the pretence of Business, he cou'd often see *Zara* at her Mother's House: Those opportunities were not lost; she was of an Opinion that Cohabitation makes a Marriage; she wou'd have given ten times her Fortune, if she had had it, that *Mosco*, as he sometimes gave her hopes, wou'd leave his Wife and cohabit with her,

her; not that he ever intended it, but Men do not use to say disagreeable things to those that they came to be happy with; he cou'd have been very well contented if she had lov'd him something more discreetly, her fondness began to be very tiresome to him. She was one Day at dinner at *Hernando*'s, *Mosco* arriv'd unexpectedly; she was forc'd to withdraw to the Air of the Window in the next Room, or she had swooned away; tender *Louisa* follows to assist her, she even leaves her dinner to administer what was in her Power towards her recovery; they got together into the Garden, where, having no Witnesses but themselves, *Zara* no longer restrain'd her self, but gave way to a great Passion of Tears: when that was over, and *Louisa* had intreated her to let her know the cause of her Afflictions, and assur'd her of secresie. She began thus,

You see here, my dear *Louisa*, the most lost undone Maid that ever liv'd. I love *Mosco* to that height, that nothing but his Love can satisfie me! alas! that's a thing impossible to gain from so unconstant a Person! yet has he a thousand, and a thousand times persuaded me, that his Passion was mutual! I cost him none of those Cares and Troubles, by which other Women are brought to oblige their Lovers; the Work was all done to his Hand; I even lov'd him before he distinguish'd me: I was the Agressor! I am the Sufferer! how dear am I going to pay for those few Moments of Delight I have pas'd with him? Those charming Pleasures are no more! I cannot bear to live without him! Doubtless, *Louisa*, you wonder to hear me en-

Q 4   tertain

tertain you at this rate; but it is not with us, as with you; we think mutual Love and Consent makes a Marriage; we stand not in need of the Priest's Ceremony; when once we give our Faith, it is inviolable; it wou'd be a mortal Crime to swerve from it: And tho' *Mosco* was marry'd before, leaving his Wife to cohabit with me, (as he has a thousand times promis'd) is sufficient Ceremony; all that we require to make a Marriage and render *Zara* happy: but he's cool'd! his fainting Ardors retain nothing of their first Sweetness! he ev'n avoids me! whilst I love him to that transporting height, I am not Mistress of my self! You saw it was not in my Power to suppress those Disorders his presence gave me. What must all the World think of my Folly? am not I mad? 'tis impossible I shou'd live under this Disease of Soul! I must put an end to all my Uneasiness: But alas! that is not to be done without putting an end to my Life.

Louisa hearing a Story so very parallel with her own, wept in Consort; she was afraid of the same Inconstancy, tho' *Hernando* was still kind and Generous. *Zara* had Beauty, Youth, and Fortune; yet were not these any Articles towards her Happiness: The capricio of Men carry 'em above all consideration; *Louisa*'s Love-sick Heart was languishing with the same Distemper. *Zara* had found out a Confident who lov'd as much as she, and therefore was not like to give her any good Advices towards her recovery: however, she said and did all that was in her power to comfort her, she ev'n advis'd her to absent her self from *Mosco*, if it were

were true, that he was really become unkind, a generous Difdain ought to be her Cure; but probably fhe might miftake, Bufinefs, unlucky crofs Affairs, might make her mifinterpret him; Men were not always difpos'd; Love feldom was confider'd in them after a time, but as a leifure Employment, an unbending of the Soul, a fweetning of fatigue, and 'twas Wifdom in Women to give way to thofe Cruel Hours, and wait with patience for the Tender.

Hernando and *Mofco* appear'd in the fame Walk; *Zara* beg'd the favour of *Louifa* to entertain the former, whilft fhe got a moments-Difcourfe with the other; this was a Service no way difagreeable to her, nor *Hernando*, but 'twas not the fame with *Mofco*, he wou'd have his Brother not to leave him to be baited by *Zara*'s fondnefs; he laugh'd, and told him he had much hurt done him, now he had an opportunity to entertain *Louifa* he wou'd not lofe it, let him look to himfelf as well as he cou'd. Thus *Hernando* and his Miftrefs, having both the fame defign, quickly ftruck into another Walk, and left that to the difconfolate *Zara*. She came up to her Lover, who inquir'd of her Health, and what had occafion'd her fudden ilnefs? As if you are a Stranger to it, Sir, there are fome Perfons who fo wholly poffefs our Souls, that we can't hear their very Name without Perturbation! their fight, unexpected, influences 'em as yours did me: But what fhall I fay? alas! I give you none of thofe Diforders; if all be not calm within you, it is becaufe Hate, and not Love, difquiets you: Why did you encourage the Follies of a Maid that might have been happy, had fhe never feen you?

you? Alas! I was Innocent! I knew none of those Arts by which, I am since inform'd, the Women of the World prolong and heighten their Lover's Passion! I thought it was a Merit in me to love what seem'd so meritorious: I shou'd have believ'd it a fault unpardonable to have dissembl'd it: I was bred in the plain road of Sincerity my Heart corresponds with my Manners: I know nothing so base and guilty as dissimulation; therefore, speak to you for the last time; things are come to that height, I can't bear to live and not possess you all. Will you do as you promis'd? Will you live with me? Shall I have that Sanction for my Passion? my Fortune may be wholly at your disposal: I will ev'n do all that's necessary to please my Mother, in whose Power it is to double it; she will no longer oppose my Inclinations, when she finds you give me that proof of yours. You have but to cohabit with me to make you Master of hers, as well as mine: I am asking you no new thing: 'Twas but what your self, first, propos'd; the Artifice by which you drew me to give you the last Proof of my Love, and without which I shou'd have believ'd that Concession highly criminal. Persons of our Persuasion, promise nothing but what they are sure to perform; you well know their very Word to them is a Law; I was never use to converse with any Deceivers, therefore you need not wonder I took so little precaution against you: Upon the whole, if you acquit your self as you ought, there is none I wou'd change Conditions with. You have screwd me, by your delays, up to the very height; you must now stop, or I break and
fall

fall to pieces: To morrow carries yours, and your Brother's Family from our *Villa* for the whole Winter. I can't support your absence, unless you'll totally destroy my hopes: Tell me you hate me, that I may cease to love you. Restore my Affairs to the posture they were, when I first ingag'd with you; give me back my Writings and my Effects; let me see that you will have no further Correspondence with me, and I will endeavour either to be easie or die. To this long Speech, *Mosco* return'd as long an Answer; Stufft with false assurances of Love, and performance of his Promise; he wou'd but put his Affairs in a posture, not to fear his Wife's anger, and then he'd devote himself wholly to her; mean time he'd often take opportunities to see her, they were discharging their own Lodging, and he wou'd henceforth take up his at her Mothers.

By this, the other (as fantastically married) People had join'd them, *Zara* became a little less Splenetick; she stay'd late that Night, because it was the last, which neither *Hernando* nor *Louisa* thank'd her for in their Hearts; because they were apparently going for a long time, to take their leaves of meeting in the same Bed together.

Louisa prov'd with Child, which alarm'd 'em both; she grew apparently big; *Hernando* bid her not disquiet her self, he wou'd take a House for her, and she shou'd be accountable to none but him for her Conduct.

This

This Lady undone with Love, confented to the Propofal; fhe valu'd not the World's Opinion which fhe was going to lofe, nor being abandon'd by all the good, to fhut up her felf in Infamy, to devote her felf to a Paffion, that poffibly might quickly meet its dofe in too full Poffeffion; but fhe doating on to the extremety, found Fame and Honour, Riches and Content, in his Arms.

Mr. *Wilmot* renew'd his Addreffes; he had engag'd his Coufin to propofe him to *Louifa* for a Lover. She had been much furpriz'd at her intended Separation, nor could imagine what a young Creature fhould take a Houfe to live alone by her felf; fhe fancy'd fome Myftery, but far from the right; however, having, to fpeak in favour of Mr. *Wilmot*'s Paffion, fhe came foftly and unexpectedly to *Louifa*'s Chamber; there was no body there; fhe heard fome talking in the little Dreffing-Room, which being upon the jar, fhe faw her falfe Husband upon his Knees, kiffing *Lonifa*'s Hand, and heard him entreat her, that fhe would admit him to her Chamber, when the Houfe was at reft; he would pretend to lie alone, and tho' there was not the fame conveniency of Windows, as at the *Villa*, yet fomething ought to be hazarded for fo great a Happinefs: *Louifa* was apparently confenting, when Lady *Volpone* made a third; you may guefs how acceptable was her Company: She loft her ufual Moderations: Tears, Grief, Rage, Reproaches, all that could agitate a Wife Jealous and convinc'd: She upbraided *Louifa* of breach of Hofpitality; of violating the Laws of Friendfhip, fhe that had been as a Mother to her;

'twas

'twas more than Adultery, 'twas Inceſt, and Paracide; ſhe not only ſeduc'd her Husband, but would murther her, ſince 'twas impoſſible ſhe could ſurvive the loſs of his Affection.

Fernando would not ſuffer *Louiſa* to reply, leaſt the *Ecclarciſſement* of the double Marriage ſhould be a double Scandal to him: But taking her by the Hand, he bow'd to his Lady, and told her his *Ward* ſhould wait upon her at another time, when her Temper was better, and ſhe more ſenſible of the Honour ſhe receiv'd by ſo deſerving a Perſon's Converſation. So leading her down Stairs, he went with her into a Coach, and diſpos'd her to her ſatisfaction, in a Friend's Houſe of his, 'till her own was fitted-up.

Throughly convinc'd of the Doctrine he had taught her, that Plurality of Wives were lawful: She manag'd her ſelf no more as to the World's Opinion, forſaking that, before it could abandon her. She lay-in at her own Houſe, and no longer pretended to keep her Commerce with *Hernando* a Secret: She conſider'd her ſelf as his Wife, and perſiſting ſtill in her beloved Opinion, indulg'd the enchanting Poyſon, which deſtroy'd her Fame, and intoxicated her Reaſon.

Mean time the afflicted *Zara* wrote ſeveral Letters to *Moſco*, to ſummon him to the performance of his Promiſe; ſhe fatigu'd; ſhe perſecuted him; he heartily wiſh'd any favourable Accident would tranſport her to a more happy Region; neither her height of Paſſion, Youth, nor Beauty, could reſtore loſt Appetite, or prevent a loathing. She perpetually talk'd of dying, but he knew that very few deceas'd of that Diſtemper. The Flower of Beauty apparently

faded,

faded, neither the Rose nor Lillies retain'd their native Colour: Her Dress she neglected; Diversions were no more; Sorrow, nay Despair, were her inseparable Companions; all she hoped and wish'd was, that they would quickly terminate her pain. In this manner she entertain'd those who pretended to comfort her: They found her deplorably Melancholy, but could not divine the Cause, and vainly strove to divert her, but that was beyond their Sphere. She argu'd with her self, that could she see him but once more, to know his final Resolution, it would determine hers; to obtain that satisfaction, she resolv'd to write again; but whether to move him, by her submission, to compassionate her Sufferings, or to threaten him into a compliance; the former method had not been successful, therefore in Words that resemble these, she resolv'd upon the latter.

Tir'd out with Love and Disdain, too cruel Friend and Husband, I have resolv'd to suffer no more in private, but will proclaim my Woes, and your Delusions, even to the Woman the World believes your Wife, tho' I only am such, and will not fail to make my Claim within two Days, at Angela; if before that time be expir'd, thou dost not comfort and relieve thy affectionate, and most despairing,

Z A R A.

Mosco could by no means relish a Visit of that nature; he rais'd not any great Ideas of delight from such a Scene; he had too much Wisdom to let it work up to that height, therefore

fore since he saw Promises were no longer a Specie that would pass current with *Zara*, he resolv'd to undeceive her, tho' it might possibly take her Affairs out of his Hands, and with it inconvenience his; yet her Persecutions were more intollerable, and he would be at rest from so troublesome an Amour. 'Twas in vain to wish that he had not engag'd her so far; these are among the things, which when once done, cannot so easily be repair'd, he took Horse, and arriv'd the same Night at the *Villa*. She was all Joy, and new Transport to see him; 'twas as if she had never been in pain. She told him he must lie there that Night: He said nothing to contradict her. They supp'd with her Mother, who afterwards withdrew to order the Linen for his Bed. All the good Nature he was Master of could not force him to shew Tenderness where he had so strong an Aversion. He ask'd himself whence it came, that a Person of her Youth and Charms, with all that's endearing in the Sex, excess of Truth, and excess of Love, could not in the least sway his obdurate Heart to a return? He found the fatal Secret, he had been happy, and that prevented him from being still so; Satiety and Loathing succeeded; his Reason could not preside over his Appetite; he could eat no more however delicate was the Banquet, and therefore it must be remov'd: 'Twas hard to tell a Lady so that had oblig'd him, but it was ten times harder for her to suffer in continual torture. Therefore having summon'd all his Resolution, he ask'd her if they should take a Walk by the River-side. The Servant was above ordering his Bed, but he was

afraid

afraid what he had to say, would make her so outragious, that the Family would hear her, and he, in the first Gust of her Passion, should be exposed, as well as her self. *Zara* consented to every thing that was agreeable to him. They began their Walk by the pale Glimm'rings of the Moon, and the agreeable noise that arose from the gentle Dashes of the Water. Leaning of his Arm, which she eagerly press'd, with the Raptures of a Passion over-joy'd, Thou shalt never, my Dear, says she, forsake me again: I have told my Mother of my design to take you for my Husband: We will begin this very Night to co-habit together; my Despair and Melancholy has drawn her at length to consent: Do but utterly forgo that Woman you call your Wife, and we require no more for making mine; (in our opinion) a lawful Marriage: We are above the little Censure of others; the Law nor Magistrates do not frighten us: I make you absolute Master of my Fortune, only upon these Conditions— My Dear! Why do you not speak? Thou art not come here to disappoint me: I beseech you to answer me. Alas! beautiful *Zara!* What can I answer? nothing, I fear, but will be disagreeable to your Expectations. You don't know the World; you are ignorant of Mankind: 'Tis in our power to marry our selves but once, that is a fundamental establish'd Law, as long as that Wife shall live; I did not doubt but you knew this, and when I first gain'd the Pleasures of your Love, said the contrary, only to allow your Virtue that pretence for yielding; but we must be both utterly void of common Sense, to go to pass such a Marriage upon the World;

World; me to abandon a Lady by whom I have so many Children, and other Benefits, to ruin my own Reputation and yours, for an airy Notion, by which we make our selves obnoxious to the Laws, and hated by Mankind. You will object the Promises I made you, it would be much greater Madness to perform 'em, neither did I think you seriously expected it; no wise Woman reckons upon the performance of those extravagant things that are said to gain her: Be contented with my Love; there's nothing I shall omit to please you; I will lose no Opportunity to entertain you with it, provided you are discreet, and do not expose us both: He was going on, when *Zara* not able to hear any more, funk upon her Knees, and catching hold of his Coat, with both her Hands, interrupted him thus, Kill me upon the instant; I have something more than the Pains of Death upon me; whatsoever are call'd the Pains of Hell and Damnation, I feel yet more, Words cannot express 'em. O! if ever you intend to meet Mercy, (as certainly you'll one Day stand in need of it) have mercy upon me, a Creature undone by Love (agoniz'd by Passion) and tortur'd by Despair: Kill me, or comply with my Request. I shall never live, I cannot live to see another Day: Pity me, pity the lost the expiring *Zara*; *Zara* that adores you; *Zara* enchanted by your too powerful Magick; *Zara* that even now dies, and can be no more without some kindness. Here her Sobs choak'd her Words. He striving to get loose from her; she grasping to retain him, Spleen join'd his Aversion; he saw he could not bring her to Reason, and therefore since they muſt quarrel, the breach had beſt be made in the open Fields, where no body could hear 'em: He would take the pretence, and burſt from her, never to be plagu'd with her Importunity again. You would do well, Madam, ſays he, aiming to unlock her Hands, to leave me in peace, and go home to compoſe your Brain, by ſleep: You happen to be amorous, and fantaſtically mad, and I muſt be the ſufferer. True, you have oblig'd me, I promis'd to make a Marriage after your faſhion, by Cohabitation: I do not think fit to perform it; what of that? Are you the firſt Woman that have gone upon a wrong Principle? My Family and Reputation are not to be ſtaked for Trifles: Be more moderate, or aſſure your ſelf I'll never, from this inſtant, ſee you more. Here he threw abroad her Hands, and broke from her; ſhe fell her length upon the Ground, then getting up as faſt as ſhe could, ſtrove to follow him, but he was at too great a diſtance. Revenge and Deſpair work'd her up to the height of Lunacy: She tore off her Hood, her Coif; her Gown that hung looſly about her, trampling it under Foot, and calling after him, Turn, turn but a moment; turn and ſee what Love and Rage can do; return and behold what *Zara* can perform: Frantick, loſt to Hope, and Love, loſt to Life; Ruin, Deſpair, Deſtruction, Death, eternal Miſery, overtake me: Heaven, Earth and Hell revenge me; Heaven, Earth and Hell are conſcious of my Wrongs. I devote my ſelf to Miſery eternal, in view of returning in the moſt afrighting Form to haunt this Barbarian: Let me mingle among all the

Traitor's

Traitor's Pleasures; let him attain to no Honours, but what may be blasted by the remembrance of *Zara*; let him reproach himself; may the World for ever reproach him; let me, a Ghost, pursue the Traitor with never-ending Reproaches: Receive me, Oh hospitable Flood! into thy cold Bosom; receive a devoted Wretch whose Flame thy Waters can only quench—— Here she flounc'd, with all her strength, into the River, to the last moment persisting in a desire of speedy Death: She held her Breath, and was immediately stifled, without swallowing any of the Water. 'Tis very much a Question if he did not hear the fall of the Body; possibly not believing a Woman's Love could work her to such a prodigious height of Frenzy and Resentment. He had made the best of his way to his Lodging; or take it for granted that he both suspected and heard her Destiny; it was scarce safe for him to return, unless he could have propos'd to have flung himself in soon enough to save her Life, which the consequence has assur'd, had been impossible, for she was stifled in a minute, even before a Gulph of Water could be swallow'd.

Next Morning the Body was found down the River, where the Stream had carry'd it, and *Mosco* upon the Road, in his return to *Angela*: The Truth hath been thus reported by many of his Friends, without finding Credit, because the World oftner condemns than acquits. Hers have advanc'd, That he had the Improvement of her Fortune in his Hands, which amounted to a considerable Sum, and was not known to any but her self: That his Affairs wou'd not then permit him

him to reftore it; which, if fhe had liv'd, and they had became Enemies, he muft have done; and therefore to appropriate that, and rid himfelf of a troublefome Amour, in conjunction with two more of his Friends, they had firft ftrangled, and then thrown her into the River.

But we cannot fee a fwifter inftance of Divine Vengeance, than in the Punifhment that here on Earth befell *Zara*, for beftowing her guilty Affections upon a Perfon marry'd to another.

By this time *Louifa* had two Children: nor can fhe be call'd much more happy than *Zara*; for tho' fhe did not furvive her Lovers Kindnefs, fhe fuffer'd by it: Neither her Charms, nor the Obligations fhe had laid upon him, could confine him wholly to her Arms: He got but an ill Prefent among fome of his Women, which not knowing himfelf tainted, he imparted to both his Wives. The firft (recover as fhe could) was not to be made acquainted with it; her Temper would never fuffer her to live eafie with him afterwards: But for *Louifa*, all Remedies were vainly apply'd; fhe was Heart-broke at his Inconftancy; and tho' by her Brother's Death fhe was become a confiderable Heirefs, yet her Melancholy would fuffer her to take no Pleafure in Life: Not that fhe ever had any Remorfe for abandoning her felf to a marry'd Man, becaufe *Poligamy* was an unfhaken Article of her Faith; but in her Tafte of Love fhe was nice, and delicate; for as fhe had wholly devoted her Heart and Perfon to him, fhe believ'd his, both by Merit, and by Promife, were wholly due to her;

but

but having receiv'd so fatal a Proof of his wandering from both, she took it to Heart, which Joining to an ill Habit of Body, carry'd her from this Life, a Martyr of that Passion to which she had been devoted; persisting to the last moment in an Opinion, that in regard to *Hernando*, she had done nothing but her Duty.

His first Lady, ignorant of her Distemper, yet longer surviv'd: But when it was come to a *Crisis*, and that Death was apparent, he seem'd to attone for all his former Irregularities by an exact Behaviour: One would have thought that he had been inconsolably afflicted; he saw no Company but in her Chamber; he receiv'd that little Sustenance that was absolutely necessary for Life, by her Bed-side: Whether he really had, or only seem'd to have Remorse, he said and did things that was necessary to approve himself a tender Husband; and departed not from that Behaviour, till her Death most obligingly set him free, and left him at full liberty to pursue, without controul, his Amours and his Ambition.

These two Brothers, renown'd for their Ascendency over the Ladies, have this in their Character, That they only desire to be heard: In their Tongues there is such Delusion, that 'tis impossible for any Women they attempt, not to be inchanted and undone by 'em.

Hernando made a Truce with Love, and apply'd himself more closely to Business: He past all the Preferments of the Long-Robe, till he had attain'd to the greatest; when once *Grand President*, by an infinite Natural Capacity, and but a superficial Knowledge of the Laws, he
ac-

acquitted himself with Applause. That Lady who last left the *Prado* (though but an inconsiderable Fortune) he marry'd amidst all his Grandeur; the Charms of her Wit and Convesation attach'd him to her. She had the good fortune to fix, as well as to survive this wandering Star; though it must be own'd, That *there are Follies like some Stains, that wear out of themselves, among which, Love is generally reckon'd to be one.*

F I N I S.